Beyond the Walled Garden

Beyond the walled garden

Wendy Fletcher-Marsh

a·r·t·e·m·i·s

ENTERPRISES

Beyond the Walled Garden
Subtitle

Published 1995
artemis enterprises, RR#2, Box 54, Dundas, Ontario L9H 5E2

Editor: Gertrude Lebans
Production: Ann Turner

Every effort has been made to secure copyright permissions where
required.

Canadian Cataloguing in Publication Data

Fletcher-Marsh, Wendy, 1963–
  Beyond the walled garden

Includes bibliographical references.
ISBN 1-895247-16-0

1. Women in the Anglican Communion – History –
20th century.   2. Women priests.   3. Anglican
Communion – Clergy.   I. Title.

BX5005.F44 1995   283'.082   C95-932984-6

I dedicate this book to my father, John Henry Fletcher,
who told me as a child that God was with me,
that I would be in the world who God made me to be,
and that I could do in the world
that which I chose to do.

Contents

PART THREE
REVOLUTION FAILS IN ENGLAND

PART FOUR
COMPARISON AND CONCLUSION

Chronology

Stage One (1920–1967)

1920   Lambeth Conference

1921   General Synod of the Church of England in Canada, Hamilton,
       Ontario
       • enacts deaconess canon

1924   General Synod, London, Ontario

1927   General Synod, Kingston, Ontario

1930   Lambeth Conference

1931   General Synod, Toronto, Ontario

1932   House of Bishops Committee on Women's Work formed

1934   General Synod, Montreal, Quebec

1935   House of Bishops Report on Women Workers in the Church

1943   General Synod, Toronto, Ontario
       • Report on Women's Work in the Church

1946   General Synod, Winnipeg, Manitoba
       • first women delegate attends General Synod

1947   Canadian Council of Churches Report on Women Workers

1948   Lambeth Conference

1949   General Synod, Halifax, Nova Scotia
       • Report on Women's Work in the Church

1952   General Synod, London, Ontario

1955   General Synod, Edmonton, Alberta
       • Report: Future Patterns of Women's Work in the Church

1958   Commission on Women's Work convened

1959   General Synod, St. Anne de Bellvue, Quebec
       • Report of the Committee on Women's Work in the
         Church

xii ◆ Beyond the Walled Garden

1962   General Synod, Kingston, Ontario
- Report of the Commission on the Status of Deaconesses
- Report of the Commission on the Training of Women
- Report of the Committee on Women's Work

1963   Church of England in Canada becomes Anglican Church of Canada

1965   Consultation on Women's Work (February 1965)
General Synod, Vancouver, British Columbia
- Report of the Committee on Women's Work
- Report of the Council on Full-Time Women Workers

1967   General Synod, Ottawa, Ontario
- Report of the Committee on Women's Work
- Sociological Analysis of Women Workers in the Church
- Primate's Commission on Women established

Stage Two (1968–1978)

1968   Lambeth Conference

1969   Commission on Women supports ordination of women to priesthood
General Synod, Sudbury, Ontario
- ordination of the first women as deacon
- Anglican Registered Church Workers Association (ARCWA) formed
- Dr. Helen Milton's Article on "The Ordination of Women to the Priesthood"
- Conference — Council for Full-Time Women Workers

1970   House of Bishops forms the Committee on the Wider Ordained Ministry
Primate convenes the Task Force on the Ordination of Women to the Priesthood

1971   Anglican Consultative Council at Limuru, Kenya (ACC-1)
- opens the door to women in the priesthood
General Synod, Niagara Falls, Ontario

1972   Majority and Minority Reports of the Primate's Task Force on the Ordination of Women to the Priesthood released

1973   General Synod, Regina, Saskatchewan
- votes to affirm the ordination of women to the priesthood in principle

Anglican Consultative Council, Perth, Australia (ACC-2)
- produces a report on women in the priesthood

1974   House of Bishops Meeting
        • discusses and studies issues around implementation of the
          ordination of women

1975   House of Bishops Meeting prior to General Synod
        General Synod, Quebec City, Quebec
        • reaffirms the principle of the ordination of women to
          the priesthood
        • motion to proceed with implementation of the
          ordination of women
        • motion to adopt a Conscience Clause
        September: *Manifesto on the Ordination of Women to the Priesthood*
        October: House of Bishops Meeting

1976   May: House of Bishops Meeting
        • agree to proceed with ordinations
        • conscience clause affirmation
        Anglican Consultative Council (ACC-3)
        November 30: first ordinations of women (6) to the presbyterate in the
        Anglican Church of Canada

1977   12 more ordinations of women to the priesthood

1978   Lambeth Conference

CHURCH OF ENGLAND

Stage One (1920–1967)

1920   Lambeth Conference
        Archbishop of Canterbury's Report on the Ministrations of Women
        League of the Church Militant established

1930   Lambeth Conference
        Society for the Equal Ministry of Men and Women in the Church
          (SEMWC) established
        Anglican Group for the Ordination of Women to the Historic Ministry
          of the Church (AGOW)

1931   Convocations of Canterbury and York discuss deaconesses

1932   Archbishop of Canterbury convenes Commission on the Ministry of
        Women

1935   Report of the Archbishop's Commission on the Ministry of Women

1941   Church Assembly — Archbishop's Report on the Ministry of Women

1944   Ordination of Deaconess Li Tim Oi in the Hong Kong diocese
        • ensuing correspondence between Hong Kong and the
          Archbishop of Canterbury

1945   Church Assembly
        • Report of the Committee on Training for Women's Church
          Work

1946   Inter-diocesan Certificate of Recognition (IDC) established by the
        Central Council for Women's Church Work

1948   Lambeth Conference
        • proposed Chinese Canon on the Ordination of Women to the
          Priesthood
        Church Assembly
        • Report on Women in the Church, by the Central Council for
          Women's Church Work (CCWCW)

1957   BBC Broadcast on the ordination of women

1958   Pamphlet on the Ordination of Women to the Historic Ministry of the
        Church (AGOW)

1960   Church Assembly
        • condemnation of BBC Broadcast

1962   Church Assembly
        • receives Archbishop's Commission Gender and Ministry
          report

1964   World Council of Churches Study on the Ordination of Women

1967   Church Assembly
        • receives Archbishop's Commission Women and Holy Orders
          report
        • Working Party on Women's Ministry established

Stage Two (1968–1978)

1968   Anglican-Methodist Commission report on Women and the Ordained
        Ministry
        Lambeth Conference

1969   Church Assembly
        • no discussion of Lambeth resolutions on women and the
          priesthood

1971   Anglican Consultative Council in Limuru, Kenya (ACC-1)
        • opens door to women in the priesthood

1972   Christian Howard's Report GS 104: "The Ordination of Women to the Priesthood: A Consultative Document Presented by the Advisory Council for the Church's Ministry (ACCM)"

1973   General Synod
- refers key motions to the dioceses

1975   General Synod
- affirms no objections to the ordination of women as priests and defeats a motion to implement such ordinations
GS 252 "The Ordination of Women: Report of the Standing Committee on the Reference to the Dioceses"

1976   GS Misc 53, "The Archbishop of Canterbury's Correspondence with Leaders of Other Churches on the Ordination of Women," 1976

1978   Lambeth Conference
General Synod defeats a motion to ask for G. S. Standing Committee to prepare legislation to proceed with removing legislative barriers to the ordination of women to the priesthood and episcopacy
GS Misc. 87, "The Ordination of Women: Arrangements for the 1978 Debate"
GS Misc. 87, "The Ordination of Women: Reports of the Anglican Orthodox Joint Doctrinal Commission, 1978"
GS 281, "Theology of Ordination"
GS Misc. 88 "The Ordination of Women: A Supplement to the Consultative Document GS 104, 1978"

List of Tables in Appendix

— Preface —

With Grace and Courage

Preface by Archbishop Edward W. Scott

I tend to approach things from an historical perspective and I have often wished that a book would be written about a particular development with which I have been involved. Occasionally, my wish has been fulfilled but sometimes when it is, I am dissatisfied with the contents of the book! This is NOT the case with *Beyond the Walled Garden: Anglican Women and the Priesthood.*

This book, about an extremely important decision made within the Anglican Communion, is far more comprehensive and far better researched than I would either have anticipated or dreamed possible! For this I give thanks to the author and to God. I hope that the care that has been taken in researching documents in many parts of the Communion and in undertaking oral history interviews with a wide range of persons who were involved in the process will become a model for many others who write about the Anglican Communion in the future.

As I read the manuscript, I realized that I was becoming much more intelligently aware of the breadth of what had taken place in the time span covered by the book and also of the significance of what had happened in particular provinces of the Communion on the Communion as a whole. The "bonds of affection" which hold the Anglican Communion together in spite of differences and tensions became clearly apparent. The author helps us to remember that history is a continuing reality — it does not stop, it has not stopped! We are encouraged to reflect upon and deepen our understanding of what has happened in relation to a particular concern. We are also challenged to give careful thought to things that still need to happen both in relation to this particular area of concern and also to other concerns which call out to be addressed. Wendy Fletcher-Marsh helps us to be more consciously aware of the dynamics of change within society and within the Anglican Communion, and thereby reducing the fear of change which often makes it difficult for us to respond to God's call.

As we read, we understand the very important part that "context" played in the process of making one of the most important changes that has ever been made in the life of the Anglican Communion. We recognize both the "general" context which affects the whole communion and also become aware of the influence of the "particular" contexts with which each Province grapples. These are important insights for any person who desires to understand the Anglican Communion and the dynamics of its life, because they are operative not only in relation to the issue being addressed but in virtually every facet of the life of the Communion.

I strongly urge Anglicans, and any others who would like to understand the Anglican Communion better, to read this book. It will enable them both to be better informed about how the Communion dealt with a particular issue of tremendous import for its future life and also to better understand the very nature of the Communion.

Even though there will be those who will not be particularly interested in all the detailed reports included, this careful reporting of details is important because it gives clear evidence of the extent and care with which research has been undertaken. It gives credibility to the process which was taking place and to the integrity with which the decision to ordain women to the priesthood was undertaken.

The credibility and integrity of the process adds great weight to the author's firm conviction — one that I share — that the decision was in fact made in the context of one of the very great prayers of the Church: that it might both perceive and know what it ought to do and that it have the grace and courage to enable it to do God's will. Both of these are required if difficult decisions are to be made.

I am sure that many of you, like me, share Wendy Fletcher-Marsh's hope: "May the Anglican Communion ever continue to pray this prayer!"

Edward W. Scott,
Primate of the Anglican Church of Canada, 1971–1986

An Episcopal Reflection

Preface by The Rt. Rev. Victoria Matthews

Beginning in 1976, the Anglican Church ordained women to the priesthood. The action caused an immediate change in the role of women in the Church and, to a surprising extent, a transformation of their historical identity. Priests celebrate the sacraments and are themselves a sacramental presence in the Christian assembly and in the wider community. What happens when women as well as men are ordained to the diaconate and priesthood?

First of all, there is a change in the perceived role and identity of women in society and nowhere more so than among women ourselves. Human beings come to know and understand themselves in part by recognizing themselves in others. When a woman recognizes not only a sister, but herself in a priest, something also happens in her understanding of God, Jesus Christ, the Holy Spirit and the Body of Christ. Women priests around the globe have opened new and different doors onto the sacred. God does not change, but perceptions of God certainly do.

In Canada and elsewhere, as the role and identity of Anglican women has changed, the Church also has changed. New doors opening onto sacred truths invite new and different light upon the mystery of the Godhead, transcendent and incarnate. Such new perceptions are both exciting and daunting for the Church.

It is tremendously important for the Body of Christ to have individuals who are able to help us understand historical developments as they unfold. Wendy Fletcher-Marsh has done just that in this overview and analysis of the decision making process and actions of the Church. She helps us to reflect on the significant roles played by those who hold Synodical power, by role models and those who represent advocacy groups. In her presentation of the events leading up to the decisions, the very distinct route taken by Canada becomes clear.

The range of recorded reactions by dioceses and bishops across the country also reveals the unique nature of the Canadian Church. It is worth noting how many bishops who either opposed or hesitated about the ordination of women, subsequently changed their minds. Even more telling is the change in liturgical language in recent Anglican prayer books. The future remains uncertain but the signs point to an increasingly inclusive description of the mystery of God in our prayers, hymns and proclamation.

Lastly, a word about the prophetic role of laywomen throughout the years of debate leading to and following upon the ordination of women. Each step has seen lay women present themselves as articulate advocates, and in some countries lobbyists, for the resolutions. Since the ordination of women, a significant voice has continued to be heard from the laity, especially progressive feminist theologians. The full importance of this aspect of women's ministry is a story that awaits its telling.

The Rt. Rev. Victoria Matthews
Bishop of the Credit Valley, Diocese of Toronto

Foreword and Acknowledgements

I began the research for this book several years ago. At that time, the situation with reference to the ordination of women within Anglicanism looked different than it does today; the Church of England and many member churches of the Anglican Communion had not moved to accept the ordination of women. Currently, the Church of England, a primary focus of this study, does ordain women to the diaconate and priesthood, as do a majority of Anglican provinces. Given the rapid change which has occurred during the period in which this study was researched and written, it is important for us to remember that this is an historical study which is being presented, rather than a contemporary commentary. The genre of twentieth century history runs the risk of being understood as journalism, rather than historical analysis. To clearly maintain the genre of critical history, the time frame under examination and the analysis are specifically limited to the period between 1920 and 1978. The history of the ordination of women in Anglicanism between 1978 and the present is a project with different aims and objectives than the one presented here.

I wrote this book for my church, that it might begin to know and understand its own story in new ways. I also produced this study for the larger academic community as an initial exploration into a previously untouched area of women's history. No historian writes history from a completely objective stance. As a historian, I have attempted to approach this subject and time period with objective eyes, employing the critical method of comparative and multi-factoral analysis and oral history, and I have struggled to bring a critical hermeneutic to bear on the data. As a woman who is ordained in the Anglican Church of Canada, I am also a subject by association in this study, with a clearly subjective bias about the place of the ordination of women in Christian history, and the valuable role which feminist theology has played in contemporary ecclesiastical life. Given the ground-breaking nature of the historical narrative provided, it is clear that one of the primary tasks of this study has been to document the narrative of an aspect of the history of women previously unknown. However, it is impossible to construct any historical narrative without also engaging in analysis. As such, *Beyond the Walled Garden* provides some initial analysis of the story of the ordination of women in both an intentional and an incidental way. It is my hope that these first generation findings will provide a seedbed for the later cross-fertilization of ideas and new interpretations of the material by other historians.

A study of this type is possible only with the support and input of many people. I would like to express my gratitude to those individuals who shared their time, wisdom and expertise with me as I compiled this study; to Dr. Thomas McIntire of Trinity college for his support — his guidance and enthusiasm were essential to the successful completion of this project; to all, more comprehensively listed in the bibliography, who shared their journeys through interview and those who shared their personal papers; to all archival staff, and especially the staff of the Archives and Library of the Anglican Church of Canada, the Church of England Records Centre, the Trustees of the Lambeth Palace Library, and the Sarah Fawcett Library; to those who shared the struggle — my mother, Joyce Fletcher, my aunts, Vera Robertson and Doris Day; Karen Ivey, Catherine Hutchman McWilliam, Theresa Corrigan-Holowitz, David Fletcher, and John and Betty Marsh; to my colleagues at Huron College for their constant encouragement and moral support; to Sandra Rice and Kathy Shaugnessy for their superb clerical assistance; to the publishers of artemis enterprises who see the importance of history affecting the lives and work of women and are willing to support it. Finally, I would like to thank my family, John, Joshua, Rachel, and Anna who lived with me through this project, every day and every hour. Their love, patience and trust gave me the will to finish and the courage to dream.

Wendy Fletcher-Marsh, London, Ontario

Anglican Synodical-Episcopal Polity

In order to navigate the complex waters of Anglican ecclesiastical polity, we must understand something about the form of Anglican governmental structures and decision-making processes. Anglicanism functions with a synodical-episcopal polity. What this means, in theory, is that Anglicanism has both bishops and synods with overlapping authority who together form the government of the church. Synods exist at the diocesan, provincial, and national levels in each province of the Anglican Communion.

A synod is an elected body with representatives from all parishes in the case of dioceses, and in the case of provincial and national synods, lay members and clerical members are elected as representatives of their diocesan synods. Synods are comprised of three houses: the House of Bishops, the House of Clergy and the House of Laity. On a regular basis, synods are held over which the senior bishop or bishops preside; it is in the synods that policy directions are adopted. The clergy members of synod can be drawn from either the category of priest or deacon, as the Anglican church's ordained ministry is the three-fold order of bishop, priest, and deacon.

The relationship between bishops and synods is a complex one. In theory, the diocesan bishop is the source of primary authority with Anglicanism. In a sense, his or her authority is absolute. However, by entering into a synodical arrangement, the diocesan bishop limits his or her own power, and becomes mutually accountable with the elected lay members of synod and the clergy of synod for the government of the church. Technically, a diocesan bishop can choose to override a decision of the synod. In practise, however, such a move is uncommon in Anglican life.

Some areas of action and policy are solely determined by the bishops. These areas of responsibility are unique to each national church and diocese, and are elaborated in the canons (ecclesiastical laws) of each diocesan, provincial or national synod. In the synod, members vote by houses; in other words, clergy, laity, and bishops vote as three separate groups. Percentage of support needed in each house for passing motions is determined by the content of the motions themselves — different areas need different levels of support (i.e. a simple majority, or two-thirds) and these particulars are again spelled out in the canons of the synod in question.

PART ONE
BACKGROUND TO CHANGE

Introduction:
Professions and Perspective

The ordination of women to the priesthood has been one of the most controversial issues to arise in Christian circles during the twentieth century. For Anglicans, this issue is not simply a matter of past history; for many it is an issue of ongoing debate. Although the admission of women to the threefold order of ministry has been on the Anglican mind in some form or another since 1920, the active decision-making processes by which ecclesiastical structures have attempted to make a formal decision on the admission of women to priesthood is a much more recent phenomenon. As of 1978, only four national churches were ordaining women as priests: Hong Kong, Canada, New Zealand, and the United States. As of March, 1994, nearly two-thirds of the provinces in the Anglican Communion (19 out of 29) were ordaining women to the priesthood and had women priests working in their midst, or had voted to proceed with such ordinations. The remaining ten provinces either had rejected the notion or had not yet made a final decision on the issue.

The Anglican Church of Canada and the Church of England represent two differing responses to the ordination of women up to 1978 — one national church which consciously chose the ordination of women and one national church which intentionally rejected the ordination of women. The Anglican Church of Canada was one of the first national churches in the Anglican Communion to ordain women to the priesthood. Women were admitted to the office of priest there for the first time on 30 November 1976. The decision to ordain women to the priesthood was preceded by the decision to admit women to the office of deacon in 1969, with the first formal diaconal ordination of a woman taking place late that year. The Church of England decided not to ordain women to the priesthood within a time frame which paralleled the decision-making process of the Anglican Church of Canada. Indeed, the Church of England did not decide to admit women to the office of deacon until 1985, with the first diaconal ordinations of women taking place in 1987. That church did not agree to ordain women as priests until 11 November 1992, 16 years after the Canadians.

The parameters in time explored here are set by two Lambeth Conferences. It was the Lambeth Conference of 1920 which formally raised the issue of the admission of women to the threefold order of ministry for the first time in the decision-making bodies of the Anglican Communion. By Lambeth 1930, women and the priesthood had been expressly named as an issue. It was at the Lambeth Conference of 1978 that the most volatile discussions took place, as Hong Kong, Canada, New Zealand and the United States had proceeded with the ordination of women to the priesthood, while many were still strongly opposed. It was at Lambeth 1978 that the bishops of the Communion agreed to live together in their disagreement over this issue, divided according to conscience but united in their commitment to each other.

The two Lambeth Conferences were central to this issue. Without the initiatives at the international level, it is conceivable that national discussion of the issue would have unfolded differently.

The period from 1920 to 1967 represents the first stage of this issue in the life of the Anglican Communion. During those years the issue was raised several times but no final decision was made about it. The period from 1968 to 1978 represents the second stage of this issue in the life of the Anglican Communion. During those years some decisions were made on the subject of the ordination of women to the priesthood at Lambeth. Interestingly these boundaries in time also reflect the rhythm of the historical processes of the two national churches chosen for examination. It was after the Lambeth Conference of 1920 that both churches began to grapple with the question of women and Holy Orders. It was the Lambeth Conference of 1978 that brought the issue to a close, at least as a decision-making process, in the Canadian church; Lambeth 1978 also heralded the defeat of a motion to ordain women in the Church of England.

There are two related questions of relevance here: why did the Anglican Church of Canada choose to ordain women as priests by 1978, and why did the Church of England not? An exploration of these questions will be realized through a consideration of several areas.

The situation in the Anglican Communion as a whole will be examined in chapter one. In chapter two, the relationship of women to ecclesiastical structures in the Anglican Church of Canada between 1920 and 1967 sets the stage for the drama of the 1970s. In chapter three, the actual decision-making process by which the Anglican Church of Canada chose to ordain women is explored. In the fourth chapter, a profile of all diocesan decision-making processes on the issue fleshes out the national profile provided in chapter three. Chapter five opens the door on the English story through an examination of the relationship of women and ecclesiastical structures between 1920 and 1967. In chapter six the process by which ordination is rejected in the 1970s is documented, and an in-depth analysis in chapter seven concludes the pictures of the English drama. An illuminating comparative conclusion in chapter eight weaves startling points of contrast and commonality in the Canadian and English situations.

ADMISSION OF WOMEN TO THE PROFESSIONS

The issue of the ordination of women is a phenomenon dependant on many factors. It was precipitated by radical shifts in the place of women in civil society in the western world. From the mid-nineteenth century social barriers against female employment began to weaken and the range of occupations and educational opportunities open to women widened.

By 1900 women had access to most professional careers in Canada at least in theory. In 1875 Mount Allison University in New Brunswick granted a Bachelor of Science degree to Grace Annie Lockhart. It was the first university in the British Commonwealth to graduate a woman. By the mid-nineteenth century, women began to be employed in public schools; by 1900 elementary school teaching in Canada was done almost predominantly by women. In 1880 Emily Howard Stowe was finally granted a license to practise medicine in Ontario. She had graduated from the New York Medical School in 1867 after being denied admission to the University of Toronto. Stowe's daughter, Emily, was the first woman to graduate in medicine in Canada, receiving her degree from the Toronto School of Medicine in 1883. In 1897 Clara Brett Martin was the first woman to be admitted to the Law Society of Upper Canada. In 1893 Caroline Louisa Josephine Wells graduated from the Royal College of Dental Surgeons of Ontario, the first Canadian woman to graduate from a dental college.

By the last quarter of the nineteenth century women in England were lobbying for equal access to education and employment. They met with some success. Opportunities in public school teaching provided white collar employment for women. In the 1880s, the 'lower ranks' of government civil service opened its doors to women. In 1919, a group of women formed the Women's Engineering Society in order to help women and girls who wanted to become engineers. Also in 1919, the Sex Disqualification Removal Act abolished many of the legal barriers which had previously prevented women from entering certain occupations. In the 1920s following the Act of 1919, the proportion of women in professional work in Britain rose sharply. Women had access to most professions in England only after the Act of 1919.

Early increases in the numbers of women in professions in both countries were short-lived phenomena. Between 1901 and 1980 there was an increase in the numbers of women in the Canadian labour force, in both real and percentage terms. During the same period, however, the numbers of women as a percentage of the professional labour force actually decreased from 42.5 percent to 41.3 percent.[1] Similarly while numbers of women as a percentage of the total enrollment in university undergraduate programs increased dramatically between 1920 (16 percent) and 1968 (35 percent), there was a significant decline in the numbers of women as a percentage of the total enrollment in post-graduate programs from 25 percent in 1920 to 18 percent in 1968.[2] Despite early gains in the professions for women in Britain in the 1920s, they soon levelled off and began a slight decline in the 1960s.[3] By 1975 the number of women in the major professions such as law, engineering, medicine, and government administration, was minuscule. For example in 1972 only 44 out of 3,281 (1.3 percent) university professors in England were woman, and over half of those were teaching at London University.[4] These statistics regarding women's participation in the labour force, higher education and the professions are an interesting parallel to the ecclesiastical situation. Recent studies demonstrate that women were a numerical majority in Anglicanism throughout the period under discussion, but not a proportional representation in the church's leadership. In this sense the ecclesiastical circumstance mirrored the reality of women in the larger societal context in both countries.

In both England and Canada, the issue of the ordination of women was discussed in the wake of major shifts in the accepted sphere of women's participation in society. Although it appears that significant proportional advances have not been made for women in the professions of either country, access at least in theory was granted prior to any decision in either country on the ordination of women. The Anglican Church was a latecomer to the idea of equal opportunity employment by gender.[5]

ORDINATION OF WOMEN IN A
CROSS-DENOMINATIONAL PERSPECTIVE

The ordination of women is an issue of cross-denominational significance. Throughout the twentieth century, largely as a by-product of women's changing position in civil society, all mainline Christian denominations have become aware of the need to respond to the issue of women as ordained persons.

While for most churches the ordination of women has been a twentieth-century issue, some Protestant denominations have never denied the possibility of women being set apart for leadership. At different times there have been Baptist, Methodist Episcopal, Methodist, Protestant, and Pentecostal women ministers leading congregations, although these women were always the exception to the rule. They were individual women, exceptional women who attained a position and status which their female peers did not share. In the Quaker tradition which has no specific 'ordained' ministry, there were women preachers from the 1650s onward, first in England and later with immigration also in North America. These exceptional cases stand out as atypical in the Christian world.

The gradual movement in most western societies to enfranchise women and open the doors of universities and professions to them precipitated a similar movement in Christianity. From the mid-nineteenth century onward, most Protestant denominations began to develop opportunities for paid work for women and at varying speeds began the process of lay enfranchisement. In most cases it was not until significant advancements were made in women's lay participation that access to the clerical establishment was granted.[6] The Anglican decision-making process on the ordination of women issue was part of an international, cross-denominational phenomenon moving in Christian institutions.

In 1970 the World Council of Churches collected data from 15 major denominational groupings on all seven continents in an attempt to document the global situation on denominational policy regarding the ordination of women at that time. 1970 is a crucial period as it falls in the active decision-making phases of both national churches examined here. Table 1 graphically depicts the global situation in 1970. As we can see on the graph, no Anglican churches ordained women in 1970. Also the Roman Catholic Church, the Eastern Orthodox Church, the Oriental Orthodox Church, the Independent churches and the Pentecostal Church did not ordain women at that time. The remaining eight Protestant categories did ordain women at least in some places. There were Baptists in Australia, West Europe, East Europe and North America who had an ordination policy which did not exclude women. Congregational churches in Africa, Australia, West Europe and North America likewise had moved to accept the full ministry of women. The Disciples' churches ordained women in Africa, Australia, West Europe and North America. The Lutheran Church ordained women in West Europe, East Europe and North America. The Methodists ordained women in all locations noted but East Europe. The Reformed Church ordained women on all seven continents. The United churches ordained women in Africa, Asia, West Europe, and North America. As of 1970, of the denominations surveyed, 72 churches ordained women and 143 did not. Also the Roman Catholic Church globally did not.

By the time the Anglicans began to make a decision on the ordination of women, many Protestant denominations had accepted women as ordained ministers.

Endnotes

1. Alison Prentice et al, eds., *Canadian Women: A History* (Toronto: Harcourt Brace Jovanovich 1988), Table A.15, p. 423.
2. Prentice, p. 326.
3. Christian Howard, "Women and the Professions," unpublished paper, 1975, p. 106. (ACCM/OW/3)
4. Howard, p. 111.
5. This study does not provide an analysis of the significant arena of women's voluntary labour. Although women's voluntary organizations were important in shaping attitudes and expectations around womanhood, they were not directly a part of the ordination question.
6. Rosemary Ruether and Rosemary Skinner Keller, eds., *Women and Religion in America* Vol.3 (San Francisco: Harper and Row, 1986), p. 337.

1
Division and Dialogue

The issue of the ordination of women in Canada and England unfolded within the context of the specific denominational group known as the Anglican Communion. The relationship of each of the national churches to the Communion, as well as the relationship of the provinces to each other, influenced how decisions were made on the issue of women's ordination to the priesthood in each case.

The Structure of the Communion

Anglicanism began as a distinct denominational grouping during the time of the Reformation. English Christianity pre-dated the formal evolution of the Anglican denomination from as early as the middle of the third century, although the actual point of origin is uncertain. By 1535, the Christian Church in England had formally separated from its Roman origin, and gave birth to the Church of England. Through the activity of British imperialism and colonization, from the sixteenth to the nineteenth centuries, the Church of England became the mother of what is now identified as the Anglican Communion. As of 1994, this is a group of twenty nine distinct provincial churches, of which the Anglican Church of Canada and the Church of England are members. The Church of England's status as mother of the Communion is not accompanied by any effectual power, except possibly that of example, esteem, and persuasion where some provinces are concerned.

This group of related provincial churches has referred to itself as the

Anglican Communion since the late nineteenth century; however, defining an Anglican identity is not a clear cut task. Although all Anglicans can point to the Church of England as the source of their life, all have moved in their own direction. An apt phrase currently used to describe the Anglican reality is "unity in diversity." In other words, the provinces of the Communion agree to live in relationship with each other but are not bound by common doctrine or practice. This diversity is extremely important in relation to the issue of the ordination of women, as it has allowed each province to make a decision for itself on the issue without any being bound by the conscience of the other. Although diversity is perhaps the most distinctive Anglican characteristic at this point in the Communion's history, there are common points of reference which have served as a focus for unity. Among these, the periodic Lambeth Conference has considerable unifying power.

The Lambeth Conference has brought together bishops of the Anglican Communion approximately once a decade since 1867. The purpose of these conferences originally was to provide some basis for communication among the provinces and some way of making and communicating authoritative pronouncements for the Anglican rule of life. Increasingly, it has been a focus of dialogue. In other words, the Lambeth Conference does not have any authority to make or enforce legislation in the provinces represented at it. As of 1994, Lambeth has served as a place where all of the bishops of the Communion can gather together and address key issues affecting the life of the Communion. While it does pass resolutions, it should be noted that these are not binding, and each province retains the right to respond to them, interpret them or implement them any way that it chooses. The ordination of women to the priesthood is just one issue which has been divisive and controversial at the Lambeth Conferences. The selection of the dates for this study demonstrates the significance of the Lambeth Conference to this issue. Without the agenda of the Lambeth Conferences, it is conceivable that national decision-making processes would have adopted a different timeline and character. From 1971, the Lambeth Conferences received support from the newly formed Anglican Consultative Council (ACC) another unifying power in the Communion. This Council is a consultative body made up of clergy, laity, and bishops, including some women, which studies and reports to Lambeth on significant issues, such as the ordination of women.

STAGE ONE: 1920 – 1967

In the first stage in the life of the Communion with regard to this issue, three Lambeth Conferences of significance took place. The actual issue of women's ordination to the presbyterate did not arise until 1930. The issue of deaconesses, however, raised the question of women in the three-fold order of ministry.

Lambeth 1920

At the Lambeth Conference of 1920, the issue of women's ministry as deaconesses arose. While deaconesses had served in the Church of England since 1861, and in some of the provincial churches from about the same time, ecclesiastical structures had not made any pronouncements on the nature of their life and work. It was generally felt that some guidelines needed to be instituted for this order by bishops and deaconesses alike. The 1920 conference devoted considerable attention to the topic of the Restoration of the Order of Deaconesses. A committee presented a report on the status of these women workers and made six recommendations defining the office, outlining its functions, and suggesting a form for "making deaconesses." Perhaps most significantly, it stressed that the office of deaconess was the one and only order of ministry for women to be recommended for recognition by the Anglican branch of the Catholic Church.[1] The recommendations of the committee with regard to deaconesses were passed as resolutions at the 1920 conference. Considerable confusion, however, still existed over the status of deaconesses. Some wondered whether the 1920 resolutions had created a Holy Order of deaconess similar to that of deacons. The specific conflict revolved around the wording of resolutions 47 and 48:

> Resolution 47: The time has come when, in the interests of the Church at large, and in particular of the development of the ministry of women, the diaconate of women should be restored formally and canonically, and should be recognized throughout the Anglican Communion.[2]

> Resolution 48: The order of deaconesses is for women the one and only order of the ministry which has the stamp of apostolic approval, and is for women the only order of ministry which we can recommend that our branch of the Catholic Church should recognize and use.[3]

The suggestion that the office of deaconess might be the same as the office of deacon caused considerable conflict; some bishops and clergy argued that women never had been and should not be allowed in Holy Orders in the Anglican Church.[4] They maintained that because women were insufficient for ordained ministry, the office of a deaconess should be clearly delineated and kept distinct from that of deacon.[5] The issue here was whether or not women could be admitted in any way to the threefold order of ministry. Some feared the concession that women were in a diaconal ministry would mean the "thin edge of the wedge" with regard to the other two orders of ministry.

At the Lambeth Conference of 1930, specific resolutions were made which put this tension to rest. Those who had argued that particular mention should be made that women were not in the same diaconal orders as men won their case. According to Resolution 67 of Lambeth 1930, the office of deaconess, the only order of ministry open to women was declared to be *sui generis*, or distinct to the female gender. Resolution 69 went on to say that the office was not equivalent to the male order of deacon.[6] A certain logical contradiction was present in these resolutions as they effectually established a fourth order of ministry while defending the threefold order of apostolic tradition.

Lambeth 1930

The 1930 Lambeth Conference also discussed the question of the ordination of women to the priesthood. The Lambeth 'Committee on the Ministry of the Church' reported that it had received deputations from two separate sources supporting the idea of women in the priesthood. The first was from the newly formed Anglican Group for the Ordination of Women (AGOW) in England. The second group who wrote the Committee was comprised of a small number of women who felt a vocation to priesthood. Unfortunately, these deputations were not preserved. The Committee on Ministry agreed that the matter warranted serious consideration but did not feel qualified to issue a statement on the subject. The Archbishop's Commission which produced the report "The Ministry of Women in 1935" was appointed in part for that purpose. In its report to the Lambeth Conference in 1930, the Committee on Ministry stated that changing gender roles in society did not constitute sufficient grounds for changing the tradition of an all male priesthood.[7]

The resolutions and discussions of the Lambeth Conferences of 1920 and 1930 are important to a discussion of the ordination of women to the priesthood as they reflect the mind of the episcopate at that time. The admission of women to the priesthood was not acceptable to the episcopate, and the admission of women to the diaconate was expressly rejected. It should be remembered, however, that at the global and provincial levels of the Anglican Communion, it was always stressed that the issue of women and the priesthood was a separate and distinct issue from women in the diaconate. Nevertheless, in every province which ordained women to the priesthood as of 1978, the issue of the ordination of women to the diaconate was decided positively before a decision was made on women and the presbyterate. The decisions of Lambeth did not put an end to tension around this issue. From 1920 onward, there were differing opinions about the 'nature' of the deaconess.

Lambeth 1948

The Lambeth Conference of 1948 raised the issue of the ordination of women as priests. In 1948, at the initiative of Bishop R. O. Hall who had previously ordained a woman to the priesthood 'uncanonically', the General Synod of the Church in China brought to Lambeth a proposed canon which it had received from the Diocese of South China (which included Hong Kong). It proposed that a twenty year experiment in the ordination of women to the priesthood be undertaken. The conference responded to that proposal by saying that it felt that such an experiment would be, "gravely against that tradition and order (Anglican) and would gravely affect the internal and external relations of the Anglican Communion."[8] The conference then reaffirmed its statement of 1930 that the office of deaconess was the one and only order of ministry open to women in the Anglican Church.

The bishops of Lambeth acknowledged that there were some people who wanted the question of women's ordination considered. Resolution 115 referred to the fact that the Archbishop's Commission in the Church of England, 1935, had concluded that the time had not come for further, formal consideration of the topic and Lambeth concurred with that conclusion.[9] Two things are interesting about this resolution. It is clear from the statement that in 1948, there were people such as members of the AGOW who wanted to talk about and were promoting the possibility of women in the priesthood. The highest levels of Church hierarchy, however, did not concur and therefore formal discussion did not happen. Secondly, Lambeth deferred to the findings of a Church of England Commission. This indicates the extent to which the mother church was more than just primus inter pares in the Communion. In a very real sense, the inclinations of the Church of England at that stage still set agenda and determined direction for the whole Communion. By 1978 that had changed.

The Lambeth Conference of 1958 did not raise the question of women and Holy Orders.

STAGE TWO: 1968 – 1978

Lambeth 1968

The Lambeth Conference of 1968 was the last conference to be held before women were constitutionally ordained to the priesthood in the Anglican Communion. At that conference, such ordinations were not sanctioned, nor were they forbidden, although Lambeth had no authority to "forbid" in any case. The ordination of women to both the priesthood and to the diaconate were discussed in 1968, and Lambeth passed five resolutions on the subject of women and Holy Orders.

The Lambeth Conference of 1968 was a pivotal turning point in Anglican deliberations on the topic. Why did the Lambeth Conference discuss and vote on the ordination of women to the priesthood in 1968?

The work of the Lambeth Conference is supported by a series of committees. The Committee on Ministry was responsible for monitoring and reporting on important issues in preparation for the formulation of the agenda of each conference. It named the topic of women and Holy Orders. The issue of women and Holy Orders was not new to Lambeth. From 1920 Anglican bishops were aware of the issue. Some arguments can therefore be made for the idea that simply the time had come to resolve the issue at the international level.[10] The specific catalyst, however, appears to have been related to the discussions held by the Church of England.

The Church of England report on "Women and Holy Orders" published in 1966 and the report on Women in Ministry produced in 1968 by a Church of England working party on the place of women in the work of the church, and a preparatory essay by English scholar, Alan Richardson, were three primary foci for the discussions of the issue by the specific Lambeth conference committee which reported to the larger body on the issue. The Committee on Ministry reported to Lambeth that it found, "no conclusive theological reasons for withholding the ordination of women to the priesthood as such."[11] In its report the committee stated that the changing place of women in society demanded that the church discuss the issue of the inclusion of women in the ordained ministry.[12] The committee recommended the discussion of women in the diaconate and the priesthood.

The impetus for these discussions then came from an awareness by bishops who participated in Lambeth that they lived in a rapidly changing world. Also the role of the English church appears to have been formative. Although the English church had not itself made a decision on the issue, it had discussed it a year earlier at its Church Assembly in 1967. As such it had reference materials readily available. The formal decision-making process of the Church of England itself did not begin until Lambeth asked all provinces for a decision.

With Resolution 32, Lambeth 1968 reversed the position taken in 1930 on women in the diaconate. By a vote of 221 for and 183 against, Lambeth declared that women who had been made deaconesses through an episcopal laying on of hands should be declared to be within the diaconate.[13] With this resolution, the bishops at Lambeth opened the threefold order of ministry to women for the first time. It did not settle the question of the admission of women to the other two orders.

At the conclusion of the debates in 1968, it was agreed that there were no conclusive theological arguments for or against the ordination of women to the priesthood. In other words, the arguments on either side were insufficiently strong to sway the majority of opinion. Resolutions 35, 36 and 37 were passed. The resolutions asked all of the provinces to study the issue and to then report their conclusions to the newly created Anglican Consultative Council (ACC), which would meet for the first time in Limuru, Kenya in 1971. The council was formed to be a body for consultation and included laity, clergy and bishops from all provinces of the Communion. The Anglican Consultative Council was asked to initiate conversations with other denominations, both those who ordained women and those who did not, and then to distribute its findings throughout the Communion. The bishops at Lambeth then recommended that any national or regional church or province which was considering such ordinations should seek the advice of the ACC before acting.[14] Hong Kong was the only diocese in such a position.

In the Lambeth report on "Renewal in Ministry," an interesting comment was made from the deliberations of the bishops:

> The tradition flowing from the early Fathers and the medieval Church, that a woman is incapable of receiving Holy Orders, appears to reflect biological assumptions about the nature of men and women which have been generally discarded today. If the ancient and medieval assumptions about the social role and inferior status of women are no longer accepted, the appeal to tradition is virtually reduced to the observation that there happens to be no precedent for ordaining women priests.[15]

The Lambeth Conference recognized that the world view which demanded the exclusion of women from Holy Orders reflected an ideology which was no longer held as valid. Such a recognition demanded an extensive re-thinking of theological assumptions around the nature of God, men, women and their relationships to each other.

In a sense discussion on the issue had only just begun in 1968, and yet clear directives were laid out for further action in individual provinces. These directives were carried out by those who ordained women in this second stage, and most notably by the Anglican Church of Canada. The Anglican Church of Canada responded to the request of Lambeth to study the question. That study of the question led relatively quickly to the actual ordinations of Canada's first women priests. Without the initiative of Lambeth in raising this as an issue for study, these ordinations might never have happened at the point in history that they did. The request for study by Lambeth 1968 opened a door through which the Canadian Church chose to walk.

Anglican Consultative Council (ACC), 1971

The meeting of the Anglican Consultative Council at Limuru in 1971 was perhaps more crucial than Lambeth 1968 in the decision-making processes of those first four provinces who agreed to proceed with the ordination of women to the priesthood. Meeting in 1971, the ACC received reports that eight provinces had begun a study on the Lambeth Conference request concerning the ordination of women, but no formal decisions were received. The remaining nineteen provinces did not give a response. It also received through the Council of South-East Asia (a body which represented the Anglican bishops and people from all dioceses in South-East Asia), a communication from the Bishop of Hong Kong who, following the approval by his dioc-

esan synod of the principle of the ordination of women to the priesthood, wanted to ordain two women to the priesthood.

After lengthy discussion, the ACC passed two resolutions. As a general response to the issue, it was agreed that many churches felt that this
was an urgent matter. As such, all provinces of the Communion should
be encouraged to study the issue and report their views to the next ACC
which would meet in 1973.[16] In a more specific motion the ACC responded to the request for direction from the Bishop of Hong Kong,
Gilbert Baker, saying that his action and the action of any other bishop
who was moving forward with the approval of his Synod and Province would be acceptable to the Anglican Consultative Council. Further, the Council stated that it would encourage all other provinces to
remain in communion with those dioceses which might ordain women.
This motion was passed by a very small majority, with 24 in favour and
22 opposed.[17]

Ordinations in Hong Kong

The Bishop of Hong Kong did not wait until the next ACC meeting to
take further action. That same year, 1971, he ordained two women to
the priesthood. In the autumn of 1969, the Bishop of Hong Kong, Baker,
set up a working party to study the matter in his diocese. Two parishes
and the Women's Service League put forward a resolution to the diocesan synod which asked for the ordination of women to the presbyterate,
and the motion was remitted to parishes for their opinion. When the
Synod met again in January of 1970 it found that only one parish in the
diocese was opposed. The synod voted overwhelmingly in favour of the
principle of ordaining women to the priesthood.

Before action was taken, the matter was referred to the Bishops of
South East Asia and through them to the Anglican Consultative Council. Baker felt that he had been encouraged by implication through the
resolutions of the ACC; the members of the Council of the Church of
South East Asia did not agree. They refrained from commenting until
after the opinions of the Communion had been more widely received in
1973. The clerical delegates on the Council of the Church of South-East
Asia had decided unanimously through an earlier meeting to oppose the
ordination of women to the priesthood. The original motion in the diocese of Hong Kong came from the 'grassroots'. The idea was then supported by all but one parish.[18] In that unique situation, bishop, priests
and laity were of one mind on the subject.

Despite the opposition expressed by his provincial council, Baker followed the common conscience of his diocese and decided to ordain two women. On Advent Sunday, 1971, he ordained Jane Hwang, a native Chinese woman educated in China and the United States, and Joyce Bennet, an English CMS missionary, to the priesthood. In his charge to the Hong Kong diocesan synod in November of that year, he had defended his decision with the following words:

> If humanity is to be fully represented before God in the priesthood it is logical to suppose that the ministry which is not limited to people of one tribe or race should not be limited to one sex.... Christ himself raised the whole status of women by the way in which he talked with them naturally and on equal terms.... Christianity has had a profound influence on the emancipation of women, not least in China.... My hope is that Hong Kong will present to the Church some living experience of women in the priesthood so that others will be able to base their studies on something more than mere speculation. Someone has to make a start, and it may be that because of our peculiar position as the only active diocese in the Chung Hua Sheng Kung Hui, God is enabling us to act where others might find it difficult ...[our action] must be determined first by the pastoral needs of the Church in Hong Kong. What others think, though not unimportant, comes second.[19]

This lengthy quote serves to give some sense of the mindset of the man who, second only after his diocesan predecessor, was the first to break with long established tradition and ordain women to the priesthood. Baker was willing to act on his authority as a diocesan bishop in isolation from provincial approval. This act distinguished the actions of Hong Kong from the processes by which women were ordained in Canada, New Zealand, and the United States. In the other three provinces, provincial approval preceded the act of ordination, with the exception of the irregular ordinations in the Episcopal Church of the United States of America in 1974.

Baker argued that the action which he took was within the Canons and Constitution of the diocese, which protected the ultimate authority of the diocesan bishop.[20] He had waited until after Lambeth 1968 and until after the ACC of 1971. He then acted according to his own conscience and his perception of the pastoral needs of his diocese.

Anglican Consultative Council (ACC), 1973

In 1973, the Anglican Consultative Council met again, this time in Dublin. At that meeting, it was noted that the Bishop of Hong Kong had ordained two women to the priesthood and that no Church or Province had ceased to be in communion with that diocese. While not all agreed with the action, all respected Baker's right to act after Limuru 1971.[21]

Several other reports were received by the ACC at Dublin. The churches of the provinces of Burma, New Zealand, and Canada reported that they had approved the ordination of women in principle. The Church of England, the Church of Wales, the Episcopal Church in the USA and the Church of England in Australia reported that preliminary action on the matter had been taken and final action was pending. The South Pacific Council and the Province of Central Africa indicated that it would not be opportune to take action in their areas. The South Pacific felt that most of its people were not ready to accept women as priests, while Central Africa did not feel the time was right to proceed with any proposal. The remaining provinces did not report to the ACC.

After discussing these reports, the ACC passed three resolutions. First, the ACC agreed to recommend that no break in the Communion should be caused by one or more of its autonomous provinces proceeding with the ordination of women (50 in favour, two against, with three abstentions). Secondly, the ACC acknowledged that any decision on women's ordination would have important ecumenical repercussions, but that issues of ecumenism should not be determinative. The Anglican Communion had to make up its own mind and act according to its own conscience (54 in favour, 1 against, with no abstentions). Finally the ACC requested that all provinces which had not responded to the request for an opinion on the matter produce one by the meeting of the ACC in Perth, 1975.[22] The next Council actually did not meet until 1976 in Trinidad.

Anglican Consultative Council (ACC), 1976

When it met in Trinidad in 1976, the Anglican Consultative Council prepared a report on the ordination of women to the priesthood. The report did not debate the issue. Those gathered at Trinidad felt that the Communion should face what was actually happening with regard to the issue, rather than continue to debate it. The report noted that there had been considerable movement on the issue and then discussed that movement. It found:

- that one diocese had ordained women (Hong Kong),
- that nine provinces (Anglican Church of Canada, Church of England, Episcopal Church in Scotland, Church of Wales, Church of the Province of the Indian Ocean, Church of the Province of New Zealand, Episcopal Church of the USA, Church of Ireland and the Church of South India) had approved the ordination of women to the priesthood in principle,
- seven provinces had taken some preliminary action but had not yet made a decision (including the Church of the Province of Southern Africa, Episcopal Synod of the Province of Central Africa, Church of the Province of the West Indies, the Anglican Church of Australia, Church of the Province of Burma, Church of the Province of West Africa, Church of the Province of Kenya),
- that four provinces had decided against it (Council of the Church of East Asia, the Church of Ceylon, Japan Holy Catholic Church, Episcopal Church of Brazil),
- that the South India Synod declared men and women eligible for ordained ministry.[23]

The ACC concluded from these reports that there was an increasing acceptance of the principle that women might be ordained to the priesthood, although opinions against were still strongly held by some. Again, all members of the Anglican Communion were urged to continue in dialogue, fellowship and communion with one another.

All three sessions of the Anglican Consultative Council which met up to 1976 were primarily concerned with maintaining unity in a conflicted situation. The extent to which the ACC actually debated the issue and made theological pronouncements was limited. The Communion was sufficiently divided on the subject that different members were moving in different directions. The key issue then became, how do we remain unified in the midst of such diverse opinion and action? The ordination of women to the priesthood was accepted 'in the doing.' Once it had been done, it was dealt with as something which was *fait accompli*.

After the ACC met in Trinidad in 1976, three more provinces proceeded with the ordination of women to the priesthood. The first of these was the Anglican Church of Canada (1976), the second was the Protestant Episcopal Church in the U.S.A. (1977), and the third was the Church of the Province of New Zealand (1977).

Episcopal Church in the USA

The most striking aspect of the process by which the Episcopal Church in the USA decided to ordain women to the priesthood is its uniqueness. It was glaringly different from the decision-making processes in Canada and Hong Kong. The words of an American historian on this topic reflect this difference, "Canadian women accepted as gift what American women demanded as right."[24] While the implications of this comment for Canadian women are worthy of debate, it does make an important statement about the relationship between the decision-making process and women. From 1970 onward there was an overt and organized lobby by organized women's groups for the ordination of women to the priesthood in the Episcopal Church in the USA. Historians such as Suzanne Hiatt have argued that without this organized, and in some ways external, pressure a decision to ordain women would not have been made in 1977. However one chooses to interpret the process, one thing was clear: there was a great deal of tension involved in the process and accompanying the outcome in 1977.

It was in 1970 that the Episcopal Church in the USA admitted women to the diaconate. This decision followed on the heels of the resolutions of the Lambeth Conference of 1968. At the same General Convention, however, a motion was defeated which would have admitted women to the priesthood and episcopacy.[25] While the first motion came slightly after the decision of the Canadian church in 1969 to permit the ordination of women as deacons, this second motion dealt with material that Canadians were only beginning to discuss. The second motion demonstrates the fact that there were people who had been discussing and planning for the ordination of women to the priesthood, but that the general mind was not prepared for it. While the General Convention was in session, the Episcopal Women's Triennial, a women's caucus, was also meeting. The Triennial, which had no legislative power, voted 222–45 in favour of the ordination of women to all three orders of ministry.[26]

After the meeting of the Anglican Consultative Council in 1971, the Episcopal Women's Caucus, which also included male clergy, laymen and bishops, was formed, "to actualize the full participation of women at all levels of ministry and decision-making in the Church." This group was comprised of deacons, lay women, and seminarians. The Master of Divinity program at the Episcopal Divinity School in Cambridge, Massachusetts opened its doors to women in 1958. This group chose the issue of women's ordination to the priesthood as its immediate priority.[27] In

1972, a House of Bishops meeting took a poll favourable to women's ordination (74-61, with five abstentions).[28] That body could not admit women to the priesthood without the concurrence of the General Convention.

By the time of the 1973 General Convention, more organization was evident on both sides of the women's ordination issue. A motion to ordain women was again defeated in the House of Deputies: Clergy: 50 yes, 43 no, 20 divided; Lay: 49 yes, 37 no with 26 divided.[29] It was therefore not passed on to the House of Bishops. Historians have attributed this failure to pass the motion in 1973 to three things. First, those who supported the idea had seriously underestimated the growth of the opposition during the three years since 1970. Second, the issue was not a central concern of the institutional church. Third, it was felt that ordaining women would be "more trouble" than not ordaining women.[30]

By 1976 this attitude had apparently changed. At the 1976 Convention, the House of Bishops voted in favour of the canonical change which made ordination canons equally applicable to men and women. The House of Deputies agreed with this move, albeit by a narrow margin; 58 clerical votes and 57 lay votes were needed for the canonical change to be made. The margin of affirmative votes was two clergy and seven lay votes.[31] Historian Suzanne Hiatt argued that faced with the same questions in 1976, the delegates decided it would mean more trouble not to ordain women. Seven months before the General Convention, a New York Times article written in February, 1976 noted that the priesthood and the Book of Common Prayer, "have been crucial in shaping the way Episcopalians walk the middle road between Roman Catholicism and Protestantism. The General Convention delegates (in September) will be asking to what extent these two elements of the church must be altered to meet new conditions."[32]

Why did the institutional church change its mind between 1973 and 1976? Historians argue that this change was due in large measure to the actions of women working together as an active lobby group. Meeting in February 1974, the Episcopal Women's Caucus agreed to split into three smaller groups which would each tackle a different aspect of the issue. These three groups reflected three different opinions that were present within the Caucus on how best to handle the issue. One group focused on educating the church to women's issues and sexism, which was the traditional work of the Caucus. A second group decided to focus specifically on the upcoming 1976 convention and to build a national grassroots network. This group evolved into the National Coalition for the Ordination of Women to the Priesthood and Episcopacy. The third group, which evolved into Women for Ordination Now (WON), "decided that educational efforts and political organizing were insufficient either for their own lives in answering their calls or in forcing the Episcopal Church to recognize this urgency and importance of women priests in its clergy."[33]

It was the third group which sought immediate ordinations and as a result became the most famous of the three. Throughout the spring of 1974, several women deacons pursued ordination with little progress. Their cause received a "shot in the arm" in June. Dr. Charles Willie, a trustee of the Episcopal Divinity School in Cambridge preached a sermon in New York calling for, "the immediate ordination of women priests by any brave bishops who could be found."[34]

Several bishops responded to these pleas and agreed to be part of an ordination service. There were about thirty women deacons at the time; 11 chose to participate in the service. The ordinations were held on 29 July, 1974, the feasts of Saints Mary and Martha of Bethany, at the Church of the Advocate in Philadelphia. The three ordaining bishops were all retired; two were not from the diocese of Philadelphia, and Robert DeWitt was the retired bishop of Philadelphia.[35] In an open letter to the church as to why they were proceeding with these uncanonical ordinations, the women said:

> We are certain that the church needs women in the priesthood to be true to the gospel understanding of human unity in Christ. Our primary motivation is to begin to free priesthood from the bondage it suffers as long as it is characterized by categorical exclusion of persons on the basis of sex. We do not feel we are 'hurting the cause', for the 'cause' is not merely to admit a few token women to the 'privilege' of priesthood. We must rather reaffirm and recover the universality of Christ's ministry as symbolized in that order.[36]

The three bishops gave their motivation as, "believing that a dramatic act of obedience to the Spirit would most clearly present to the Church the urgency of the question."[37]

The ordinations were immediately condemned by the church's hierarchy. They were called irregular by the American House of Bishops as the bishops who ordained the women did not have the permission of the diocesan bishop in Philadelphia, nor did any of the women have the permission of their bishops or standing committees. The House of Bishops met in an emergency session two weeks later at Chicago's O'Hare Airport and declared the ordinations not only irregular but invalid. Presiding Bishop John Allin concluded that, "the ladies are indeed not priests."[38] The ordinations in Philadelphia were followed by another set in Washington, D.C. that same year. Despite the declaration of invalidity, the women continued to function in their priestly ministries.

The orders of these first American women in the priesthood were regularized in 1976 after the decision by the General Convention to allow women as priests. The first regular ordinations of women to the priesthood in the Episcopal Church of the USA took place in January, 1977.

The work of the three sub-groups of the original Women's Caucus continued between 1974 and 1976. The third shifted its focus to supporting the newly ordained women and was often in conflict with the second which focused only on the vote scheduled for 1976 through education at the 'grassroots.' This National Coalition for the Ordination of Women to the Priesthood and Episcopacy worked toward canonical and constitutional change, which Women's Ordination Now (WON, the third group) resented as they felt that the debate should be a dead issue as women priests were already a reality.[39]

The historians who have written on this subject so far, credit the organized activity of the women with breaking down the barriers which stood in the way of women's ordination. It is impossible to determine in retrospect whether the necessary canonical change would have passed in 1976 without the actions of the women, particularly the uncanonical ordinations. What can be said is that the organized actions of women were an integral and major aspect in the decision narrowly made in 1976 to allow for the ordinations of women to the priesthood and episcopacy in ECUSA.

Church of The Province of New Zealand

The Church of the Province of New Zealand was the fourth church to ordain women to the priesthood during the stage under examination here. The bill which allowed the ordination of women to the priesthood was passed by the General Synod in March, 1974. The procedural rules of the synod required that, after this passage, the bill should be submitted again to the diocese before a final decision was made on the matter at the next General Synod. At the General Synod of May 1976, the bill was again passed, but after the passage it was required that the church wait a year before implementing the bill. That year of waiting was to allow for the possibility of an appeal which could be made to a Tribunal, established by an Act of Parliament in 1928. In November 1977, the Tribunal heard an appeal which was dismissed by more than the required two-thirds majority. Within a month the church proceeded with its first ordinations. By December 1977, there were five women ordained to the priesthood: Jean Brookes, Wendy Goldie, Heather Brunton, Cherie Baker, and Rosemary Russell.[40]

Some contend that the Church of New Zealand resembled the Canadian church in so far as key leaders demonstrated openness and support for the matter. As in Canada, the ordination of women to the priesthood was not raised as an issue until after the Lambeth Conference of 1968. It has been argued that while the Church in New Zealand is generally affirming of human sexuality and advocates an equality of opportunity for gender in its constitution and synod, it has remained an essentially male-dominated institution. Most members of synods, both clergy and lay are male, and most committees of the church are still dominated by a predominantly male membership and viewpoint.[41]

From this brief profile there is evidence that the processes by which different provinces decided to ordain women to the priesthood were highly individual. The character of each process was shaped by the constitutional structure, the attitudes of individuals, and the cultural methods of its own situation. Nonetheless, the processes were all connected to the rhythm and actions of the larger Anglican container within which they found themselves.

Lambeth 1978

When the Lambeth Conference met in 1978 it was confronted by a Communion which was strongly divided in opinion and action on the ordination of women to the priesthood. It was *fait accompli* in four provinces but not in 23 others, some of whom passionately rejected it. The threat of actual division within the Communion was a real one. Because of this, it was the most pressing issue in the hearts and minds of many of the gathered bishops. Ultimately, however, the desire for unity was stronger than the division of opinion and a way forward to the future together was realized.

Two resolutions, numbers 21 and 22, were passed in 1978. Resolution 21 dealt with women in the priesthood. It acknowledged that since the Lambeth Conference of 1968, four provinces had ordained women as priests, while others were still in the process of making a decision and others had rejected the idea. It acknowledged that there was pain on both sides of the issue which the bishops had a primary responsibility to help heal. It encouraged all members of the Communion to remain in dialogue with one another, directing the Anglican Consultative Council to use its resources to encourage dialogue between provinces and as far as possible in ecumenical relations with churches outside of the Communion.

The Conference declared its acceptance of those provinces that did ordain women as well as those that did not. It acknowledged that the Roman Catholic, Orthodox and Old Catholic churches might be disappointed by the acceptance of the ordination of women, but that the Anglican Church was reflecting its heritage as a group which was bound together by the principle of diversity in a unity of faith. It affirmed that those bishops and churches which participated in ordaining women believed that such ordinations were a part of the historic ministry of the church, and expressed hope that ongoing ecumenical dialogue could be maintained. Finally, it was urged that further discussion on this issue should take place in the larger context of theological discussions on ministry and priesthood.[42]

In Resolution 22, the question of the consecration of women to the episcopate was raised. It recommended that such consecrations be undertaken only with the full support of the dioceses involved, "lest the bishop's office should become a cause of disunity instead of a focus of unity."[43] It was not until the Lambeth Conference of 1988 that a request was made for an Archbishop's Commission on the subject.[44]

Between the years 1920 and 1978 the issue of the inclusion of women in the threefold order of ministry came to life in the Anglican Communion. As early as 1930 and more directly in 1948, 1968 and 1978, the specific issue of the ordination of women to the presbyterate was an ongoing struggle for the bishops of Lambeth. While Lambeth itself did not make universal decisions on the subject, its invitation to study the question in 1968 opened the door which moves continually wider. A movement toward the ordination of women to the priesthood within Anglicanism was begun in 1968. One by one, Anglican churches have moved to adopt such ordinations, while some have continued to resist.

Endnotes

1. *Lambeth Conference Reports and Resolutions 1897 to 1930, London,* 1949, pp. 177–179.
2. Underlining is added for emphasis here.
3. *Lambeth Conference Reports and Resolutions 1897 to 1930, London,* 1949, p. 78.
4. These sentiments were recorded by the local press. For example, *The Guardian,* 5.5.21.
5. Lambeth, p. 181.
6. Lambeth, pp. 60–61.
7. *Lambeth Conference Papers,* LC 114 (1920), p. 208.
8. Roger Coleman, ed. *Resolutions of the Lambeth Conference 1867-1988,* Toronto, 1992, p. 119.
9. Coleman, p. 120.
10. Oral history interview with Archbishop Edward Scott, 29 January 1993. Archbishop Scott thought that the bishops simply believed that the time has come to resolve the issue.
11. GS 104, p. 2. GS 104 is the title of a numbered document produced by the General Synod of the Church of England.
12. *Lambeth Conference, 1968 , Preparatory Essays,* p. 295.
13. Coleman, p. 163.
14. Coleman, resolutions 34-37, pp. 163–4.
15. *Lambeth Report 1968,* "Section on Renewal and Ministry," pp. 106–7.
16. Report of Actions, p. 2 in Scott Papers (M101).
17. Report of Actions, p. 3 in Scott Papers (M101).
18. *Hong Kong Diocesan Synod Journal,* 1971, p. 6.
19. Excerpt from Bishop's Charge, *Hong Kong Diocesan Synod Journal,* 1971, p. 8.
20. GS 254, Appendix IX, p. 2.
21. ACC-2 Report, 1973, p. 39.
22. ACC-2 Report, 1973, p. 41.
23. ACC-3 Report, "Ordination of Women to the Priesthood", 1975, pp. 45–46.
24. Suzanne Hiatt, "How We Brought the Good News from Graymoor to Miineapoli-An Episcopal Paradigm" in *Journal of Ecumenical Studies* 20:4, Fall 1983.
25. R. Ruether, McLaughlin, eds., *Women of Spirit (Female Leadership in the Jewish and Christian Traditions),* New York, 1979, p. 358.
26. Mary S,Donovan, *Women Priests in the Episcopal Church: The Experience of the First Decade,* Cinncinnati, 1988, p. 6.
27. Ruether, p. 359.
28. John Howe, *Highways and Hedges: Anglicanism and the Universal Church,* Toronto, p. 229.
29. Howe, p. 229. The motion had also been defeated in the House of Deputies in 1970. In that House, a divided vote counts as a vote against. Each diocese has one clergy and one lay vote. Each diocesan delegation consists of four clergy and four laity. If clergy and laity are divided three to one, then the majority control the vote. If they are divided two to two, the vote counts as a negative vote.
30. Hiatt, p. 579 and Heather Huyck, "Indelible Change, Women Priests in the Episcopal Church", in *Historical Magazine of the Protestant Episcopal Church,* V.L1,#4, Dec.1982, p. 386.
31. Howe (1990) p.313. Clergy: 60, yes and 39, no, with 15 divided; laity: 64, yes and 36, no. with 13 divided.

32. *New York Times*, Feb.7, 1979, 48:1.
33. Huyck, p. 390.
34. Hiatt, p. 580.
35. Huyck, p. 391. Ordained to the priesthood were Merrill Bittner, Alla Bozarth-Campbell, Alison Cheek, Emily Hewitt, Carter Heyward, Suzanne Hiatt, Marie Moorefield, Jeanette Picard, Betty Schiess, Katrina Swanson, and Nancy Witlig. A fourth bishop participated but did not ordain any of the women. The bishops who ordained were Daniel Corrigan, Robert DeWitt, and Edward R. Welles II.
36. Donovan, p. 8.
37. Donovan, p. 8.
38. Huyck, p. 391. The vote declaring invalidity was 129 votes to 9, with 8 abstentions.
39. Hiatt, p. 581.
40. Howe, p. 314. These names were collected by me from New Zealand by telephone and facsimile.
41. Janet Crawford, "Attitudes to Female Sexuality in the Anglican Church in New Zealand", in *Women, Religion, and Sexuality*, WCC, 1990, p. 257.
42. Coleman, pp. 186–7.
43. Coleman, p. 188.
44. Coleman, p. 193.

PART TWO
THE CANADIAN
REVOLUTION SUCCEEDS

2

Crisis and Women's Work

The story of the Anglican Church of Canada's active decision-making process on the ordination of women is confined to the period between the Lambeth Conference of 1968 and the Lambeth Conference in 1978. However, the period prior to 1968 provides the backdrop against which the ordination question was debated and resolved.

WOMEN AND THE ECCLESIASTICAL STRUCTURES IN THE ANGLICAN TRADITION OF CANADA, 1920 – 1967

Between 1920 and 1967, women were not allowed to participate in the traditional forms of ministry as defined by ordination in Canadian Anglicanism. Women who wanted to serve the church as paid employees often found themselves serving in ministries which were a creative response to the pastoral and social needs of different areas of the country. They fashioned outreach ministries in places where the church had chosen not to involve itself or where clergy would not serve. Paid women's ministry in twentieth-century Anglicanism gradually came to be characterized in no small measure by the willingness of women to work where no one else would, on the fringes of society.

The backdrop to the active phase of Canadian decision-making which began in 1968 is comprised of the story of the place and role of women; the story of those who served as deaconesses and bishop's messengers is of particular relevance, as it was from that group that the first women were ordained to the priesthood. The backdrop is further illuminated by a consideration of the attitudes toward the ministry of women promoted by the predominantly male hierarchy of the ecclesiastical structure, and the findings of those committees which studied the place and circumstances of paid full-time workers in the church.

GENERAL SYNOD 1921

When the Lambeth Conferences of 1920 and 1930 asked member churches to report decisions of Lambeth in their national settings, the Canadian church complied, and what emerged from the reporting was the adoption of parallel ecclesiastical legislation.

In 1921 at its ninth session, the General Synod in Canada enacted a Deaconess Canon to govern the participation of deaconesses in the church. After the example of the Church of England, which ordained its first deaconess in the diocese of London in 1861, there were women serving in the Canadian church as deaconesses from the late nineteenth century onward. In 1893, Canadian Anglican Evangelicals established a home for the education and training of women who wanted to serve in the church as deaconesses. The impetus for this home, known as the Church of England Deaconess and Missionary Training home until 1956 came from a group of Toronto Evangelicals who wanted to offer women an opportunity for service in the church other than as female religious.[1] From 1930 the Home was known informally as the Anglican Women's Training College (AWTC). This name was formally adopted in 1956. Although this home was in existence under the direction of Miss Sybil Wilson from 1893, the decision-making bodies of the church did not formally address the existence and work of the deaconess until after the Lambeth Conference of 1920 had done so and asked that its member churches also standardize the office of the deaconess.

The deaconess canon passed at that 1921 General Synod of the Church of England in Canada meeting at Hamilton, Ontario, reflected the basic ideas of Lambeth. It stated that the ministry of the deaconess was one of "bodily and spiritual succour, especially to women," for which women would be set apart through the laying on of hands by a bishop, after receiving at least two years of formal training. The criteria for admission to the office of deaconess were spelled out. These included a minimum age requirement of 25 years and the admonition that she must be a woman of devout character who was an Anglican communicant in good standing. The canon defined the parameters of her work. The deaconess was an assistant to the incumbent of a parish, who served by license of the bishop in whose diocese she worked. Under the direction of the incumbent, she was to minister to women and girls, care for the sick, and assist with Christian education and social service work, including "moral reform."[2]

The Canadian canon differed from the Lambeth deaconess canon in only one significant respect: deaconesses in the Canadian church were to remain celibate. If women married after assuming the office of deaconess, they were expected to vacate the office. This policy was a dramatic shift away from both Lambeth and the Church of England. Both of those bodies stated that women could marry and retain their diaconal office, as could their male counterparts in the ordained ministry.[3]

The enactment of the deaconess canon was the first significant piece of ecclesiastical legislation dealing with women's paid labour in the Canadian Anglican church. It was the first attempt of the General Synod to address the relationship of women's ministry to the ecclesiastical structure; it was initiated after the example of Lambeth. The canon was limited in scope; it discussed women only as deaconesses. The assumption of an essential difference between men and women undergirded the emphasis on the distinction between the office of deaconess and the male order of deacon. That women might be included in the full ministry of the church was not considered at that point in the Canadian church's history.

The office of the deaconess was the only form of ordered ministry for women preceding the ordination of women as deacons and priests. Interestingly, it was from the category of deaconess that most of the first women ordained to the priesthood came in the Anglican Church of Canada.[4] In light of that, the importance of that ministry cannot be underestimated.

GENERAL SYNOD 1931 TO GENERAL SYNOD 1943

At its twelfth session, in 1931, the General Synod meeting at Toronto, Ontario, addressed the larger issue of the place and ministry of women. This discussion was held in light of the preceding debates at Lambeth, 1930. The discussions of the Synod led to the passing of three motions in both the House of Clergy and the House of the Laity. The purpose of these motions was to take steps toward the implementation of resolutions passed at the Lambeth Conference the preceding year.[5] The Synod formed a committee to deal with women's work. That committee subsequently began working on a report which would study and comment on the work of women in the church for the General Synod.

The General Synod of 1931, also discussed the place of women in the councils of the church. Resolution 66 of Lambeth 1930, which called for a real partnership of women with those who "direct the work of the church," led the Canadian church to question the exclusion of women from its councils. The wording of Resolution 66 implied that women were not formerly in full partnership with the church, but full and equal partnership was not what Resolution 66 called for. Instead, it asked that women be brought into partnership with "those who direct the work of the church," and not that women themselves lead the church.[6]

The Canadian church was sympathetic to that view. The Committee on Women's Work which began after the General Synod of 1931 published its conclusion in a report in 1935. That report outlined the situation of women's work in the church and gave special attention to the question, "How best can we enlist the Womanhood of the Church behind the work of the Church?"[7] The report raised this question with regard to both paid women workers and the larger area of women's endeavour, women's voluntary work. Acknowledging that women had not formerly participated in a genuine partnership within church structures, the Committee expressed the desire to bring, "church women engaged in various philanthropic and social activities" into real partnership with those who directed the work of the church. It concluded by recommending that women's participation in the councils of the church should be encouraged as long as the women served as representatives of women's organizations, rather than as delegates elected in parishes and dioceses.[8]

In 1935, the Church of England in Canada did not discuss the issue of the ordination of women as priests. In fact, it barely discussed the issue of full-time women's labour at all. The primary focus of its concern was with issues of voluntary labour, that aspect of women's efforts which was predominant. In keeping with that predominant role, women might participate in church structures as long as they served as representatives of the traditional women's sphere such as voluntary groups engaged in philanthropy and social activities.

From its establishment after the General Synod of 1931, the Committee on Women's Work remained in place until the issue of the ordination of women came up after Lambeth 1968. Prior to 1968, it never addressed the issue of women's ordination. That issue was simply nowhere on the horizon of its world view. Instead, it consistently addressed the concerns of paid women workers and women's participation at synods. In the Canadian scenario a progressive inclusion of women unfolded. Before women were considered for ordination, their full enfranchisement within ecclesiastical structure had to be realized.

In 1943, the General Synod accepted the recommendation of this committee to allow women to represent the Diocesan Synods in the Lower House of the General Synod.[9] At the following session of General Synod held in Winnipeg, the first woman delegate participated in the proceedings: Mrs. Roberta E. Wodehouse, representing the Yukon.[10]

THE WOMEN CHURCH WORKERS

Who were these women workers to which the Committee on Women's Work responded, and what did they do? A lack of numerical data on these women workers is frustrating. No groups, committee, or ecclesiastical department kept a consistent count of the actual numbers of women who were at any one time employed in church work. That reality is complicated by the fact that the women themselves studied in several different places. Some women studied at the Deaconess Home (AWTC) in Toronto, others studied in the United States and came north; others studied in England and came west, and still others studied in the theological faculties which trained men for ordination. To the diversity of educational background is added the fact that several different employers hired these women once they were trained. Individual dioceses hired some; individual parishes hired others. Some were employed by the Women's Auxiliary of the national church, and the labour of still others was paid for by missionary societies based in England. Subsequently, an accurate numerical profile of these women simply cannot be compiled. Nonetheless, some comments on numbers can be made.

The above mentioned diversity of education and employment might lead one to speculate that the numbers of women serving as paid full-time workers and as deaconesses in the Canadian Anglican Church was large. The numbers of women who at any one time were actually employed in full-time church work appears to have been comparatively small but nonetheless significant.

Canadian Council of Churches Report, 1947

In 1947, the Canadian Council of Churches collected information on women's work in all of the major denominations in Canada. The Council's survey concluded that for some denominations, including the Anglican Church, the question of women's work was not a lively issue. It did, however, find that in all denominations women made a significant contribution to the life of the whole church. According to the report, the Anglican Church had the largest number of women in voluntary organizations, but was second to last in terms of numbers of paid workers.[11]

The voluntary organizations of the Anglican tradition in Canada during this period included the Women's Auxiliary of the Church of England in Canada, the Mother's Union, the Girl's Friendly Society, and the Daughters of the King. The Women's Auxiliary was the largest of these and eventually came to serve as the umbrella under which all women's voluntary efforts were co-ordinated. These organizations made a large financial contribution to the church. In 1947, there were 44,400 Anglican women giving voluntary service to the church, and their givings and fund-raising efforts contributed $196,275 to the church, supplementing the general coffers in no small measure.[12]

The paid women workers were divided into six different categories. The first category considered was ordained women. Obviously, the Anglicans had none of those in 1947. The second category was that of deaconess. According to the report, there were forty-two deaconesses serving in the Anglican tradition at that time. This number is an invaluable quantitative measure, as the Anglican Church itself did not begin to collect statistics on deaconesses until after 1961. During the war, a third category was named, Chaplain's Assistants. Of the five Canadian women known to serve in this capacity, two of them were Anglican.[13] The fourth category considered was female religious. The report noted that there were two Anglican religious orders for women in Canada in 1947, the Sisters of Saint John the Divine, the first Canadian-based order for women located in Willowdale and the Sisters of the Church, also in the Toronto area.[14] No figures were collected to indicate the number of women who served the church in that capacity.

The fifth category considered was home and overseas missions. In this category, women's voluntary efforts and women's full-time labour were connected in a significant way. Anglican women's associations supported women as missionaries both at home and abroad. Because the male-dominated church mission boards would not pay to send a female missionary overseas, the Women's Missionary Society of the Church of England in Canada broke away from the general missionary society in 1911.[15] The women did this in order to have control over the significant mission dollars that they raised and thereby send women missionaries overseas. Both the Missionary Society and the Women's Auxiliary supported mission work overseas and in Canada. Approximately twice as many women workers served in missions in Canada as overseas. In 1947, twenty women worked in overseas missions supported by Canadian Anglican women's mission dollars, while forty women worked in missions in Canada.[16]

A sixth and final category was classed as "other church workers." No numbers are provided in relation to these women. This was probably because it would have been impossible to gather an accurate count as most women in this classification were individually attached to parishes and other ministries with no central collection or registration point through which they would be identified. The types of positions listed were church social workers, field secretaries of Christian education, writers and editors who worked for religious publications and in the preparation of educational materials, executive secretaries of bodies like mission boards and the principals and teachers in church schools and colleges, such as the Anglican Women's Training College in Toronto.[17]

The total number of Canadian Anglican women working in full-time ministry according to this report was 104, excluding numbers of female religious and women workers. Another important source of information at this juncture is living memory. In oral history interviews, the number 200 recurred for this period. For example, Francis Lightbourne, who worked as Field Secretary for the Anglican Women's Training College in the late 1940s, stressed that the depression era through to the 1950s was the high point in terms of numbers of women workers on the Canadian Anglican scene. Her memory places the number of graduates from the Anglican Women's Training College serving in the field during 1947 at approximately 200.[18] That figure, of course, does not include female religious. The Community of the Sisters of the Church had 18 women living in their community at its high point in Canada in the 1950s, and the Sisters of Saint John the Divine had a numerical high of 38 members living in its community during that same period.[19]

The figure from the Canadian Council of Churches was probably comprised largely of deaconesses and of women in the last category, other church workers who are otherwise numerically lost to history. Of course, that figure represents women serving overseas and only women who were graduates of AWTC. Nonetheless, the figure of 200 gives us something of a picture of what the number of women workers might have been in 1947. Tables 2 and 3 attempt to graphically depict these estimated numbers. Table 2 plots the types of work and their numbers. Table 3 presents a graphic depiction of the proportion of each type. The deaconess was obviously in a minority position with the single largest category being other church workers. The women in paid work represented 13.4 percent of the total paid labour force. 1,780 clergy made up the remaining 86.6 percent.

The breadth of variety in women's paid labour in Canadian Anglicanism is impressive. Some discussion of that variety will fill out the picture of what women workers were doing between 1920 and 1967. Two broad areas of women's work present themselves, urban and rural ministry. The nature of the work and ministry of women was largely determined by their demographic location. Deaconesses were the category which straddled the two.

• *Deaconesses*

The numbers above indicate that deaconesses were not a numerical majority in terms of women workers; however, their ordained, or set apart, status makes them particularly important here. The designation of the deaconess in the deaconess canon was very specific. She was an assistant to an incumbent. In other words, her ministry was in a parish working with a clergy person, to whom she was a subordinate. Given that definition, most deaconesses worked in large urban centres in sizeable parishes which had need of extra ministerial labour. Christian education, particularly Sunday School and Bible study for women, were the deaconess's area of expertise. Pastoral visitation and, in some cases, social outreach were also on her job description. Some were administrative assistants to the incumbent. The particular focus of her work was highly individual as it reflected the needs of the parish and the expertise and ability of the woman.

• *Other Church Workers*

Unlike their urban sisters, a group of women called Bishop's Messengers served in isolated rural settings in the west. Although their work was reminiscent of the deaconess', they were technically of the category 'other church workers'. In 1928, an English woman by the name of Marguerite Fowler was commissioned by Bishop Thomas of the newly formed Diocese of Brandon for the "special task of ministering to people for whom the Church could not find an ordained man."[20] Fowler proceeded to establish the Order of St. Faith's, which became known as the Bishop's Messengers. This order of women had the unique task of following the mandate set out for Fowler in 1928. In other words, these women after being commissioned by the diocesan bishop, were sent to minister in isolated outposts of the Canadian West, primarily in the dioceses of Brandon and Athabasca.

These women functioned as incumbents of parishes, without the sacramental aspect to their ministry. They differed from the deaconess model as they were their own boss. They did not serve as assistants to male incumbents. As their original mandate suggests, they worked where no men would go.

Modelling themselves on "The Company of Women Messengers" of the Diocese of Derby, Church of England, the Messengers developed a rule of life which included vows of obedience to the bishop and the senior Messenger and regular prayer. Unlike the deaconesses, they took no vow of celibacy and were not 'set apart' or ordained. They understood themselves to be missionary in their focus. They travelled many miles in the Canadian west establishing ministries in isolated outposts. They conducted services, provided pastoral care and Christian education.[21] In other words their work paralleled that of the male clergy without the sacramental aspect. In that regard they were unique in Canadian Anglicanism. Their quasi-clerical status meant they were included in the ranks of the clergy on occasion.

A year after the Order was founded, five women served as Messengers. When the Order was dissolved in 1979, there had been 56 licensed Messengers and many others who worked with them over the years.[22]

When the first women were ordained to the priesthood in the Anglican Church of Canada, four of them were Bishop's Messengers from the Diocese of Brandon. Their ordinations as priests did not change the nature of their ministry. They continued to serve in the congregations where they had been the pastors and preachers for decades. The only difference was that they could administer the sacraments without external clerical assistance.

The Bishop's Messengers were part of the larger group of 'other church workers.' In both urban and rural settings, women known as 'other church workers' pursued ministries which had a more specifically missionary flavour. The paid church worker, variously funded, often created an innovative ministry in a non-traditional setting.

The church worker differed from the deaconess in that she was not set apart for her ministry. While her education and training were the same as a deaconess, she was not ordained to an office in the church. Rather she received a license to function in a specified parish or place by a diocesan bishop. She took no vow of celibacy, and there was no canon to govern her place in the church.

In the rural environment, the licensed church worker often engaged in education as outreach. Many women over the course of the twentieth century, although the number cannot be defined, appear to have taught in residential schools for native Canadian children. Others served as missionary teachers on native reserves. Others established "Sunday school by post" for children in isolated communities who otherwise would have had no Christian education. This work was supported by the caravan missions under the supervision of an English woman by the name of Eva Hasell. The caravan mission began in the early 1920s and still exists in some places of the Canadian west funded by diocesan budgets. Every summer, the caravans travelled to isolated areas and set up Sunday school programs for the education of children and adults alike. This mission took place in several dioceses, with individual caravans covering over 2,000 miles each.[23] The circuit riding preachers of a century before most closely parallel the work of these caravans.

In urban centres, licensed women workers developed creative missionary work among various ethnic groups. After World War I, several women worked with immigrants, helping them with the language and life skills essential to relocation in their new Canadian context. As early as 1930, carrying on into the 1960s, some women workers and deaconesses worked in "Jewish Missions" in Montreal which were designed not only to aid Jewish immigrants in relocation, but also to convert them to Christianity. On the west coast, women were found from the late nineteenth century onward serving in missions to immigrants from Asia and, during and after World War II, working with Japanese Canadians who were relocated and dispossessed during the war. Missions to native Canadians in large urban centres flourished with the support of women workers. Urban centres from coast to coast were the home of mission work among single girls and women through the establishment of residences and fellowship groups. Other licensed workers served in poor urban neighbourhoods with inadequate housing, and still others along with many parish deaconesses visited in hospitals and prisons.[24]

FINDINGS OF THE COMMITTEE ON WOMEN'S WORK

Although women were engaged in active and varied ministries in the church between 1920 and 1967, women's work was plagued by many difficulties. In its 1949 report to General Synod, the Committee on Women's Work identified areas of special concern. It named two "matters of grave urgency": wages that were often well below those of the male deacon, and the lack of a pension plan for full-time women workers.[25] Those women workers who were employed by the Women's Auxiliary apparently were paid wages that were more or less in line with a curate's stipend and received retirement support as well. Those who worked for the church at large, however, often suffered from poverty, particularly after retirement. The Committee spoke of the need for a regularized wage system and for the implementation of a pension plan.

The disparity of compensation between ordained and non-ordained workers reflected the extent to which women's paid labour was a marginal concern within the church. It also highlights the fact that women who worked for the church were not seen in any way as a part of the same category as male clergy. Women's work was not considered to be as valuable as the work carried out in the male sphere of church life. Women's lack of financial well-being and security created a situation of "grave urgency."

In its report to the Synod of 1949, the Committee on Women's Work also stressed the value of women's participation in the councils and governing bodies of the church. It asked the Synod to give careful attention to [this] issue.[26] Although women had previously been admitted to the General Synod of the church, their actual participation in it was limited by the willingness of diocesan synods and parishes to allow the full participation of women in their own bodies. By definition, one could only be a delegate to General Synod if one served as a delegate at a diocesan synod and was elected there to the General Synod. In turn, one could not be elected as a delegate to the diocesan synod unless one was previously elected to a parish council. The dioceses and parishes needed further encouragement before they would allow women as full voting members of the church.

This synodical reality had implications for deaconesses and paid women workers. Although they served in full-time ministry, they were functionally ineligible to represent themselves in the decision-making processes by which the future of their church was decided. The decision-making process by which the Anglican Church of Canada chose to include women in the threefold order of ministry, had some women participating as lay delegates to General Synod, but these were a minority as a result of the short history of female inclusion. Of course there were not any women in the other two orders and as such, women had no voice at that level.

THE FUTURE PATTERNS REPORT

After the General Synod of 1952, the Primate appointed a Task Force to study and make recommendations about the place and work of women in the church. Its report in 1955, entitled "Future Patterns on Women's Work in the Church," pointed out the extent to which women were still excluded from the councils and synods of the church. Its findings are significant. At the grassroots level, the Anglican Church in 1955 had not accepted the full participation of women in its ministry. The "Future Patterns" report, however, was circulated widely and served to open the door to a gradual re-definition of gender-based spheres of participation in Canadian Anglicanism. That process of re-definition for which a need was noted in 1955 continued to go on through the 1990s.

In its opening remarks, the "Future Patterns" report noted that women were still doing "what is accepted as women's work," while men were making decisions and forming policies that would direct the affairs of the church.[27] The Task Force discovered that in 1954 women were eligible for and were elected to the diocesan synod in six dioceses. In two dioceses, women were eligible but were not elected. In seven dioceses, the matter was not discussed. In a further nine dioceses, the resolution was brought in but was defeated. In one other, the motion to allow women in the synod passed and was then vetoed by the diocesan bishop.[28]

Three dioceses reported that they did not have deaconesses. Fifteen dioceses stated that their deaconesses had no status in the synod. Women workers were generally found to have a confused status that varied from diocese to diocese. It was noted that in one case a licensed deaconess had the same status as licensed clergy. In others, however, deaconesses were not licensed at all and had virtually no position of authority within parochial or diocesan structures.[29]

Apparently considerable opposition existed to the inclusion of women in synods. This opposition was based on two very different arguments. The first argument reflects the extent to which gender-based discrimination was alive and well in the church in 1954. According to it, women were totally unsuited to take part in such gatherings and were not interested in participating anyway. Others argued that if women were eligible, they would swamp the meetings.[30] In an inverse way, that fear acknowledged the fact that women were actually a significant majority in the church. Women were more numerous and had the ability and gifts necessary to shape their own destiny. In many ways, they did that through the exercise of their own unique ministry; they were not, however, allowed to shape that destiny as full participants in those structures that set the course for the future of the whole church.

The "Future Patterns" report recommended full and equal status for all deaconesses and licensed lay workers in the synods of the church, adequate compensation for licensed workers and full pension plans for all who were engaged in paid labour for the church. The report stated that the future must look different than the past for women in the church. While there was never any reference to the idea of ordination, either to the diaconate or the priesthood, it stressed that women should no longer be kept from full participation in church life. The General Synod and indeed the whole church were asked to recognize that communicant standing in the church should be sufficient criteria for full participation in its governing bodies.[31] With that statement, however, the "Future Patterns report" did not presume to comment on the exclusion of women from Holy Orders. That would be the question for another decade.

GENERAL SYNODS 1962 AND 1965

At the General Synod of 1962, reports were received from three separate groups dealing with different aspects of the life of women in the church: the Commission on the Status of Deaconesses, the Commission on the Training of Women, and the Standing Committee on Women's Work. All reiterated the need for clarity with regard to the position and work of women. All asked for further study of the issues.[32]

At the General Synod of 1965, the imbalance of male-female relations in the decision-making bodies of ecclesiastical structures was reiterated. The Committee on Women's Work observed that, of its own ten members, nine were men and only one was a woman. In an attempt to give women greater representation, the Committee asked the Synod to form and fund a Commission on Women's Work which would include representatives from the various types of women's groups.[35] The synod agreed, and there was both a Commission and a Committee on Women's Work supported by the General Synod until after the first ordinations of women to the priesthood.

GENERAL SYNOD, 1967

At the General Synod of 1967, the Committee on Women's Work reported optimistically that only five dioceses did not permit women to serve as delegates to diocesan synods. Only six dioceses excluded women from membership on parish boards of management and select vestries. On the other hand, 21 out of 28 dioceses did not allow women to serve as church wardens. Women represented only six dioceses at General Synod.[34]

At the same General Synod, members passed resolutions asking the primate to form all existing councils, commissions and committees into a single Commission on Women. He eventually complied with the request. When that Commission on Women's Work reported to the Government Commission on the Status of women in 1967, it said in reference to full-time women workers that the, "Church in general shows little understanding or appreciation of how to make use of such women."[35]

SOCIOLOGICAL STUDY ON
WOMEN CHURCH WORKERS, 1967

A report was also received at the General Synod of 1967 from the Council on Full-Time Women Workers. This body was responsible for monitoring the life and work of paid women workers, including deaconesses. It reported that it had commissioned a sociological study of the "changing situation in Canada in relation to the employment of women and identifying implications for women workers in the Church."[36] This study resulted in a report entitled, Sociological Analysis of Women Workers in the Church, which was circulated two years later.

The Sociological Analysis contained important information on the status and experience of women workers in the church. It estimated that by 1967, there were approximately 100 women working in full-time paid ministry for the Anglican Church of Canada.[37] That figure excluded numbers of female religious but included deaconesses and 'other church workers'. It represents a 50 percent decline in the number of women from the earlier estimated figure of 200 in 1947. Table 4 demonstrates the steady decline in numbers of deaconesses between 1961 and 1978.

The estimated 100 women in 1967 is paralleled by approximately 2,775 active male clergy. The 100 women represented 3.9 percent of the church's paid ministerial labour force. As the number of male clergy went up since 1947, the number of paid women who served the church went down. This trend continued with the number of active clergy rising to approximately 2,800 in 1978, while the number of paid full time women counting deaconesses and women clergy in the same year was approximately 25, or less than one percent of the church's paid labour force.

The information gathered by questionnaire for the analysis led the framers of the report to conclude that parish work was a dismal prospect for women and a form of labour which was dying out. It said:

> What the Church is saying to its women workers…is that you are a strictly peripheral group and some kind of inferior breed that we will tolerate and use, when it suits our purposes, but inadmissible to the centres of power and decision-making.[38]

These harsh words make a clear statement about the women in the ecclesiastical structure of the Anglican Church of Canada in 1967. By the end of the first stage, 1920-1967, under examination here, the woman with a vocation to full-time ministry in the church was a marginalized person.

Deaconesses and women workers were themselves aware of the limitations and problems that plagued their employment situation. Many women graduates of the Anglican Women's Training College found their task in ministry to be poorly supported by the church's hierarchy. These women noted poor wages, lack of status, non-supportive rectors, and a general lack of recognition in congregations. They expressed hurt over the gradual disillusionment of their vision of a life of service in the church.

ANGLICAN REGISTERED CHURCH WORKERS ASSOCIATION

Disheartened by this reality, women workers chose one of several options. Some left church work entirely; others continued to work quietly and faithfully in oppressive circumstances, and still others continued to work in the church but began to organize among themselves to lobby for better working conditions. Eventually some formed the Anglican Registered Church Workers Association (ARCWA) in the late 1960s. This association of women workers and deaconesses sought to study the crisis of women's work and then to bring these problems to the church's conscious mind. They consistently asked for better working conditions for women, arguing for improvements which would include greater recognition and higher status within church structures. Their mandate, however, was not to change church structures, but rather to press for better working conditions within the existing institutional forms.

ARCWA as a group never entertained the idea of promoting the ordination of women to the diaconate or priesthood. Indeed, in retrospect, many declared themselves to be opposed to it as for them it represented the co-optation of women's gifts into a patriarchal and oppressive structure. Some deaconesses from that period state that the question of ordination to the priesthood simply did not enter their heads. Others stress that even if they had felt a vocation to ordination, they would never have admitted it for fear of being rejected by the system in which they were serving.[39]

By 1967, the crisis of women's work was clear. The church did not know what to do with its women workers. At the same time, it was gradually opening up the traditionally male sphere of church life to women. Access for women to membership on councils and synods was underway. As of 1967, however, that access did not include any discussion of the possible inclusion of women in Holy Orders.

Endnotes

1. Alison Kemper, "Deaconess as Urban Missionary and Ideal Women" in G.S. 76-15, Box 25.
2. G. S. *Journal of Proceedings* (1921), pp. 186–187.
3. G.S. *Journal of Proceedings* (1921), p. 187.
4. See Table 6.
5. G.S. *Journal of Proceedings* (1931), p. 143.
6. *Lambeth Conference Reports and Resolutions* 1930 (London: Church Press, 1930) pp. 60–61.
7. Report of the House of Bishops on Women's Work (1935) p. 3.
8. House of Bishops Report (1935), pp. 59–61.
9. G.S. *Journal of Proceedings* (1943), p. 55.
10. G.S. *Journal of Proceedings* (1946), p. 258.
11. Canadian Council of Churches Report on Women's Work in the Church (Toronto: 1947), pp. 6–12.

12. Canadian Council Report (1947), p. 12.
13. Canadian Council Report (1947), p. 6.
14. Canadian Council Report (1947), p. 7.
15. Alison Prentice et al, eds., *Canadian Women—A History* (Toronto: Harcourt, Brace, Jovanovich, 1988), p. 171.
16. Canadian Council Report (1947), pp. 7–8.
17. Canadian Council Report (1947), p. 9.
18. Oral History Interview with Francis Lightbourne, 11 December 1992.
19. Oral History Interview with Sister Anita, Community of the Sisters of the Church, 11 November 1992.
20. Diocese of Brandon, "Bishop's Charge," Diocesan Synod *Journal of Proceedings* (1976), pp. 18–20.
21. Barnett-Cowan, pp. 3–7.
22. Barnett-Cowan, p. 4.
23. Grace Hallenby, *Anglican Women's Training College—A Background Document* (Toronto: AWTC, 1989), pp. 60–61.
24. Hallenby, pp. 49–59.
25. G.S. *Journal of Proceedings* (1949), p. 258.
26. G.S. *Journal of Proceedings* (1949), p. 259.
27. Future Patterns of Women's Work in the Church Report, (1955), p. 1.
28. Future Patterns Report, pp. 1–3.
29. Future Patterns Report, pp. 3–6.
30. Future Patterns Report, p. 5.
31. Future Patterns Report, p. 7.
32. G.S. Journal of Proceedings (1962), pp. 340–367.
33. "Report of the Committee on Women's Work," *Journal of Proceedings* (1965).
34. G.S. *Journal of Proceedings*, (1967), pp. 451–452.
35. G.S. *Journal of Proceedings*, (1967), p. 452.
36. "Report of the Committee on Women's Work," *Journal of Proceedings* (1965), p. 483.
37. *Sociological Analysis of Women Workers in the Church* (Toronto, 1967), p. 3.
38. *Sociological Analysis of Women Workers in the Church* (Toronto, 1967), p. 3.
39. These observations are based on extensive oral history interviews with women workers and deaconesses who served in the church between 1940 and 1960, conducted by me between 1988 and 1990.

3

Gender Questions to a New Vision

The process by which the Anglican Church of Canada made the decision to ordain women to the priesthood was brief. It was not until the Lambeth Conference of 1968 asked the members of the Communion to report their views on this issue to the Anglican Consultative Council which met in 1971, that the wheels were set in motion for a formal discussion on the question. This formal discussion of women in Holy Orders began in the General Synod of 1969, and was completed by the General Synod of 1975 when the members voted to proceed with the ordination of women to the priesthood. Members of the House of Bishops carried out these ordinations, beginning on 30 November 1976. What happened in the life of the church and in the ecclesiastical decision-making process between 1968 and 1976, up to and including the Lambeth Conference in 1978?

THE CANADIAN DECISION-MAKING PROCESS, 1968 – 1978: REVOLUTION FROM ABOVE

When the Lambeth Conference of 1968 raised the question of women's ordination to the priesthood, the Anglican Church of Canada was ready to take up the theme for consideration. The procedure was significant. If the process is viewed in terms of a hierarchical structure, it was the 'top' level of the hierarchy within the Communion that raised the issue first for Canada, although a formal stand was not taken. The matter was then referred to the national churches for comment. This is similar to the process which occurred in Canada on a smaller scale; the General Synod discussed and then took a stand on the issue. It then referred the issue to the dioceses for study and comment.

Twentieth century Italian philosopher Antonio Gramsci discussed the relationship between those who lead and those who follow in his *Prison Notebooks*. He argued that in any revolution there is an intellectual elite which leads the mass of the population forward into its next stage of historical evolution. A historic bloc is only successfully formed out of the revolution when the "organic intellectuals" are able to lead the people to a place where they are willing to go. In other words, the successful leader has a vision with which he/she will take his/her people into the future which is simultaneously visionary and grounded in the passion and experience of the people. No historic bloc can be successfully maintained without a certain amount of consensus. Extensive use of force or coercion will not hold the new society together effectively for any length of time. Ultimately people will rebel against the force which makes them live in a way that they do not want to live.[1]

Intellectuals in Gramsci's theory are not simply highly educated individuals. All who exhibit any mental or intellectual activity are understood to be intellectuals. What distinguishes all intellectuals from the intellectual elite which provides leadership is function. The intellectual elite of a society or institution is that group which provides organization and leadership, having been formed from a long and difficult process of integrating theory and practice. The function of organization and leadership makes the designation of intellectual elite applicable to the episcopacy in this case.[2]

In the Anglican Church of Canada between 1968 and 1978, there was a revolution from above with regard to the ordination of women to the priesthood. While the ordination of women represents a 'revolution' in an institutional and thereby limited sense, the concept of the intellectual which Gramsci articulated is illuminating for this analysis. The Primate, the titular head of the church, and the House of Bishops, a college of those in episcopal office, formed a leadership which took the church into a new era. The ordination represented a radical break with preceeding Christian tradition. The movement forward would not have been successful if it had not been sufficiently grounded in the passion and experience of the church to form a historic bloc. In other words, the actual ordinations did not precipitate a revolt or irreparable schism. They have become an accepted part of everyday life in the Anglican Church of Canada. Unpacking the complexity of this process of action and decision-making is the task to which we now turn.

THE COMMISSION ON WOMEN

When the Canadian bishops returned from the Lambeth Conference the Primate asked its Commission on Women to begin discussion on the issue of women's ordination.

In its turn, the Commission on Women asked Canadian scholar Dr. Helen Milton to write an article on the issue of women's ordination to the priesthood. This article helped the Commission and ultimately the Canadian church to 'dabble its feet' in the issue in an exploratory way. As a New Testament scholar, Milton confined herself predominantly but not exclusively to a discussion of the New Testament's view of ministry and of women. No conclusion was reached with regard to women's ordination, and indeed the writer did not engage in a debate on the subject. Rather, she examined the roots of the ministry of the whole people of God, the idea of *diakonos* and the place of women in early Christian communities. She noted the lack of uniformity in the role of women. Milton concluded first of all that women had exercised important leadership throughout Christian history, but that there was a lack of substantial evidence within the whole tradition for women's exercise of ministry in cultic roles, in other words, no precedent for a priestly function by women.[3]

As was noted earlier, the first time that any branch of the Canadian Anglican Church put this issue on its formal agenda occurred in 1969, the year following the Lambeth Conference. At a meeting of the Commission on Women, held on 12 February, 1969, a motion was carried which stated that:

Members of the Commission on Women want to go on record as expressing their conviction that women should be eligible for ordination to the priesthood in the Anglican Church of Canada. The first motion was followed by a subsequent one which read as follows: Be it resolved that the Primate be requested to initiate action on a study of the ordination of women to the priesthood to establish the position of the Anglican Church of Canada in this matter and to report to the General Synod in 1971.[4]

At the same February meeting, the Commission noted that women workers expressed frustration that there was little acceptance of them and their work by clergy. Although dioceses such as the diocese of Brandon had "large numbers" of women workers at the time, it was felt that they, as with other women workers, had little or no status in the structure of the church.[5]

GENERAL SYNOD, 1969

The General Synod of 1969 was a landmark in the Canadian church in more ways than one. In light of Resolution 35 of Lambeth 1968 and the request from the Commission on Women it was resolved that the Synod request that the Primate initiate, through a task force or commission, a study of the question of the ordination of women to the priesthood for report to the next session of General Synod. This motion carried in both houses. Perhaps even more significantly the following resolution was made:

> Be it resolved that in regard to women presently ordained as dea-
> conesses in the Anglican Church of Canada, the Primate be asked
> to initiate any steps which may be necessary to ensure that those
> who are so ordered may belong to the diaconate.[6]

This motion resolved the conflict which had existed in the church since the Lambeth Conference of 1920, as to whether or not the deaconess was actually in diaconal orders. Apparently there was very little conflicted discussion on this issue at the synod. Many felt that since there were women already competently performing essentially diaconal functions there was not any issue to debate.[7] Some of those who had no problem with the idea of women deacons ultimately expressed strong dissent over the idea of women priests.

With this motion in 1969, the General Synod passed the recommendation which it received from Lambeth 1968 for the full acceptance of women into the diaconate. At its November meeting in 1969 the House of Bishops endorsed this decision by passing the following resolution:

> That this House considers that the action of the 1969 General
> Synod has established for the Anglican Church of Canada the
> fact that duly ordained deaconesses are to be regarded as being

members of the diaconate in the Church and that the bishops be asked to establish this in the life of the Church, requiring of the candidates the same qualifications and commitments as the men being so ordained.[8]

Apparently the bishops had differing attitudes as to whether a second laying on of hands was necessary to complete this 'transition' to diaconal orders. The Reverend Mary Mills became the first female deacon in the Anglican Church of Canada, ordained by the Right Reverend George Luxton of the Diocese of Huron on 12 December 1969.[9]

While these motions with regard to ordination questions were passed in 1969, the synod tabled subsequent motions regarding women workers. Following up on the findings of the Sociological Analysis of Women Church Workers and the concerns of the Commission on Women and the Council for Full-time Women Workers in the Church, motions were made which advocated equal pay for work of equal value for women so that women workers would receive salaries equivalent to those of the clergy they worked with as well as voting participation in diocesan synods for women workers, parallel to clergy.[10]

HOUSE OF BISHOPS, 1970 – 1972

In October, 1970 at the House of Bishops annual session, the Bishop of Nova Scotia, William Davis, presented a report on the place of women in the diaconate and subsequently moved that the House approve the use of the regular service for the ordering of deacons contained in the Book of Common Prayer (1962 Canadian) as suitable for ordaining to the diaconate, women who had the same qualifications as the men being so ordained.[11] The acceptance of the ordination of women to the diaconate was formally accomplished, even though it had been a practical reality since the General Synod of 1969.

At this same session, the House of Bishops formed a sub-committee on "Wider Ordained Ministry." The committee members were Bishop Edward Scott of Kootenay, Bishop Douglas Hambidge of Caledonia, and Bishop John Frame of the Yukon. Its original terms of reference were to consider Resolution 33 of the 1968 Lambeth Conference, which stated that men could be ordained and work in a lay occupation, and to see if there were any other recommendations that needed to be brought before the House of Bishops or General Synod. Various additional mandates were added over the course of the ensuing year including the request of the Primate that the committee on the "Wider Ordained Ministry" give consideration to the matter of the ordination of women to the priesthood, in consultation with a special task force in the Maritimes appointed for that purpose, known as the Primate's Task Force on the Ordination of Women to the Priesthood.

With regard to the ordination issue, the Wider Ordained Ministry committee made the following statements. It reminded the House of Bishops that the church was already ordaining women, to the diaconate. This committee made the distinction between theological objections to women's ordination and other objections. Throughout the debate over women's ordination to the priesthood this distinction was obvious. While ultimately most agreed that there were no theological objections, some were still held back from supporting such a move because of their concerns over other considerations—sociological, psychological, ecumenical, practical and pastoral. Until all of these issues were responded to there was division with regard to proceeding with such ordinations. In fact, 'other' objections were not fully put to rest and continued to arise from those clergy and laity in the Anglican Church of Canada who remained opposed to the ordination of women.

The Wider Ordained Ministry committee of the House of Bishops also addressed the 1969 decision to accept women in diaconal orders. It advocated that several steps be undertaken to fully implement that decision. These included the licensing of women as deacons in the same fashion as their male counterparts, the admission of deaconesses to diocesan synods in the House of Clergy, the implementation of a salary scale for deaconesses which was on a par with deacons, and the admission of deaconesses to the clergy pension fund with accompanying fringe benefits.[12] While this represented an important shift in church policy, it was only relevant to ordained women. Those women who were full-time women lay workers were not included in these measures, and they continued to exist as an interesting 'dilemma' for the church which it only solved by phasing them out in favour of ordained women.

The Primate did convene a task force that was to study the question of women's ordination to the priesthood and report its findings to General Synod in 1971. In keeping with the General Synod practice of using regional committees to work on issues for the national church, Archbishop Clark asked a group in the Diocese of Nova Scotia to be the Task Force on the Ordination of Women to the Priesthood. The appointed group was a diocesan committee on women's ministry which was then asked to focus its deliberations on the issue of women and the priesthood. There was a representation of diverse opinions and backgrounds in the committee. Henceforth this group is referred to as the "Primate's Task Force." These seven members on the Primate's Task Force were both lay and clergy. They began reading widely on the subject and invited corresponding members from across the country to work with them in the capacity of consultants. They also sought communication with representatives from other communions, particularly the Swedish Lutheran, the United Church, and the Roman Catholics.

Given the breadth and depth of its mandate, the report was not ready until 1972, and it was not until the Synod of 1973, that the report of the Primate's Task Force was received and discussed. At the General Synod of 1971, however, the Primate's Task Force moved that study guides based on the Lambeth Conference be prepared and that dioceses and parishes be encouraged to study them, as well as other relevant material while the Task Force continued its work.[13] It is unclear to what extent the dioceses undertook this study. It appears that most dioceses did not undertake an extensive study of the question at the diocesan or parish level at that juncture.

While the Primate's Task Force worked on its report, the House of Bishops began a new era in its life with the installation of a new Primate, Archbishop Edward Scott. With his leadership, the House of Bishops continued and expanded discussion about the ordination of women to the priesthood for the Canadian church. At its annual session in 1971, held in Edmonton, Primate Scott gave a report on the first meeting of the Anglican Consultative Council previously held in Limuru, Kenya. The Limuru meeting produced a report entitled "The Time is Now." The Primate discussed the report referring particularly to Resolution 28, which stated that each province had the right to make its own decision on the issue. He noted that the Council agreed that while the Communion was divided, there were no fundamental objections to the ordination of women and it would not stand in the way of a province, diocese or bishop who felt moved to ordain a woman. Scott then referred to a letter from Archbishop Dean of the East Asia Council which stressed that, while his council did not support Resolution 28, it did not forbid Hong Kong, which had brought the matter before the Limuru meeting, from going forward with such ordinations if it felt it was right to do so. Scott then noted to the House of Bishops that the Canadian church had a Task Force which was dealing with the issue. They agreed that no further action needed to be taken by the House of Bishops at that time.[14]

The interactions then occurring represented the best of what is to be found in Anglicanism. In the Limuru case, we see a respect for the other which is so profound that unity in diversity held even in the midst of extremely divided opinion. In the Canadian situation, the House of Bishops allowed a group appointed for the purpose to offer some direction before it proceeded to take further action. A mutual process of study and decision-making was unfolding.

REPORT OF THE PRIMATE'S TASKFORCE ON THE ORDINATION OF WOMEN TO THE PRIESTHOOD, 1972

By the time the House of Bishops met the following year, the Primate's Task Force had prepared its report on the ordination of women to the priesthood, and it had been distributed in anticipation of General Synod. The report was comprised of two separate reports, the *Majority Report* and the *Minority Report*. At the conclusion of its work, the Task Force found itself divided on the issue. All members of the Task Force except one supported the ordination of women. The *Majority Report* was written from the perspective of those who supported such ordinations, and the *Minority Report* was written by the one person who opposed the issue.

The *Majority Report* was divided into three primary sections: Scripture, Tradition and Other Considerations. This report supported the ordination of women to the priesthood, and toward that end, dealt with a series of points relating to women and Holy Orders under the three categories. The central points made in the *Report* reflect the key ideas on the "*pro*" side of this issue in the Canadian church.

The *Majority Report* stressed that Scripture was the fundamental norm of the teaching and practice the church. It argued that the question of women's ordination did not arise from Scripture, but rather from our cultural and historical experience. The movement from experience to its testing through Scripture was considered to be normative and, therefore, acceptable as a criterion for determining the teaching of the church.

The *Report* established several premises. It was agreed that Scripture has traditionally been interpreted as prohibiting women from Holy Orders. This prohibition is found in passages such as *I Corinthians* II: 2-16, *I Corinthians* 14: 34-35, and *I Timothy* 2: 8-15. These passages all appeared to argue for the headship of man over woman and are commonly used as the basis of evangelical and Catholic arguments which have sought to justify the exclusion of women from leadership positions in home, church and society. On this view, in I Timothy, the woman is taught to be submissive and also to seek her salvation through motherhood. In *Corinthians*, Paul seemed to write that women should not address a congregation, which would make preaching and liturgical leadership impossible. The framers of the *Majority Report* concluded, however, that Scripture nowhere explicitly prohibited women from exercising ordained ministry in the church; rather this prohibition was inferred from the other passages about teaching, silence and the headship of man.

While recognizing the force of these passages, the Primate's Task Force rejected them on what it termed exegetical and evangelical grounds. It stressed that this rejection had to be decisive and final in light of the larger message of liberation and justice which was present in the gospel, just as those passages which might be seen as condoning slavery had to be decisively and finally rejected. The rejection of these passages was based on the Primate's Task Force's use of then current critical exegetical methods which argued against literal interpretation of Scripture. The rejection of such passages was based on the powerful themes found in Scripture regarding creation, redemption, reconciliation, ministry and membership in the church which it was agreed encouraged the admission of women to ordained ministry. The report argued that the seeds of the destruction of the theory about women's subordination were sown in Scripture.[15]

The Primate's Task Force then went beyond this and presented its case in favour of women's ordination based on Scripture. It argued that the theological case for admitting women to the ordained ministry of the church was put and agreed to when the first woman was baptized into the church, and thereby into the body of Christ. Scripture demonstrated that apostleship, discipleship and ministry overcame a person's racial, social or natural status. If the argument that Christ appointed no women as his apostles was carried to its logical conclusion, then one must argue that only Jewish males, and at any one time, only twelve Jewish males could be admitted to Holy Orders. Finally, the Task Force stressed that the images of God found in Scripture were not solely male. Images of all aspects of human life, rather than simply maleness, have been used to talk about God, for example, generosity, self-givingness and creativity could be applied to both men and women.[16]

Tradition has proven to be the thorniest problem for those in episcopal traditions who have attempted to justify the inclusion of women in Holy Orders, but the Anglican tradition does allow for the contravention of its own precedents. The Primate's Task Force found that the traditional practice of the church was overwhelmingly against the exercise of ordained ministry in the church by women. That being said, it then posed the question: was tradition alterable, and if it was, were there sufficient reasons for altering it in light of traditional Anglican teaching on authority? The Anglican position on authority, as with many other things is difficult to define universally.

The Primate's Task Force argued that the Anglican position on authority was essentially defined in the Thirty Nine Articles. Article 21 stated that General Councils of the church may have erred and have erred in the past. It asserted the right of every national church to change, abolish and ordain according to its own conscience. If it could be shown that the prohibition against women's exercise of the ordained ministry was not scriptural, then the practice of the church could be altered by a national church or ecclesiastical province. The Primate's Task Force concluded that the existing position of the church with regard to the ordination of women was alterable because the usual scriptural justification for it was faulty.[17] The ordination of women was neither taught by, nor prohibited by, nor repugnant to Scripture, and therefore was allowable.

Reasons for proceeding to change the tradition were offered. These included the belief that the theory of women's subordination was untenable, the fact that women were becoming massively involved in the world at all professional levels, and the reality of the growing struggle to end social, economic, and legal discrimination against women. A further reason was the new theological emphasis on the ministry of the church as the activity of all people who are the church. All agreed that there was a logical contradiction in allowing women's full participation in the church, except in ordained ministry. The *Report* felt that all of the above were sufficient grounds for abandoning the traditional prohibition of women from the ordained ministry.[18]

The *Majority Report* incorporated the best insights of feminist scholarship into its findings. While recognizing that there were forceful passages of Scripture which might be and indeed had been used to exclude women from a full participation in the life of the church, it rejected them using the tools of current exegetical scholarship, just as it rejected those passages which might have been seen to condone slavery. It also rejected the previous popular notion of the subordination and inferiority of women, and affirmed that the gospel of Christ called for a community of full and equal disciples who lived in service to one another and the world.

Those who supported the ordination of women to the priesthood at all levels, including bishops, priests, and laity, would not allow a biological determinism to direct the ministry of the church. The simple affirmation that WOMAN CAN BE PRIEST AS CAN MAN, is a statement which reflects a commitment to gender equality and the formation of a community based on mutual discipleship. Somehow those individuals who voted for the ordination of women had incorporated the idea that femaleness was not a disqualifying characteristic for ordained ministry.

Although I found through interviews that the word 'feminist' often caused individuals difficulty, the sentiments they expressed supported the equality of men and women. Much scholarship has been generated which debates diverse meanings of the term feminist. Different scholars define the word differently. Here the word is understood in its most elemental form. The feminist position is one which is based on a belief in the fundamental equality of women and men. In the Christian context the feminist commitment to gender equality is reflected in its invitation to mutuality and inclusivity, whereby all human beings are understood to be creatures of God. Separation of human beings into a hierarchical system of superior and inferior, with the criterion of differentiation being external genitalia defies the fundamental invitation of Jesus, which is an invitation to loving relationship in a community of mutual service. However much people may have wanted to avoid the label of feminist, those who supported the ordination of women to the priesthood represented an essentially feminist understanding of life and ministry.

The *Majority Report* of the Primate's Task Force also responded to "other considerations" which those who were opposed to the ordination of women often put forward as prohibitive. All agreed that these "other considerations" were of little weight in the actual case against women's ordination. Some in the church hoped that new forms of ministry would be developed in which women could take full part, instead of participating in ordained ministry. Some argued that the ordination of women would compound the present confusion felt by many regarding the ministry of the church. The Primate's Task Force responded to these concerns by stating that it felt that withholding ordination from women imposed barriers to full experimentation and inhibited the development of new forms of ministry.[19]

The issue of ecumenism was also a major pillar of the opposition's argument. Many opponents expressed doubt that a national church of one denomination could presume to change the tradition which it had inherited from the larger church. It was felt that such a decision could only be made in concert with the rest of christendom. In reply, the Primate's Task Force stated that the ecumenical consequences would be grave either way. While the Roman and Orthodox churches did not ordain women, many Protestant denominations had experienced extensive female leadership for decades, and in some cases longer. The Task Force stressed that it did not feel that the issue of women's ordination lay at the heart of what divided the churches as they had been divided for many centuries preceding this subject. Furthermore, there was currently no authoritative body in existence by which a universal decision on this issue could be made. In keeping with the meeting of the Anglican Consultative Council in Limuru the preceeding year, the Primate's Task Force understood that within the Anglican tradition it was agreed that each national church should initiate a process whereby it might make its own decision, and the Canadian church needed to do just that.[20]

The final area of concern to which the *Majority Report* responded was the possibility of internal division within the Anglican Church of Canada and the Anglican Communion. Some had apparently argued that the ordination of women would prove to be divisive to the church and the resulting conflict dehumanizing to the women priests themselves. While the Primate's Task Force stated that it could imagine extreme division might result, it was possible that these fears were groundless. This has proven to be the case; however, it did note that that type of attitude would certainly prevent the church from taking a stand on, or making a decision about, any number of other potentially divisive issues. Finally, it concluded that ultimately a woman should be free to make up her mind as to whether or not she was willing to take the risk of the possible conflict which might follow her ordination. The report stated, "The hope which goes with such a step is at least as great as the apocalyptic visions which have been listed above."[21] The *Majority Report* recommended that the church proceed with the admission of women to the threefold order of the church's ministry.

One member of the Primate's Task Force was opposed to the ordination of women to the priesthood at the conclusion of its work. Because it was felt that all voices on the Task Force should be heard, Peter Andrews was invited to submit a *Minority Report* outlining his perception of the negative arguments on the question. The report was actually longer than the pro report and argued against the ordination of women on the basis of Scripture, christology, ecclesiology and ecumenism. The foci of these issues are noted above.

From the beginning of the *Minority Report*, the author asserted that there was a categorical distinction between ministry and priesthood and that it was from the sacramental priesthood that women must be barred. This reflects what has been categorized in the English case as the basis of the Anglo-Catholic opposition which would allow a woman to offer liturgical leadership through preaching and prayers but not as presider at the sacraments. He referred to the teaching of Paul in *I Corinthians* and *Timothy*, as the writers of the *Majority Report* had, and stated that these were justifications for excluding women from priesthood. He named those who support women's ordination as modernists who willingly disregarded Scripture and tradition in favour of current desire. From the christological perspective the maleness of Christ was seen as essential; a woman could never represent Christ at the eucharistic table because she was not a man.[22] The issue here was one of ontology rather than function. The very nature of a woman, her femaleness, prevented her from engaging in a particular function.

The *Minority Report* held that the headship of the church must be male. This assertion was based on the writer's interpretation of apostolic heritage—Jesus only called men to be his disciples/apostles. Throughout the report the author stressed that we cannot be selective in our interpretation of Scripture and tradition. Rather we "must accept the reality of what has been handed down to us."[23]

The views of those opposed to the ordination of women as expressed in the *Minority Report* and elsewhere in the Canadian church can be summarized by four key points:

1. Women could not represent a male Christ.
2. Women could not have headship over a man.
3. There is no precedent for such ordinations in the Christian tradition.
4. Ecumenical relations with the Roman Catholic and Orthodox churches would suffer.

The first two arguments reflect one interpretation of Scripture. The first of course, means simply that Christ was a man, and therefore a woman cannot be his representative at the altar. Those who opposed this point argued that biological sex was not the determinative characteristic of Jesus which the priest represented. Rather, the redeemed humanity of Christ was what the priest represented, and that transcended all biological categories.

The second argument held that Scripture did not permit women to exercise authority over men. The metaphor of the patriarchal household taught that the man was head of the house and in turn the priest/church/ God maintained a position of authority over humanity. As such, the priest had authority over the people in his pastoral charge. As a woman could not have authority over a man, a woman could not be a priest. Those who objected to this line of reasoning denied that there was something different about a woman which would make her incapable of leadership. Others who objected to the idea, rejected the whole hierarchical world view it embodied, saying that the Christian community, if it sought to be faithful to the teaching of Jesus would be a more circular model, with men and women acting as servants of each other.

Both of these arguments against the ordination of women were ontological rather than functional. They disqualified women because of who they were rather than what they were able to do. The arguments were not that women were incapable of being priests because of lack of ability, but because of their person, the fabric of their being. There was something about the female person which meant that she could not represent the ultimate dimension of life in Christian terms — God.

The view that the female could not represent the ultimate dimension of existence grew up in the container of a patriarchal society. Plato and Aristotle had left their mark on the consciousness of the society into which Christianity was born. The societal structure of Jesus' day reflected the hierarchical model of Platonic thought. For Plato, the material represented only a pale image of the divine. The flesh was the prison of the soul. While Christianity affirmed the fact that human beings were made in the image of God and therefore good, it also internalized the subliminal message of its time that spirit was good and matter was evil. In keeping with the basic principles of Aristotelian thought, male was equated with spirit and female was equated with matter, or the aspect of lesser value. Woman was simply a defective male. As the subject of lesser value, woman was not only barred from representing the divine, SHE was equated with evil. SHE became, in the words of Tertullian, the devil's gateway.

The God which Christians inherited from Judaism was a sole male authoritarian figure. Although God was occasionally represented by feminine imagery in the Hebrew Bible, it was the male principle and its attributes which were predominant. As Christianity experienced a metamorphosis from its status as a reform movement within Judaism to an autonomous religious institution, women were excluded from positions of responsibility and authority in the ecclesiastical structure. This brief comment on the origins of the attitude of Christianity toward women is intended to highlight the fact that the opposition to the ordination of women as it was expressed in the first two arguments, had a lengthy precedent. As a patriarchal religion, Christianity bore the fruit of misogyny and restricted women from full access to all dimensions of life in the faith.

The third argument on the side of the opposition was that there had been no precedent for the ordination of women to the presbyterate in Christian tradition. While this may have been true after the second century, those who disagreed with this argument stressed that the first century of ministry after the time of Christ was a time of ministry of charism. There were no specific orders for men or women. Both apparently had ministries of service and prophecy, and both figured prominently in the communities of which they were a part. The argument that by the apostolic tradition Jesus appointed only men to be his apostles is brought into question by those who would argue that the first apostle was Mary Magdalene. If an apostle is someone who has seen the risen Christ and has been sent to proclaim that witness, it was Mary who first met that criteria. Jesus greeted her at the tomb and sent her to tell the others that he lived.

This third argument demanded the perpetuation of a patriarchal tradition of exclusion. It argued that the wisdom of the church had excluded women for almost two thousand years because they were incapable of being priests by virtue of their person; they were inferior or different because they were women.[24] That tradition was seen as a justification for continuing exclusion. Ultimately then this argument was an argument which was derived from the ontological perspective. It was the perpetuation of the argument from the nature of women.

The fourth and final major argument held that it was wrong for one branch of Christianity to proceed to make such a fundamental break with tradition on its own. While this argument has continued to cause concern for those in the Anglican Church of Canada who remain opposed to the ordination of women, some may rest easier knowing that the action has not caused an irreparable split between Anglicanism and other world churches. Our distance from the Roman Catholic Church and the Orthodox Church is commensurate with what it has been for much of the twentieth century, and we are closer to those denominations who have chosen to ordain women than in earlier decades. Those who espouse the fourth argument are making a choice, a choice to maintain something which may be theologically or morally wrong in favour of ecumenical relations.

Primate Scott observed that in the educational process whereby the church discussed this issue, the arguments against the ordination of women were put to rest one by one. The one argument which could not be put to rest was the argument that a woman was simply incapable of being a priest by virtue of her femaleness. There was no argument which could change that prejudice. The next question then became, "Is that a view that we want our church to promote?" The answer to that question was, "No."[25]

The reports of the Primate's Task Force were ready for circulation in 1972. Bishops, clergy and laity alike had access to their findings prior to the General Synod of 1973. The House of Bishops had a lengthy discussion on the subject at its April-May meeting of 1973. They agreed that differences between the sexes were a key aspect of the issue. Practical problems such as women in the chaplaincy of the Armed Forces were named. The bishops agreed that there was no shortage of clergy in the Anglican Church of Canada. Some bishops felt unable to accept the idea of women in the priesthood even after lengthy discussions. It was agreed that if the General Synod accepted the ordination of women to the priesthood there would have to be a conscience clause to accommodate those who felt that they could not ordain women. Someone expressed the concern that no woman had been involved in those discussions which were about them — "Women have had no voice in the discussion." There was also a division of opinion about the authority of individual bishops. Could a bishop proceed to ordain a woman immediately following a General Synod decision in the affirmative? Although the answer was technically, 'yes,' the House agreed that it would continue its discussion on the subject after the General Synod of 1973.[26]

Before the reports were debated in the General Synod of 1973, another piece of commentary was also put before the members of Synod. Andrews, who produced the *Minority Report*, wrote to the Primate expressing procedural concerns about the work of the Task Force. Andrews wrote that the Task Force had been too limited in its composition to be representative and thorough. Firstly, only one member of the group was an academic theologian, while the others had only limited and varying degrees of theological knowledge. Secondly, there was no national representation. The members of the group were drawn only from the Halifax area. Thirdly, Andrews noted that the Task Force met with only three outside sources, of whom two were for and only one was against the ordination of women. He claimed that none of these spoke with any authority as representatives of their various churches, and that he was unaware of any contacts having been made with other national churches, or other persons across the country as the *Majority Report* claimed. There was no mention of these concerns at Synod although all members of Synod received a copy of Andrew's letter in their convening circular.[27]

GENERAL SYNOD, 1973

At the General Synod of 1973, the Bishops' Committee on Ministry presented the reports. Before motions were put dealing with this issue, small group study time was allotted. The houses of Synod were given a resource paper by the Rev. Dr. William Crockett of the Vancouver School of Theology entitled, "The Ordination of Women to the Priesthood." Stating that its purpose was not to present a case for or against the issue, the author of the paper hoped simply to provide an overview of the key elements of the issue.

Eventually a resolution coming out of the work of the Commission on Women was put by Miss Ruth Scott and Bishop David Somerville of the Diocese of New Westminster, "That this General Synod accept the principle of the ordination of women to the priesthood, and this decision be communicated to the Anglican Consultive Council." Before the motion was voted on, it was agreed that the vote on any motion on the principle of the ordination of women to the priesthood should be by orders.[28]

Before the synod voted on the actual motion, a motion to refer was made. It was moved that the question of the principle of the ordination of women to the priesthood should be referred to the dioceses for study and discussion, with a view to action at the next session of General Synod.[29] In other words there were some members of Synod who wanted the matter discussed in the dioceses before a national decision was made. The House of Clergy defeated the motion. The leadership on this issue was thus set at the national level rather than at the 'grassroots.'

Several motions to refer were being formulated at the Synod. After the defeat of this first motion, those who wanted to delay a decision held a caucus in an attempt to consolidate the motions to refer. Ultimately, the Reverend Murray Stockall, later to be known as a leading proponent of the movement against the ordination of women, and Bishop Robert Seaborn moved:

> That this General Synod request the Committee on Ministry to promote the study of the question of the ordination of women to the priesthood to the end that each diocese vote on the matter and report the results of its decision to the National Executive Council through the Committee on Ministry prior to the next General Synod with the best possible references being provided for study.[30]

This second referral motion was again defeated in the House of Clergy. There were obviously some who felt that the General Synod was not ready to make such a historic decision. The House of Clergy, however, felt it was ready to proceed with the vote. This did not necessarily mean that all clergy were ready to endorse women's ordination, but rather that they were ready to make their voice heard on the subject. Eventually the 1973 Synod passed a motion on this issue which had been amended several times. It was finally agreed to approve the ordination of women to priesthood in principle, and then refer the issue to the dioceses for study. The amended motion read as follows:

> That this General Synod accept the principle of the ordination of women to the priesthood, that this decision be communicated to the Anglican Consultative Council, and that implementation not take place until the House of Bishops has worked out a pattern for the Canadian Church that would include an educational process for the Church. {ACT 31}[31]

The compromise which the Synod worked out held that the Synod supported women's ordination in principle but that the church would not proceed with such ordinations until the House of Bishops developed a pattern for implementation and some plan for education at the diocesan level.

CONSTITUTIONAL STRUCTURE

Interpreting the implications of this deferral to the House of Bishops is dependent upon some understanding of the constitutional structure of the Canadian Anglican church. The Church of England in Canada existed under the direction of the Church of England during colonial times. By the mid-nineteenth century, many Canadians were saying that the time had come for an autonomous and self-directed church. From 1893 the individual provinces of the Church of England in Canada formed themselves into a self-declared independent province with a General Synod as the focus of its unity. From 1896, the Church of England in Canada had its own constitution which articulated the balance of powers between national, provincial and diocesan synods and their relationship to diocesan bishops and their collective form as embodied in the House of Bishops.

Between 1922 and 1967 many changes were made to the Constitution. In 1931 a document entitled the Declaration of Principles was constructed which articulated the jurisdiction and theoretical basis of the General Synod in relation to the other bodies which comprised the church structure. The General Synod did not have the right to interfere with or take away the rights, powers or jurisdiction of the provincial or diocesan synods. Having said that, the Declaration of Principles identified eight areas of jurisdiction which it claimed. In 1952 the place and ministry of women in the church was added to these areas of jurisdiction. It was stipulated that any change affecting the canons dealing with the doctrine, discipline and worship of the church (including ministry of women) would have to be passed by two successive General Synods, and that a change in the Declaration of Principles itself would require a two-thirds majority in each of the three orders to pass.[32]

Given that 1952 addition, it was the General Synod which was expected to deal with issues of women's ministry and ordination after the Lambeth Conference of 1968. At the 1969 session of General Synod a key inquiry was held before a decision was made to implement Lambeth recommendations with regard to women deacons. The Synod asked the Assessors to the Prolocutor and other relevant persons of legal expertise to make a comment on whether or not a constitutional or canonical change would have to be made before women could be admitted to the threefold order of ministry. It was agreed that no constitutional barrier then existed to the ordination of women, and as such no constitutional or canonical change would have to be undertaken. Any decision to proceed with the ordination of women could be implemented within the existing container of ecclesiastical law.[33] While the ministry canon was written in masculine language, this was understood as generic rather than exclusive terminology.

This statement by the Assessors to the Prolocutor was a key factor in the decision-making process of the Canadian church in the 1970s. It meant that no major changes to the Constitution had to be made. As such, a two-thirds majority in each house did not apply. A simple majority passing a statement of opinion at one General Synod would allow the implementation of the ordination of women. Interestingly, however, this ruling was not actually applied in the long run. As we will see, the General Synod actually voted on the issue twice, and a two-thirds majority was reached in each house. The Synod deferred to the House of Bishops in 1973 and the House in turn wanted affirmation of its mandate, and so went back to the Synod in 1975.

The powers and rights of bishops were important in this process. Section 8(a) of the Declaration of Principles states that nothing in the preceding sections shall limit or affect the powers, jurisdiction and authority inherent in the office of bishop, as it was exercised either individually or collectively. By virtue of his orders a bishop has the sole right of ordination, without limitation or the possibility of delegation. He or she may or may not ordain whomever he or she chooses; however, through original consent in the formation of provincial, diocesan and General Synods, bishops consented to work with a synodical form of government which if respected, effectively limits their choices and actions. A bishop is given power to act in the Synod by the Synod, of which he along with all other bishops are members.[34]

In the General Synod, bishops exercise collective powers as members of a separate house, along with two other houses, the House of the Clergy and the House of the Laity. The weight of each house in voting is the same. The House of Bishops does not hold unique powers. It does, however, perform important functions in the areas of education, study and policy recommendation. The bishops as a group do not possess the authority to direct the decisions of the Synod, nor to cancel a synodical act. The usual *modus operandi* between the House of Bishops and the Synod has been co-operation.[35]

HOUSE OF BISHOPS, 1973–1975

What did happen in the House of Bishops on this issue between 1973 and 1975? The issue of women's ordination to the priesthood occurred on every agenda for meetings of the House of Bishops between 1973 and 1975 except for one, 31 January – 1 February 1975. At the November-December session of the House of Bishops in 1973, the House appointed an in-House task force to deal with this issue. At the meeting of the House of Bishops held in Toronto, 10-11 May 1974, Bishop Barry Valentine gave a report on the work of the in-House task force. He noted that it was currently in the process of preparing a position paper for study at the next meeting of the House in December. At the May meeting, the discussion was structured around six different categories, namely scriptural, historical, theological, ecclesiological, sociological, and constitutional concerns.[36] These categories were important as they represented those areas which the in-House task force felt were crucial to any discussion of the issue. By agreement the groups did not report on these discussions. The next stage of the process was the weighing of priorities of the categories. Before the House closed its business on the issue, it agreed that all dioceses should be summoned to study and prayer concerning this issue and that implementing that study would be the responsibility of individual bishops.[37]

When the House of Bishops next met in December 1974, at Port Credit, Ontario, the in-House task force had prepared and distributed a report for the perusal of all members of the House of Bishops. The bishops discussed this document, simply entitled, "The Ordination of Women to the Priesthood," and agreed that it would then be circulated to the whole church for study and discussion prior to the General Synod of 1975.[38] This report contained some analysis of the issues surrounding the actual implementation of the ordination of women. The report referred to the irregular ordinations of the eleven women in Philadelphia that year, and stressed that the Canadian church should not take any "intemperate or obdurate action" which would aggravate an already complex "problem."[39] This reference was interesting as very little mention of the American situation is made anywhere in official church documents and deliberations. It also shows, however, that the issue was known and thought about. After this introductory caution was issued, the bishops identified six areas as areas for concern if the actual stage of implementation was to be arrived at in the Canadian church.

Authority was first on the list of important issues with which the house had to deal. The task force saw authority as a problem of jurisdiction. Whose jurisdiction was it to make a decision on this issue? While noting that diocesan and provincial synods, bishops and the House of Bishops all had jurisdiction in the matter, the report stressed that, "real authority ultimately rests on the ability to engender respect for decisions." The report commented that the church had evolved a decision-making process over the years which had served it well and that that process should not be abandoned because the decision on this particular issue was one of such magnitude. While the House of Bishops had decided to ordain women to the diaconate in 1969, there were many who felt that the General Synod should ratify the decision regarding priesting. This concern was noted only to demonstrate a viewpoint which was pervasive in deliberations on this issue. Although there was virtually no debate on the issue, General Synod was involved in the decision regarding women in the diaconate through the motions of the Commission on Women's Work in 1969. They also stressed the importance of staying connected with the larger Anglican Communion. It was felt that this decision should not be implemented without a clear and, perhaps more importantly, perceived involvement by all bodies of ecclesiastical authority.

The task force raised the question of study with respect to implementation. The need for people in the church to submit themselves to, "the hard discipline of discussing this matter honestly within the separable categories", to the end of mutual understanding was stressed. They emphasized the educational process recommended by the preceeding General Synod and the responsibility of individual dioceses to carry it out.

Some bishops raised the question of collegiality in the House of Bishops. In short, this section of the report stated that there would have to be a mutual expectation of collegiality between bishops. The report acknowledged that there was a division of opinion on the issue among bishops but that it would be intolerable if one bishop refused to support the action of another. This was noted as an internal problem of mutual support which the members of the House would have to work out among themselves.[40]

Closely related to the internal problem of collegiality was the larger problem of acceptance. There would be clergy and laity who were opposed to the implementation of women's ordination. The report made no suggestions about how to deal with this dissent. Rather they discussed the relationship of the church to secular society. They argued that the church should not set its policy based on the whims of society, but that it was inevitable that the wider context of the study meant that it would, "sooner or later extend to new theological insights about women and women in society."[41]

The issue of sacrifice, namely the inevitable sacrifice of those women who would be the first to be ordained, was also named. The report asked the church to respond pastorally to the particular needs of women who would make the sacrifice of pioneers, but concluded by saying that, "We are not alarmed by the prospect of sacrifice; it is an integral part of the Christian life which every member will accept and rejoice in."[42] While there is a certain theological validity to this statement, it must be approached with caution. For many centuries women particularly have been admonished that sacrifice is good for the soul, often to their detriment.

The task force considered the practical question of deployment. Stressing that ordination was a matter of function as much as of being, the report stressed that all bishops who would eventually ordain a woman also granted a jurisdiction, namely power and authority to act fully as a priest, all priests who would lay hands on her promised to serve her as a colleague and friend, and the laity who voted for the principle must support the ministry of the woman priest.[43]

The House of Bishops carried a motion which referred this matter back to the General Synod of 1975. The motions which came from the General Synod of 1973 did allow for the possibility that the House of Bishops could move forward with ordinations when they had devised a plan of implementation if they chose. At the December, 1974 meeting, however, the bishops agreed that the issue of approval in principle could well be considered a matter of Faith and Order, and as such should be ratified by a second vote at General Synod.[44] This move was directed by Section 11, paragraph two of the Declaration of Principles of the Constitution of the Anglican Church of Canada, whereby matters of Faith and Order must be passed by two General Synods.

One further meeting of the House of Bishops took place before the crucial General Synod of 1975. At that time the House formulated a plan of action. The House agreed that the Primate, Edward Scott, should introduce the subject at General Synod and attempt to set the focus for the debate and subsequent action. It was also agreed that the vote at General Synod should be made by secret ballot.

After some discussion, it was agreed that the House should send a "memorial" to General Synod. This memorial stated that after study of the resolutions circulated in the convening circular for the Synod, it felt that the unity of the church and the collegiality of the House of Bishops would be best served if a simple reaffirmation of the 1973 resolution was made. Once this principle was declared and ratified by the General Synod it should not be "rendered ineffective by improper delays in implementation."[45] As such, the House advised that the 1973 resolution be reaffirmed and that there be no further debate on the issue itself. The bishops also agreed that if the Agenda committee felt that it was impossible to make this change, the House of Bishops would make a motion to implement this change on the floor of Synod. This motion was carried unanimously; it was the only unanimously carried motion recorded with reference to this entire issue. All bishops felt strongly about trusting the guidance of the Holy Spirit and letting the chips fall where they might.

GENERAL SYNOD, 1975

The General Synod of 1975 was the determinative historic occasion at which the tides of history were turned forever, and the path toward the ordination of women to the priesthood in the Anglican Church of Canada was chosen. The Synod passed three resolutions on the subject.

The first motion reaffirmed the resolution of the previous synod. It was resolved, "That this General Synod reaffirm the principle of the ordination of women to the priesthood." The voting on this resolution was then recorded by request.[46]

	IN FAVOUR	AGAINST
Laity	88	18
Clergy	75	30
Bishops	26	8
TOTAL	189	56

The second motion the Synod made and carried provided the vehicle for actually implementing the ordination of women to the presbyterate. Prior to the vote Professor Joanne Dewart made a presentation on Christianity and feminism. This presentation invited the church to move beyond the "perversion of Christianity" which historically hindered a woman's right to relate directly and personally to God.[47] It was resolved: THAT this General Synod further affirm that it would be appropriate for women qualified for the priesthood to be ordained at the discretion of diocesan bishops acting within the normal procedures of their own jurisdictions and in consultation with the House of Bishops.[48]

The third and final motion was the most controversial from the standpoint of history. Contained within the third motion was the controversial conscience clause, which has since been revoked at the General Synod of 1986. Although discussion in the House of Bishops referred to the unqualified need for this clause, there is little record of discussion about it anywhere, in the House of Bishops, in the General Synod Committee on Ministry, or in the press. It appears with the other two motions, and in the opinion of those who participated in the preparation of this issue was of inestimable value in letting the motions in favour of women's ordination to the priesthood pass. After the fact it has been controversial because it qualified what was perceived by many to be the movement of the Holy Spirit. In any event it was resolved:

> THAT no bishop, priest, deacon or lay person including postulants for ordination in the Anglican Church of Canada should be penalized in any manner, nor suffer any canonical disabilities, nor be forced into positions which violate or coerce his or her conscience as a result of General Synod's action in affirming the principle of the ordination of women to the priesthood, and requests that those who have authority in this matter, to act upon the principle set out above.[49]

With these words the Canadian church was able to find a 'middle road' which offended the fewest possible people; it opened up the road to the future.

THE MANIFESTO ON THE ORDINATION OF WOMEN TO THE PRIESTHOOD

In the Anglican Church of Canada there was no organized lobby for the ordination of women to the priesthood. The only organized 'movement' in response to this issue was against. There was a small movement by some male clergy who were opposed to the ordination of women to the priesthood which surfaced after the General Synod of 1975.

In September 1975, a letter signed by a group of more than 200 Anglican clergymen was published in the *Anglican Churchman*. That 200 represents less than ten percent of the total number of active clergy at the time. This letter was called, *A Manifesto on the Ordination of Women to the Priesthood from Concerned Clergy of the Anglican Church of Canada*. Its purpose was to offer a public protest against the General Synod decision to proceed with the ordination of women to the presbyterate. A document of substantial length for a newspaper publication, it argued against the ordination of women, with its opposition being grounded in concerns about the maintenance of Anglican tradition and heritage, as well as ecumenism. It noted with alarm that with this move the Anglican Church of Canada was abandoning its heritage, which was grounded in the male apostolic succession of ordered ministry.

Those who wrote the *Manifesto* claimed to be, "bearing witness to the truest principles of Anglicanism." Those priests who signed the document rejected the General Synod decision "*ab initio*" as they felt that it was simply an impossibility "in the divine economy" for a woman to be a priest. The issue was one of ontology. There was something about the being of a woman which prohibited her from being a priest. The document made reference to the ordinations in Hong Kong and the United States saying that they were not a precedent and might be overlooked, as they were done in the first case on diocesan authority alone, and in the second illegally. It also referred to the Church of Sweden which had been forced by secular authorities to open ordained ministry to women, saying that it had not ceased to be a cause of division in that church. Their greatest concern was that the Anglican Church of Canada was only one small part of Christendom and should not act alone. Clearly views of the *Manifesto* echo the sympathies of the writer of the 1972 *Minority Report*.[50]

The last section of the *Manifesto* identified the struggles of those clergy who felt that they might have to leave the church because of this decision. It is clear from the wording, however, that most clergy who signed the document would not actually leave the church because of their family responsibilities, their inability to make a living in any other way, and their "love of the church". Instead they would make use of the conscience clause and withhold their support from the ordination of women in their own dioceses.[51] 22 of the 30 dioceses of the church had some clergy who had signed this document.

The writers of the *Manifesto* contacted clergy around the country asking for their support of the document before it was published; publication appended the names and dioceses of supporters. Once it was published the only further action taken by this loosely formed organization was to address the House of Bishops at its October meeting through an open letter to the House in order that it might defend the publication of the *Manifesto*.

The *Manifesto* precipitated a large amount of correspondence from several interested parties. In a pastoral letter dated 17 November 1975 the Primate affirmed the integrity of those clergy who had signed the *Manifesto*, and stressed that he respected the deep concern and struggle over the issue which was reflected in their signing of the document. No formal statement had been made to the Primate or to the House of Bishops up to that point which declared the displeasure of the clergy with the ongoing movement toward women's ordination, although it was acknowledged all along that there was disagreement over the issue at every level of the debates. In his letter Primate Scott stated that he realized that individual clergy had signed for differing reasons. He then included in the letter several documents which responded to the problems raised by each of the identified positions. The tone of the letter was one of pastoral concern and conciliation, but it was made clear that it was the author's conviction that what was being done was the right path of action.[52]

Several clergy wrote answering letters to the Primate defending their action. None of these recanted their actions in any way. The letters defended the position of those who remained opposed to the ordination of women for various reasons. In the interests of ecumenism one priest wrote, "I have read the arguments in favour of the Anglican Church of Canada giving a lead to the rest of the Church, but I cannot accept them in any way."[53] Expressing opposition to the procedure by which the decision was made, a bishop wrote, "I have more and more problems accepting Synod as a decision-making body in matters which I believe rightly belong to the House of Bishops."[54] The most obviously angry tone was found in a letter from another priest. In his letter he wrote:

> I am writing to ask you to have my name removed from your mailing list. I do not wish to receive any more propaganda for priestesses in the Christian Church. It is quite obvious to me that you and your cohorts are determined to take this illegal action, and you have your position and authority to do so. We in

the lower ranks will simply have to wait patiently upon God and see what happens to us.[55]

In more than one of the letters from those who had signed the *Manifesto* the argument that, "Jesus Christ is the same yesterday, today and forever", was used to justify the argument from tradition against including women in the priesthood.[56]

While other letters of opposition were vehement in their tone, there was not a large number of them. What then can we conclude about the nature of the organized opposition in the Canadian case? The opposition lobby was framed around clergy. According to Gramsci's model this group represents the traditional intellectual class which has a vested interest in protecting the status quo. In most Anglican situations, it is the clergy who serve as a focus for the opposition to women as priests. They set themselves up as the guardians of tradition, but in the Canadian case what is most striking is the comparatively low level intensity of the opposition.

The organized opposition did not get underway until after what appeared to be a final decision on the issue had been made. Apparently some clergy did not believe that the church would actually decide to proceed with ordinations which would, "split Christendom irrevocably." Once General Synod 1975 had met, it seemed that the handwriting was on the wall, and the *Manifesto* was a last bid attempt to stop what was coming. It was too little too late to affect the decision-making process.

This opposition by clergy must also be viewed in light of the fact that most clergy, as represented by voting at General Synod and the small percentage of clerical participation in the *Manifesto*, supported the idea of women in the priesthood. In response to the *Manifesto* one priest wrote the Primate expressing his concerns. As one who was known to support the ordination of women he had not received a copy of the *Manifesto*, but rather was shown a copy of the letter by another priest. Addressing the argument 'against' from the perspective of a clergy person, he argued that in a sense he felt his maleness limited his priesthood. Referring to his colleague in the parish, a female deacon, he stressed that his ministry was enriched by her presence; she brought things to the community which a man could not. He further stressed that maleness did not qualify him as a priest, "What we seek in ordinands are precisely those qualities which allow us to become '*alter Christus*'... Our

Lord exhibited not only the 'male' qualities of his humanity, but also his female attributes."[57]

LAY SUPPORT

Clergy were not the only ones offended by the content of the *Manifesto*. Lay people who were present at the General Synod in Quebec in 1973 and who had supported the motions in favour of ordaining women wrote to the Primate. These letters expressed outrage at the contents of the *Manifesto* insisting that those who had supported women's ordination were as faithful in their commitment to their faith and denomination as anyone. These letters also refuted the arguments against women's ordination touched on in the *Manifesto*. One particular letter from a lay delegate to the General Synod referred to the fact that there had been people who had supported the ordination of women for years, but they had not been vocal about it:

> For years now those of us who believe women should be able to follow her faith into the full witness and service of priestly ministry, have waited, talked, persuaded, prayed humbly. Women were kept firmly outside the real decision-making hierarchy of the Anglican Church, that is the episcopacy. We organized no clamorous groups proclaiming we alone possessed the truth inherited through the ages. My reply to the St. James' group is — let us now test this thing to see whether it to be of God. By her fruits we will know her. As helper she has served— Often where men would not— in the north, in cities, in the west for years without much recognition. Let her serve in the priesthood and she will show you your faith and your God have been too small.[58]

This letter is important because it documents the idea that support for women's ordination preceded the formal discussion of the same in church circles. This letter supported by living memoirs shows that support among the laity for this issue did pre-exist the discussions and motions of the Synod. Moreover, this support was not concertedly expressed anywhere, until the aggressive attack against women's ordination was formulated in the *Manifesto*, and after a lawful decision had been made by the decision-making bodies of the church.

The tenor of this letter to the Primate echoed voices from oral history interviews. Women who had been actively involved in lay ministry for many years were passionate in their support of the notion of equality for women in the church. This was reflected in the lobby for just wages, pensions and status for women church workers, but not in a lobby for the ordination of women.

The fact that there was no large movement in favour of the ordination of women at any time in the Canadian context is not surprising when seen in relation to the larger picture of Canadian history. When one compares the ordination of women question to the movement for women's suffrage (1877–1918), one finds a strikingly similar pattern. Relative to other English speaking countries, Canada's suffrage movement started late and achieved its goal comparatively easily. Although the wave of feminism which promoted women's suffrage was the first massive women's movement in Canada, it never attracted a groundswell of support. At its height in 1914, the movement had only ten thousand supporters, or 0.2 percent of the adult Canadian population. Even so it was only four years later that all women over the age of twenty-one years of age had the federal vote, and most also had the provincial franchise.[59]

The Canadian *mentalité* has not historically embraced aggressive lobbying activity as part of its political milieu; and yet things change. This same *mentalité* is in evidence in the Canadian Anglican Church. The Anglican Church of Canada has virtually never made its decisions after aggressive lobbying. A pattern has emerged in the synodical decision-making. Decisions are made in the Synod quietly. When people have a conviction on any given issue, they are vocal about it when they take their turn at the microphones in Synod sessions. Groups designed to promote change, lobbying for a particular agenda item, and/or promoting the interests of a particular issue are virtually unheard of in the Canadian system. As such, the debates over the ordination of women to the priesthood were conducted in a style which was true to the form of the Anglican Church of Canada. Unfortunately, the 'quietness' which surrounds actual decision-making processes makes it more difficult for the historian to assess the relative impact of various factors and points of view.

An anecdote from the General Synod of 1973 illustrates the non-aggressive nature of Canadian Anglican lobbying activity. Three laywomen from ARCWA went to the Synod as observers. Their purpose was to set up a booth with artwork and the limited amount of feminist literature that was available so that the issues around women in the church might be promoted. They were promoting the interests of women workers but did not function specifically as a lobby group. In the hall outside the central meeting place, the three women offered apples to members of Synod commenting that, "there were two bites out of the first apple."[60] With this gesture the women supported the ordination of women to the priesthood. The dramatic difference between this form of support and the organized and highly politicized lobby which existed in the Episcopal Church of the United States is striking; aggressive grassroots lobbying was not the Canadian way.

What then do we know about the attitudes of the laity at the grassroots of the church to the ordination of women? The synodical voting figures demonstrate a greater than two-thirds majority of support, over 80 percent in favour of the 1975 re-affirmation of the 1973 vote in favour of the ordination of women. In other words, the House of the Laity had the largest margin of support in favour; the House of Bishops was second, 76 percent in favour and the House of Clergy was most opposed with 71 percent in favour. The correspondence noted above indicates that lay people were aware and supportive of the issue, although not vocal about it. In the Canadian case there was no grassroots lobby for the ordination of women, but when the ecclesiastical power-holders put the topic on the agenda, there was a great deal of enthusiastic support for the idea.

It is understandable that many lay people at the parish level would be enthusiastic about the idea of women in Holy Orders, for it is the laity who for years had been the beneficiaries of the ministry of women. In more than one diocese parishioners took the initiative in requesting the ordination of their women deacons. In both the diocese of Huron for Mary Mills, and in the Diocese of Athabasca, for Enid Longwell and Phyllis Locke, the diocesan bishops were asked by the members of the parishes in which these three women served to ordain them to the priesthood. These requests were made after a decision to proceed had been made at the national level. In both cases the diocesan bishops had already publicly declared their support for the ordination of women. These actions by parishioners demonstrate the existence of a strong support for the ministry of women at the parish level. In all three instances the parishioners stressed that the women were already priests in every sense, except for presiding at the eucharist. To ordain them to the priesthood would simply confirm a ministry which was already happening.

THE HOUSE OF BISHOPS, 1975 – 1976

The House of Bishops met in St. Norbert, Manitoba from 31 October to 1 November 1975. At that session of the House some correspondence was received which expressed sympathy with the dissent found in the *Manifesto*. These letters were an attempt to convince the House of Bishops that it should not implement the wishes of the General Synod. Although what appeared to be a final decision had been made following the lawfully established procedures of the church, those who opposed the decision realized that in an episcopal system, the final authority in ordination rested with the individual bishops. As such, the fight was not over until the bishops had proceeded with the actual ordinations.

Individual letters from opposing clergy were not the only material received by the House of Bishops. At the October meeting some clergy who supported the *Manifesto* presented it to the House of Bishops. This presentation was followed by a lengthy refutation of the points made by the Primate in his letter to those who had signed the *Manifesto*. Most important among these, from a procedural point of view, was the contention that the vote of General Synod was precipitous and unrepresentative:

> Chronologically, from your point of view, the vote does not look precipitate: theologically to us it looks like a DEATH-LEAP. But it is also precipitate and unrepresentative, we are convinced (and the response to the *Manifesto* seems to bear us out), in that the numerical figures of the Quebec vote simply do not reflect the true state of mind of the Church at large.[61]

No statistics are available to support the claim that the vote at the Synod did not represent the mind of the church. To be able to claim this, one would have to take a referendum. The breakdown by dioceses included in the next chapter indicates that a majority of dioceses were indeed in favour of, or at least not openly opposed to, the ordination of women to the priesthood. These comments apparently represented only the opinion of those who supported the *Manifesto*, a small percentage of the total number of clergy in the national church.

Bishop Barry Valentine prepared a paper for final deliberation at the request of the Agenda Committee of the House. The paper stressed that the issue, however it had arrived there, was now firmly in the hands of the House of Bishops. Although the General Synod had made its feelings known, the bishops could then choose to do whatever they felt was right. This position demonstrates the extent to which the House of Bishops understood itself to be the final arbiter of the situation.

As such Valentine outlined what he perceived to be the three possible responses which were open to the House. The first would be to reject the principle outright. In other words, although General Synod had twice affirmed the ordination of women to the priesthood in principle, the House of Bishops could choose to reject it at that point. Such a move would have re-opened the whole debate concerning the pros and cons of the issue itself. The second option was to say "Yes we accept the principle and we will do it immediately or soon." The third and final option which he addressed was to say, "Yes, we accept the principle, but we will not do it yet." After discussion the House carried the following motion:

> THAT this House reaffirms a collegial commitment to the principle and implementation of the ordination of women to the presbyterate, while not pretending to unanimity, and therefore supports the desire and intention of the bishops who after due consultation with their dioceses determine to ordain certain qualified women to the presbyterate. Further, the House requests the Primate to inform the other Primates of the Anglican Communion of this resolution, to seek their response to it and report it to other communions of our intention. This House agrees that if the responses are not overwhelmingly negative Bishops are free to proceed to the ordination of women to the presbyterate after 1 November 1976. In any case we intend to present our case reasonably and urgently to the Lambeth Conference of 1978, or an acceptable alternative and thereafter proceed to full implementation.[62]

This meeting of the House of Bishops was key in the gradual movement of the Canadian church toward the actual ordination of women to the priesthood. The motion which was passed (above) was a masterpiece in progressive compromise. It responded creatively to most of the concerns and goals of the diverse opinions represented in the House.

The action taken at this session explains the time delay between the vote at General Synod in the summer of 1975 and the first ordinations on 30 November 1976, one and a half years later. Although the House of

Bishops had full authority to proceed, one further step was undertaken, namely, direct consultation with other branches of the Anglican Communion. The House of Bishops asked the Primate to correspond with other Primates and provinces and request feedback. If that feedback had been overwhelmingly negative, the ordinations would not have gone forward at that point in history.

Following the meeting of the House of Bishops, the Primate sent or delivered a letter to all Primates or Presiding Bishops in the Anglican Communion. Fifteen of the Anglican Primates were able to meet with Scott to discuss this issue prior to the World Council of Churches meeting in Nairobi. Others responded in writing. In his letter Scott outlined the circumstances in the Canadian Church. He then addressed two questions to the Primates and Presiding Bishops which he asked them to respond to:

1. In the Anglican structure, in the light of past action by the Lambeth Conference and the Anglican Consultative Council, would you agree that each Province has the authority to act as long as "due procedure" in terms of its own canons is observed?

2. Would you personally recommend to your Province that women qualified under the criteria of the Province concerned and ordained to the Presbyterate according to the procedure of the Province, should be recognized as having been validly and regularly ordained priests? We would recognize that in other Provinces, as in other dioceses in Canada, they would not have the right to exercise their ministry without the permission of the Province or Diocese, House of Bishops or Bishop concerned (depending upon where the authority lies in each Province).[63]

In his letter Scott then assured all concerned parties that the Anglican Church of Canada had not acted "unadvisedly, lightly or wantonly." He added that the church was then in the process of seeking to develop adequate means of continuing discussions with, and providing pastoral support for those who remained opposed to the decision of the church to ordain women. There is actually little evidence of follow-up with this issue in the Canadian church.

Scott personally collected, both in verbal and written communication, the responses of the heads of provinces to both these questions. These actual responses were recorded indirectly at the meeting of the House of Bishops in February, 1976. In the minutes of those sessions we have the record of a report by Scott which related many of these responses, and the conclusion by him and subsequently the House that these responses did not indicate an overwhelmingly negative response.[64] There is very little sense of urgency. The responses showed that a gradual movement toward the ordination of women to the priesthood was underway in many parts of the Communion but had not yet been fully accomplished.

At this same meeting Scott referred to an informal report prepared by Bishop John Howe of the Church of England regarding the meeting in Rome of a group of Anglicans from the Church of England with a group of papal representatives. The discussion at the meeting led to the statement by Rome's ecumenical emissaries that if women were appointed to the priesthood, "It would not mean an end to the Anglican/Roman Catholic joint striving for unity, but that if Anglicans did proceed with the ordination of women it would constitute a new and serious difficulty and obstacle in our joint search for unity."[65]

The House reviewed recommendations on sexism from the final assembly of the World Council of Churches. In his report of the meeting, Scott stated that all Orthodox churches except the Russian Orthodox supported a motion that churches who believed God was calling them to ordain women should feel free to move, and that they should remain in dialogue with churches who did not feel so called.[66] In other words, the ecumenical implications from the perspective of Roman Catholics, Orthodox (except Russian), and the Protestants were discussed in the House and, in and of themselves, were not considered to be prohibitive as these partners in ecumenical dialogue had not shut the door on the issue.

Perhaps one of the most interesting events of that meeting of the House of Bishops was the reception of a report of an in-House task force on guidelines regarding the ordination of women to the priesthood. Bishop David Ragg of the Diocese of Huron reported that a common date for the first ordinations had been suggested, St. Andrew's Day, 30 November 1976, with a recommendation of synchronized and simultaneous ordinations across the country. The emphasis was on "normality". If at all possible there should be male and female candidates ordained at the same time. There was to be a special press release from each diocese involved, but there was to be no radio or television at the services, and the usual ordination procedures would be observed as far as possible.

While the course of the church seemed to have been set at that point, there was still considerable dissent over this issue. After the in camera session, it was argued that the Anglican Consultative Council was meeting in April of that year and that further discussion and preparations should be delayed until after that meeting. It was agreed that a special meeting of the House of Bishops should be held on 29 May 1976, to receive information from the Anglican Consultative Council and to make firm decisions about the next steps to be taken in Canada.[67]

That meeting of the House of Bishops was held at Huron College, London, Ontario. The House passed three motions. The first affirmed the decision in principle of women's ordination to the priesthood and its implementation in the Anglican Church of Canada, the second affirmed the implementation of the Conscience Clause and the third stated that the service to be used for the ordination of women presbyters was to be the Prayer Book Ordinal or the usual service of the dioceses concerned, in other words, the same for the women as for the men.[68]

The most interesting wording was found in connection with the second motion. The conscience clause was a key ingredient in making it possible for the actual ordinations to happen. Be it resolved:

> THAT the Conscience Clause passed by General Synod be reaffirmed with the understanding that this in effect, recognizes the tolerability of living with an anomaly, and removes any question of the integrity of those who while in opposition to the ordination of women to the presbyterate and unable to recognize the reality of such ordinations, are yet able to remain within the communion of the Anglican Church of Canada even as it respects the integrity of Bishops who ordain women to the presbyterate and the canonical rights and integrity of the women so ordained.[69]

This motion was a masterpiece of diplomacy.

After that meeting the only thing left to be done was the actual event of ordination. The House chose the date 30 November 1976, and those bishops who felt "so called" agreed to ordain the Canadian church's first women to the priesthood. The House of Bishops did not select the dioceses involved in the first ordinations. Rather Scott invited all bishops by letter, dated 6 August 1976, to inform him if they had women whom they were planning on ordaining that night. Some bishops wrote and responded in the negative, some said nothing, and four sent the names of women whom they planned to ordain on 30 November 1976.[70] These four were the Bishops of New Westminster, Cariboo, Niagara and Huron.

REVOLUTION FROM ABOVE

In the matter of the ordination of women to the priesthood, the House of Bishops did not claim absolute jurisdiction; neither did they abdicate leadership. In their deliberations between 1971 and 1975, the bishops studied and debated. They struggled with issues of authority and jurisdiction. Ultimately, they corporately agreed to trust the synodical process and in fact sought assurances from the Synod which by constitution they were not required to do. However, what is most notable about the bishops in this matter is the collegial manner in which they undertook to offer direction to the church, and eventually to take on the responsibility of acting on its behalf.

THE ROLE OF PRIMATE EDWARD SCOTT

The leadership of Primate Edward Scott was a key factor in the church's acceptance of the idea of women in the priesthood. His actions and initiative provided a leadership for the church which facilitated the direction the church pursued. In that sense, the decision-making process was a top-down initiative. His vision for the church was eventually actualized because there was sufficient support for it at all levels of church life; his vision was mirrored in other segments of the church's populace.

The Primate of all Canada is the titular head of the Anglican Church of Canada. His powers in essence parallel those of a diocesan bishop. He or she is an Archbishop who has chief pastoral responsibility for the care of the clergy and laity of the church. He or she has the power to ordain but has no specific jurisdiction within which to act without invitation by other diocesan bishops. In other words, he or she is a bishop without an actual diocese. In a sense, the whole church is the pastoral charge but he or she no longer has the power to act or direct dioceses — that is the responsibility of each diocesan bishop. By his or her election, the church invests the Primate with a certain spiritual authority to offer spiritual direction and leadership in the area of policy and vision for the church.[71] Whatever influence the Primate has will be determined by the extent to which he or she is able to gather support for their actions from other segments of the ecclesiastical structure. In other words, the Primate's power is persuasive rather than legislative.

Scott was strongly in favour of the ordination of women to the priesthood. He stated that conviction openly from the early 1970's onward. While he felt that he did not want to force the church in a direction that it could not go, he felt that it was the direction in which it should go.[72] As such, he supported the issue as it came up for discussion in various places. This is evident in his interactions with the dioceses. The Primate visited virtually every diocese at some point during the period when this issue was under discussion. When he was specifically asked to address the issue he offered support for it, along with a pastoral and supportive overture toward those who felt that they could not accept the ordination of women. Further, he did not initiate discussion on the topic when not invited to do so. His actions throughout were those of a diplomat who struggled to convey empathy for both sides of the argument while gently articulating his own position. He did not attempt to change the mind of a synod which was heading in a direction contrary to his own conscience.[73]

The Primate is the senior member of the House of Bishops. As such, his power and influence in that body is that of *primus inter pares*. There is virtually no written record of the comments which Scott made in the House of Bishops, but his brother bishops readily noted that he actively lobbied for the ordination of women. By their admission and his own, he always worked for a common ground of understanding. The continued unity of the House of Bishops in the face of divided opinion was always tantamount in his approach to this subject and others. Many commented that the debates in the House were carried on with a great deal of good nature humour and very little anger.[74]

One of Scott's most significant contributions to the collegiality of the House and the maintenance of unity within the church was the conscience clause. The wording of this clause was a masterpiece of conciliation and mediation. It allowed all people to live according to their conscience. While he saw the necessity of the clause, Scott also regretted its implications for the women who would be ordained. In his letter to the women ordinands prior to the first ordinations, he expressed hope that the clause would not be needed forever.[75] He conciliated the opposition and also encouraged and consoled the women ordinands. He responded to the interests of all in some fashion. A middle road was constructed without which the ordination of women might not have become a reality at that time.

The statesmanship of Primate Scott was evident from the manner in which he conducted relations with other parts of the Communion. When Scott contacted them after the General Synod of 1975, it was evident that not all Anglican Primates were in agreement about the ordination of women. After discussions with Scott, all of them agreed to support the action in so far as they respected the right of the Canadian church to make up its own mind on the matter; they also agreed to remain in Communion with the Canadian church. Scott was able to navigate the turbulent waters of international conciliation.

How does the historian assess the impact of an individual on history? With great difficulty. It can be said, however, that Primate Scott, the official leader of the Anglican Church of Canada was committed both to promoting the ordination of women and to maintaining unity at home and abroad. His diplomatic skills were notable and influential. Without his input and direction, it is entirely conceivable that history would have taken another course.

EPISCOPAL MOTIVATION

This brings us to the question: why did the episcopal leadership of the church support, and in many cases actively promote the idea of women in the priesthood? The answer to that question has several aspects to it.

Economic and Employment Factors

Economic considerations were a factor. A myth exists in the larger Anglican Communion that the Canadian church moved to accept the ordination of women readily because its 'vast wilderness' meant that it had a chronic shortage of clergy to minister to the needs of its people. Comments from the House of Bishops previously related lead to the conclusion that this was not the case. Even if there was a localized clergy shortage in places, it is clear that the perception of the bishops themselves was that there were sufficient clergy to meet the needs of the Canadian Anglican church. There is evidence, however, that practical concerns played some part in this unfolding drama. There was a labour problem in the church, and as has been noted, this problem involved the place, status, authority and remuneration of its paid women workers.

The tradition of women's work which had existed from the late nineteenth century in Canadian Anglicanism played no small part in the decision which was ultimately made to ordain women. All of the bishops interviewed for this study cited the long, strong tradition of women's work as a major factor in their acceptance of the idea of women as priests. Recurrently in the debates of the House of Bishops, the experience of women as deaconesses and paid lay ministers was referred to as evidence of the fact that women were more than competent to 'do the job.'

Some distinction must be made between deaconesses and full-time women workers. The deaconess was more clearly a direct part of the hierarchy of the institutional structure of the church than the worker. The deaconess was set apart by an episcopal laying on of hands in a service of ordination and was required to give up her orders if she married. There was controversy over whether or not these women were a part of the threefold ministry. The church said no, they were not from 1930 to 1968, and yes they were after 1969 in Canada. The reason that a distinction between these two categories must be made here is that it was from the deaconess group that the first women priests primarily came. Obviously, at least in retrospect, there was some relationship between the vocation of deaconess and the vocation of priest.

Table 6 profiles the ministry background of the first 18 women ordained to the priesthood. That table indicates that seven women were deaconesses prior to becoming deacons and then priests, four were Bishop's Messengers, one was a religious, and six were not engaged in paid church work prior to becoming deacons. These last women tended to be somewhat younger than their deaconess counterparts, coming to the vocation of paid ministry after the 1969 decision to allow the ordination of women as deacons had been made.

A majority of the first women priests then were formerly set apart as deaconesses. As such, the argument that an experience of women's ministry was related to a positive decision on the priesthood issue is viable. If one includes the Bishop's Messengers, 78 percent of the first 18 women in the priesthood were previously deaconesses. If one counts Bishop's Messengers as a separate category, the percentage of deaconesses falls to 56 percent of the total. The popular myth held by most individuals interviewed was that "the first women priests were old-timers in parish ministry."[76] 22 percent were not, but the remaining 78 percent support that myth.

What is perhaps most interesting, however, is the finding that none of the first women ordained to the priesthood came from the category of paid women workers. All with a history of parish ministry were invested in the ecclesiastical hierarchy in a permanent capacity, that is, life-long orders. This differentiated them from the licensed lay worker.

Virtually none of the first women priests, with one exception, were self-declared feminists. Many former lay workers interviewed, however, identified themselves in that way. Those who named themselves as feminists for the most part did not choose ordination. While they wanted to have a full-time ministry in the church, they also raised, as in the example of ARCWA, significant challenges for the church regarding remuneration, pensions, standardization of employment and the status of women in the church. Many of these women were lobbyists, even agitators in a mild way. These issues in their view were distinct from any question of ordination.

Herein lies a fascinating anomaly. Those women workers who did not pursue ordination were in many cases active in lobbying the ecclesiastical hierarchy for change. The women who chose ordination generally declared themselves to be inactive in the arena of lobbying for change. They did not promote the possibility of their own ordination, and, in most cases, they did not ask for structural changes related to their employment.

This connection between the women deaconesses and women priests posed some problems for women in ministry. When the church decided to ordain women first to the diaconate and then to the priesthood deaconesses were given the option of moving from their status as deaconesses to deacons and then priests. The numbers indicate that most chose this option. The number of deaconesses in the Anglican Church of Canada in 1969 was 26. In 1971, it was nine. These nine women represented those who chose to remain deaconesses rather than accept diaconal orders. In 1977, a year after the first women were ordained to the priesthood, four active deaconesses remained. Currently, the category of active deaconess is all but non-existent in the life of the church.[77] Licensed lay workers were not offered or did not choose that option.

As shown above, there were women who chose to remain deaconesses. The bishops had decided that they would not ordain any more deaconesses after the early 1970s because there was the option of diaconal and then priestly ministry. Also, virtually all other job opportunities for laywomen in the church ceased. If you wanted to remain a lay worker in the church, very few jobs were available. As a woman you either became a clergyperson or you did not have employment. In a very real sense much of the creative energy which had characterized a labour force which had been previously forced to live on the margins of church life was destroyed. In the words of one of the new women priests, the message was implied, "Fit in here girls or else."[78]

Accepting the ordination of women first to the diaconate and then to the priesthood, in part solved the employment problem of the church with regard to women. Although there is no evidence to suggest that this was a conscious factor in the decision-making process of the church's leadership, the concerns which were raised by women workers were still largely unaddressed when they became obsolete in the face of the ordination of women. Prior to the ordination of women the concerns of women workers were always on the agenda of Synods and House of Bishops meetings. ARCWA met to caucus about their concerns. After 1976, these items disappeared from the agendas of meetings and ARCWA disbanded.

The church had a structure in place for dealing with the employment of clergy. When women fit this category, the problems associated with their place in the church structure, including their authority and status, were put to rest. The Reverend Ruth Pogson commented that once she was ordained she automatically was given a respect from the laity and clergy which she had been unable to earn as a lay worker, even after a lifetime of devoted service to the church.[79]

A difference of perception exists between the views of the episcopacy and the views of those women who served the church as workers. Bishops commented that they dealt with the concerns of women workers before a decision was made to ordain women. Indeed minutes from the House of Bishops meetings bear this out. The House of Bishops, the General Synod and the Commission on Women all wanted to implement pay equity and pension plans; however, they could not legislate respect and authority in the workplace. As such, many of the women themselves argued that the real issue of the place of women in the church was not dealt with, and that the energy which was generated by their concerns for change in the church was subverted by simply ordaining some women.[80]

Changing Theology

A second response to the question posed with regard to the motivation of episcopal leadership in this issue lies in the theological change which was engaging the leadership of the church in a variety of ways. As a result of the theological shift which was happening in Western Christianity away from an atonement based theology toward the creation centred theology of incarnation noted above, the House of Bishops became involved in many questions which were in a sense justice issues. If one embraces the idea that all people are made in the image of God, and that human beings are thereby fundamentally good, one's world view reflects that. We see the House of Bishops talking about issues of justice for native peoples, concern for the poor and liturgical renewal in the same way that they discussed the ordination of women to the priesthood. The challenge to traditional hierarchical conceptions of ministry, presented by a re-affirmation of a theology of the priesthood of all believers and the whole people of God, meant discussion about Christian Initiation and the whole structure of ordained and lay ministry.[81] The world was changing and with it the theology of the church was shifting.

The Reverend Dr. Eugene Fairweather and the Reverend Dr. John Morden played no small part in the theological shift which encouraged the church to accept the idea of women as priests. These two men were highly revered in the church as theologians and were regularly asked for direction in matters involving theology. Morden, systematic theologian and principal of Huron College, London, Ontario, was openly supportive of the ordination of women from the beginning of the debates. He had served on the Committee for Ministry of the national church and had prepared a report commenting on the arguments in both directions of the issue. Fairweather, systematic theologian at Trinity College, Toronto was not as supportive of the ordination of women originally. At the General Synod of 1973, he did not declare a position, but after struggling with the issue in the context of the Diocese of Toronto and his teaching at Trinity College, he declared at the 1975 General Synod that, in his view, there were no valid theological reasons for excluding women from the priesthood. This individual's decision apparently influenced the thinking of much of the church's leadership as bishops, clergy, and laity alike remember being influenced positively by his declaration of support.[82]

What is perhaps most interesting about the theological shift which encouraged an openness to women as priests is that the ordination of women moved women into a clerical caste rather than using their energy to transform the whole structure. The impact which women will have on the church as they participate in that traditional clerical structure is a question for future study. Perhaps the next generation of historians will be able to derive some objective measure by which the implication of women in the priesthood for change and continuity might be assessed.

The Reverend Virginia Lane wrote a thesis for her Doctor of Ministry degree from the Episcopal Divinity School which attempts to analyze the role and attitudes of female rectors in the Anglican Church of Canada between 1981 and 1986. She found in her study that women rectors, in general, have adopted a traditional clerical *persona* as a means of coping with the stresses of living in the institutional hierarchy.[83]

Social Change

Some bishops stated that they moved to support the idea of the ordination of women because of the changing times both inside and outside the church. Primate Scott, Archbishop Bothwell, Archbishop Somerville and Archbishop Hambidge were among those who noted the changing place of women in society as influential in the church's changing perception of the role of women in its midst.

No religion is immune to the needs, demands, changes and particular circumstances of its culture. Christianity is no exception. The church in every time and place is influenced by the society in which it lives. The Anglican Church of Canada was shaped at least in part by the Canadian circumstance. During the time period of this study, Canadian society changed drastically. Changes in the place and role of women were among the most drastic of the changes which had an impact on the reality of church life.

During the years that the ordination of women was debated in the Anglican church, Canadian society was experiencing a second wave of the feminist revolution. From 1969 onward, there was an organized feminist movement which drew on the support of a small number of women. The full equality of status and opportunity for women that the first wave of feminism had not included as key to its suffragette platform was now on the agenda of feminists.[84] The feminist critique of the marginal place of women in Canadian society was being heard in the church through feminist theologians. This critique was a part of the ferment generated by the 1960s push for social revolution and massive social change. Feminist theologians were few and far between in Canada between 1968 and 1976; however, feminist theological ideas did form part of the theatre within which the ordination debate was being acted out.

Secular feminism did not have a direct and immediate effect on the ordination debates. There is no evidence of direct involvement of 'secular' feminists anywhere in or around the decision-making process. However, changes in the sphere of women's involvement in society throughout the twentieth century influenced the perceptions of church members and leaders with regard to what women were competent to do.

The modern era witnessed a drastic change in the parameters of women's accepted participation in society. Statistics indicate that from the late nineteenth century onward there has been a steady growth in the numbers of women participating in the workforce, outside of the home. This growth in participation was accelerated during both of the world wars when women's labour was needed to maintain wartime industry in the absence of adult males of working age. Although numbers of women in the work force decreased somewhat when the wars ended and men resumed their traditional roles in the workforce, more women remained in the workforce than were there previously.[85] This steady but gradual increase continued, involving both single and eventually married women, although women with preschool age children were not in the workforce in any significant numbers until after 1970.

This trend parallels what occurred in the ordination case. 16 out of the first 18 women ordained to the priesthood (89 percent) were single women. The remaining two were widows with grown children. Women in the priesthood with young children is a recent phenomenon. In Canadian society it was becoming increasingly commonplace for women to work outside of the home. Table 5 demonstrates the dramatic rise in numbers of women in the Canadian labour force from 1951 onward.

There was a notable progression in both society and the church, as professions were first opened to single women, and then older or childless married women, and finally and recently to young married women with children. In this progression the church followed the lead of society. Although as early as the 1950s a significant number of older married women were remaining in the workforce of society, it was not until after the first ordinations to the late 1970s that the church hired married women, and in the 1980s married women with children. Although there was no explicit policy of exclusion, the progression in church employment mirrored what was happening in the society at large. The church was influenced by the society in which it lived. It was not until after changes began to take place in society with regard to the status and employment of women that similar changes occurred in the church. The tension between vocation versus right has been a predominant motif.

Women, lay and ordained, other clergy and bishops alike all debated whether or not this issue of the ordination of women to the priesthood was a question of vocation or of right. Virtually all bishops and ordained women stressed that their ordinations were about their vocation to serve as priests in the church. They were not ordained because they felt that it was their right, but rather because it was the fulfilment of their vocation.

The sense that someone would be ordained because of a justice issue is offensive to some. This hesitation rises from the basic Anglican theology of ministry which holds that ordination is a gift of grace. If ordination is a gift of grace then it cannot be demanded as a right. The words of the American historian, Suzanne Hiatt are again relevant, "The Canadian women accepted as gift what we Americans demanded as our right." The Canadian temperament which is hard to quantify often seems to adopt a non-conflictual stance. In politics, as noted above, this often means a non-aggressive approach to promoting a particular view or party. In the church this often means reserved promotion of a given theology or view.

While it is true that the way in which the ordination issue was handled seems to reflect the 'Canadian way,' it is a false dichotomy to set up vocation and right as opposing concepts. While Anglican theology would agree that ordination can never be earned, the vocation of women would not have been discerned if the unjust exclusion of their ministry had been allowed to continue. For most of Christian history, structures were in place which prevented the discernment of a woman's vocation beyond a specific gender restricted sphere. Women's sphere limited the role of women to domestic responsibilities or religious pursuits which were, in effect, a continuation of those hearthly duties. Although women have always found a way to exercise their gifts, as on the model of the medieval abbesses and early church prophets, a structure which did not limit the discernment of these gifts by a gender restricted code of behaviour would have more easily facilitated the action of God in history.

That the church has been able to begin the process of breaking free of the limitations of a restricted woman's sphere is due in large part to the influence of the secular realm. The Anglican Church of Canada moved to allow women as lay readers, and as elected members of parish councils and diocesan and General Synod, as well as opening the door for their participation as servers and wardens before they addressed the issue of the ordination of women. The journey by which the severely restricted sphere of women's participation in church life was opened up, by which the sphere was widened to currently include the whole, at least in theory, was a progressive journey. While one might hope that the church would be on the forefront of a movement to liberate all of humanity for the full realization of their gifts and vocation, such was not the case. From the late nineteenth century onward, the Anglican Church (first with the restoration of the order of deaconess) followed the lead of society and gradually opened its doors to a fuller participation by women in the life of the whole community.

Throughout its history the Christian church has had a conception of the world which has divided the human community into sacred and secular components. A dualism was set up between what it perceived to be godly and what was not. Unfortunately this dualism was further aggravated by the contention that the church is the guardian of the sacred, of God's action in the world. It is this world view which led bishops and women alike to reject any notion that the ordination of women was an issue of justice or right. For many, any association with the feminist movement discredits the idea of women as priests. Indeed, those who opposed the ordination of women often accused those who supported it of simply jumping on a secular bandwagon. If we reclaim the notion that all of creation is the good work of God, it is entirely conceivable that God can act through agencies other than the church in promoting Her vision for the world. Without the good work done by secular feminism, the church might never have seen the injustice of its exclusion of women from the full life of the Christian community. Yes, ordination is a matter of vocation, of gift, but without working for the establishment of a just ecclesiastical structure, the full realization of that gift will never be seen in the church or the world.

Religious Experience

In tracing the evolution of their support for the idea of women as priests, some bishops stressed their moment of personal revelation on the issue. Bishops such as David Ragg of the diocese of Huron moved to ordain women simply because he felt that God had communicated to him that it was God's will. However, the line between the two explanations should not be drawn too sharply. All agreed that something of the will of God was revealed to them as they struggled with the issue.

For the historian, revelation is a difficult concept. For centuries church historians argued that life unfolded as it did because of "God's will." As scholars committed to some measure of objective empirical historical analysis, we must acknowledge that these revelations cannot be measured or proven. As persons of faith, however, we must claim a common history of personal revelation. As such, what can be said at this juncture is that many bishops in the Canadian church felt moved to ordain women because of what they named as divine inspiration. In other words, personal religious experience and personal philosophy must be recognized as valid factors in human motivation which, in turn, contribute to the historical process.

The Impact of Churchmanship

There seems to be some evidence of a relationship between churchmanship and attitudes on this issue in the Canadian church. This division was prominent in the House of Bishops.[86] Those who were Anglo-Catholic in their orientation often opposed the ordination of women with the logic of the first and the fourth categories of argument identified earlier: a woman cannot be the icon of Christ because she is not male, and ecumenical relations. Those who were inclined to the Evangelical side defended the second category of argument which held that a women could not have authority over a man — the headship or *kephale* argument.

In the diocesan synod charges of those bishops who actively opposed the ordination of women, we see that they always expressed either the icon of Christ, the *kephale* argument, or the argument from ecumenical relations. In fact most adopted the model of opposition defined in the first category. While this tendency was not universally true, there is some evidence of a relationship between attitude to the ordination of women and churchmanship.

Those who located themselves within the broadstream were more likely to be supportive of the ordination of women than were their high and low contemporaries. The broadstream of the church was considered to be a "new wind" in the Canadian church during the late nineteenth and early twentieth century; it did not share the extremism of the two other groups.[87] The label of "liberal" is also often applied to this category of churchmanship. Those bishops who were the most active protagonists in the movement toward the ordination of women identified themselves as liberal, or broadstream in their churchmanship. This expression of churchmanship is necessarily related to the theological shifts which were precipitated by the rise of liberalism as a school of thought in the life of the church.

Various factors influenced the episcopal leadership of the Canadian church in the movement toward the adoption of the inclusion of women in the priesthood. This direction was strongly supported by the grassroots constituency of the church. The transition to a new historic form of ministry was accomplished.

THE FIRST ORDINATIONS

On 30 November 1976, the dioceses of Niagara, Huron, Cariboo, and New Westminster ordained the first women to the priesthood in Canada. The names of the individuals involved have not been collected previously. In the Diocese of Cariboo, Bishop John Snowden ordained the Reverend Patricia Reed, with the Primate preaching at the service. In the Diocese of New Westminster, Bishop David Somerville ordained the Reverend Elspeth Alley and the Reverend Virginia Bryant to the priesthood. In the Diocese of Huron, Bishop David Ragg ordained the Reverend Mary Mills. In the Diocese of Niagara, Bishop John Bothwell ordained the Reverend Beverley Shanley and the Reverend Mary Lucas.

The church at large never identified these first six women priests as a distinct unit. At all times the national office was careful not to draw an obvious distinction between male and female priests. In fact, in terms of numbers, there is only one report from this period in existence. In January of 1978, the office of the General Secretary who was the Venerable Edwin Stanley Light, chief administrative officer of the Anglican Church of Canada, reported to the Primate that there were 18 women ordained to the priesthood in ten different dioceses. The names of individuals were not recorded. For the purposes of this study the names of the 18 women and the ten bishops involved have been recovered and have served as a sample for the purposes of oral history interviews. The criterion for this selection is that they were seen as a discernable unit by the national church itself. In the eyes of the church as a group, they were the first women ordained to the priesthood. Below is a comprehensive list of these men and women, and Table 6 graphically displays the names, dates, and backgrounds of the women involved in the ordinations.

- Diocese of Athabasca: (2) — Phyllis Lock and Enid Longwell were ordained by Bishop Frederick Hugh Wright Crabb.
- Diocese of Brandon: (4) — Joy Ruddock, Thelma Tanner, Kathleen Hill and Margery Kennon were ordained by Bishop John Conlin (two of these women have since died).

- Diocese of Caledonia: (1) — Dorothy Daly was ordained by Bishop Douglas Hambridge.
- Diocese of Cariboo: (1) — Patricia Reed was ordained by Bishop J. S. P. Snowden.
- Diocese of Huron: (2) — Mary Mills and Virginia Lane were ordained by Bishop David Ragg.
- Diocese of New Westminster: (2) — Elspeth Alley and Virginia Bryant were ordained by Bishop David Somerville.
- Diocese of Niagara: (2) — Beverley Shanley and Mary Lucas were ordained by Bishop John Bothwell.
- Diocese of Quebec: (1) — Ruth Matthews was ordained by Bishop Timothy Matthews.
- Diocese of Saskatoon: (1) — Ina Caton was ordained by Bishop Donald Ford.
- Diocese of Toronto: (2) — Sister Rosemary Benwell was ordained by Bishop Allen Reed, and Margery Pezzack was ordained by Bishop Lewis Garnsworthy.[88]

As Table 6 shows, 14 out of the first 18 women (78 percent) ordained to the priesthood had served as either deaconesses or Bishop's Messengers. The other four came to church work at a later date. The 14 received their theological training prior to any discussion of the ordination issue in the Canadian church. The remaining four completed their theological studies after the 1969 decision by the General Synod to allow the ordination of women as deacons. As such, in this first unit defined by the national church, there were actually two groups, those who trained and served before ordination became a possibility and those who trained afterwards.

After this first year of ordinations virtually no mention of the subject was made again in the House of Bishops or General Synod. Prior to Lambeth 1978 it was simply noted in the records of House of Bishops meetings that it would be on the agenda at Lambeth. After the Lambeth Conference, the House of Bishops met in Mississauga between 5 and 8 November, and at that meeting the Lambeth Resolutions were discussed. The House simply noted that resolutions 20-22 dealt with the ordination of women to the diaconate, the priesthood and the episcopate respectively, and that discussion in the Anglican Communion was ongoing.[89] For the Anglican Church of Canada the story of women in the priesthood as a decision-making process was ended, and the story of women in the priesthood as a reality was begun.

Endnotes

1. Antonio Gramsci, "Problems of History and Culture — The Intellectuals," in *Selections from the Prison Notebooks*, (New York: 1971), pp. 5–23.

2. Gramsci, p. 334. Gramsci himself would probably not have applied the designation of organic intellectual elite to an ecclesiastical body, as he was highly suspect of the heavily hegemonic role of clergy in maintaining traditional structures and forms of social power. However, his definition lends itself to our application in this case.

3. "Theological and Scriptural Principles Governing the Laity and the Work of Women Within this Ministry," by Dr. Helen Milton, 1969. (G.S.76 - 15 Box 25).

4. Minutes of the February 12, 1969 meeting of the Commission on Women. (GS 76 - 15 Box 25).

5. Minutes of 1969 Commission on Women.

6. G.S., *Journal of Proceedings* (1969), p. 47.

7. Oral History Interview with Primate Michael Peers, 03 June 1992.

8. Minutes of the Meeting of the House of Bishops, November, 1968.

9. Oral History Interview with the Reverend Mary Mills, 15 October, 1991.

10. G. S. *Journal of Proceedings*, (1969), p. 48.

11. Minutes of the House of Bishops Annual Meeting, October, 1970, p. 11. (Box F 150).

12. Minutes of the House of Bishops, (1971).

13. G.S. *Journal of Proceedings*, (1971), p. 164.

14. Minutes of the House of Bishops, October 1–4, (1971), pp. 15–16. (Box F 150).

15. Majority Report of the Primate's Task Force on the Ordination of Women to the Priesthood, 1972, "Section on Scripture."

16. Majority Report, "Scripture."

17. Majority Report, "Tradition."

18. Majority Report, "Tradition."

19. Majority Report, Section on "Other Considerations."

20. Majority Report, "Other Considerations."

21. Majority Report, p. 6.

22. Minority Report of the Primate's Task Force on the Ordination of Women to the Priesthood, 1972, "Section on Christology."

23. Minority Report, "Christology."

24. Christianity has been influenced for centuries by thinkers who have affirmed the inferiority and subordinate position of women. For example: CLEMENT: "Let us set our womenfolk on the road to goodness by teaching them to display submissiveness. Every woman should be overwhelmed with shame at the thought that she is a woman." COUNCIL OF MACON: In the year 534, in Lyon, France, 43 Roman Catholic bishops and 20 men representing other bishops held a most peculiar debate: ARE WOMEN FULLY HUMAN? After many lengthy arguments a vote was taken. The results were 32 yes and 31 no. Women were declared human by one vote. JOHN KNOX (1503-1572): "Woman in her greatest perfection was made to serve and obey man, not to rule and command him." MARTIN LUTHER (1482–1546): "Women should remain at home, sit still, keep house and bear and bring up children. If a woman grows weary and at last dies from child-bearing it matters not. Let her die from bearing- she is there to do it." SAMUEL BUTLER (1612–1680): "The souls of women are so small that some believe they've none at all." AGOW Papers ORE/AEOW/A, B-2.

25. Oral History Interview, Archbishop Edward Scott, 12 July, 1992.

26 . Minutes of the House of Bishops, April 30–May 2, 1973, pp. 4–7.
27. See p. A19-20 of the Convening Circular of G.S., 1973.
28. G.S. *Journal of Proceedings*, (1973), p. 24.
29. G.S. *Journal of Proceedings*, (1973), p. 30.
30. G.S. *Journal of Proceedings*, (1973), p. 30.
31. G.S. *Journal of Proceedings*, (1973), p. 31.
32. H. R. S. Ryan, "The General Synod of the Anglican Church of Canada: Aspects of Constitutional History," in *Journal of the Canadian Church Historical Society*, Volume XXXIV, No. 1, April, 1992, pp. 52–53, 62.
33. Ryan, p. 97.
34. Ryan, pp. 82–84.
35. Ryan, p. 52 and beyond.
36. Minutes of the House of Bishops Meeting, May 10–11, 1974, p. 10.
37. Minutes of the House of Bishops Meeting, May 10–11, 1974, p. 16.
38. Minutes of House of Bishops Meeting, December 1–6, 1974, p. 18.
39. Minutes of House of Bishops Meeting, December 1–6, 1974, Appendix B, p. 1.
40. Minutes, December 1–6, 1974, Appendix B, p. 2–6.
41. Minutes, December 1–6, 1974, Appendix B, p. 7.
42. Minutes, December 1–6, 1974, Appendix B, p. 8.
43. Minutes, December 1–6, 1974, Appendix B, p. 8.
44. Minutes, December 1–6, 1974, p. 18.
45. Minutes, June 13–16, 1975, p. 33.
46. G.S. *Journal of Proceedings*, (1975), p. M-50.
47. "Christianity and Feminism," 1975, p. 18. Provided from the personal papers of Dr. Joanne McWilliam.
48. G.S. *Journal of Proceedings*, (1975), p. M-66.
49. G.S. *Journal of Proceedings*, (1975), p. M-66.
50. *Manifesto on the Ordination of Women to the Priesthood*, see Exhibit 1. *Anglican Churchmen*, v. 101. October, 1975, p. 9.
51. *Manifesto on the Ordination of Women to the Priesthood*, see Exhibit 1. *Anglican Churchmen*, v. 101. October, 1975, p. 9.
52. Letter of Primate, in Scott Papers (M101).
53. Letter to the Primate, February 1976, in Scott Papers (M101).
54. Letter to the Primate, October, 1975, in Scott Papers (M101).
55. Letter, 1975, (G.S. 81-1, Box 3).
56. Letter to Primate, January, 1976, (G.S. 81-1, Box 2).
57. Letter to Primate, October, 1975, in Scott Papers (M101).
58. Letter to the Primate, October,1975, in Scott Papers (M101).
59. C.L. Bacchi, *Liberation Deferred: The Ideas of English Canadian Suffragists 1877–1918* (Toronto: 1989), p. 3.
60. Grace Hallenby, *AWTC — A Background Document*, (Toronto: 1989), p. 101.
61. Excerpts from the covering letter to the Manifesto when presented to the House of Bishops, 21 October, 1975, in Scott Papers (M101).
62. Minutes, 31 October –1 November 1975, XII, pp. 8–9, and Appendix A, pp. 1–12.
63. Letter from the Primate to other Anglican Primates, Scott Papers, (M101).
64. Minutes of House of Bishops, 26 February 1976, pp. 4–6.
65. Minutes of the House of House of Bishops, 26 February, 1976.
66. Minutes, 26 February 1976, p. 8.
67. Minutes, 26 February 1976, p. 8.

68. Scott Papers, (M101).
69. Scott Papers, (M101).
70. Scott Papers, (M101).
71. Ryan, p. 52 and beyond.
72. Oral History Interview with Edward Scott, 12 July, 1992.
73. For example, the Diocese of Fredericton, *Journal of Proceedings* of the 100th session, (1973), p. 76.
74. Oral history interviews, with Scott, Bothwell, Hambidge, Somerville.
75. Letter, October, 1976, in Scott Papers (M101).
76. Oral History Interview with Ina Caton, 24 October 1991.
77. These figures are compiled from *Anglican Church of Canada Year Books*, 1960 to the present. See Table 4: Deaconesses in the Anglican Church of Canada.
78. Oral History Interview with the Reverend Canon Beverley Shanley, 11 October 1990.
79. Oral History Interview with the Reverend Ruth Pogson, 13 August 1991.
80. Oral History Interviews with Archbishop Edward Scott, Edith Shore, Marion Niven, the Reverend Virginia Lane, the Reverend Beverley Shanley.
81. These comments on changing theological perspective are made after reading minutes of the House of Bishops meetings from 1920 to 1978.
82. This paragraph was written after reading the written reflections which Dr. Morden and Dr. Fairweather produced for General Synod, and after listening to the comments of bishops in interview.
83. The Reverend Dr. Virginia Lane, D.Min. thesis, *A Profile of the Experience of Women Rectors in the Anglican Church of Canada, 1986–1991* (Episcopal Divinity School: Massachusetts, 1991).
84. A. Prentice, ed., *Canadian Women: A History*. (Toronto: 1988), p. 289.
85. Prentice, p. 312.
86. Oral History Interview with Archbishop Hugh Wright Crabb, 16 July 1991.
87. Phillip Carrington, *The Anglican Church in Canada*, (Toronto: 1963), p. 201.
88. This list has been compiled through research in the archives and personnel files of each of the relevant dioceses.
89. Minutes of House of Bishops, 5-8 November 1978, p. 16.

4

Profile of the Canadian Dioceses

The issue of the ordination of women to the priesthood was not solely an issue for the national level of church life. This issue was of concern to the General Synod, the House of Bishops and individual dioceses. A consideration of the ways in which this issue was dealt with at the local level does two important things: it illuminates the truth of the contention that episcopal leadership was of primary importance in the acceptance and implementation, or rejection of women in the priesthood; it demonstrates that there was no discernible relationship between geography and stances taken on this question.

A survey of the attitudes toward the ordination of women to the priesthood by diocese in the Anglican Church of Canada during the relevant period shows that every region of the country contained a mixture of support, opposition, and indifference for and to the ordination of women. The only proviso on this commonality lay in the fact that two of the four ecclesiastical provinces had been in existence before the creation of General Synod in 1893, and as such they reserved the right to decide on the issue separately. That is not to say that they were not a part of the General Synod decision-making process. Rather, they reserved the right to approve of or reject the decision in their own provincial synods afterward. These provinces did not participate in the ordinations of November, 1976. There was a time delay while the provincial synods clarified their own relationship to the General Synod process.

The ten different responses to the issue, which are elaborated in

Table 7, included: no mention of the issue; bishop and synod in favour; bishop in favour and synod undecided; bishop opposed and undiscussed by synod; bishop undecided and synod opposed; bishop and synod opposed; bishop opposed and synod in favour; bishop in favour and synod opposed; bishop undecided and synod in favour; bishop in favour and synod passes a conscience clause.

These categories were essentially represented in each of the four ecclesiastical provinces. In each province there were dioceses in which there was a strong support by bishops and people, dioceses which were strongly opposed, dioceses which were divided and dioceses in which bishops acted without the declared support or opposition of the synod. There is not a sufficient preponderance of one category or another in any region to make any claims of a relationship between location and attitude on this issue. A regional pattern of support and opposition cannot be discerned.

The lack of correlation between region and attitudes on this issue is somewhat surprising. Within the Canadian church there is a myth which is still prevalent which holds that there was a regional component to the acceptance of the ordination of women. It has been argued that Western Canada was most open to women's ordination because of their past experience with the Bishop's Messengers and other lay ministry. The frontier mentality of risk and openness to challenge has also been cited as a factor in their perceived openness. The Province of Ontario was seen as middle of the road, and the Provinces of Quebec and the Maritimes have been identified as the most fundamentally conservative on the issue. This was not the case. Episcopal leadership was the single most determinative factor in local decision-making.

In the largest category both bishop and synod were in favour of the ordination of women. There was mutual opposition in only one diocese. In six dioceses both bishop and synod expressed no conclusive opinion on the matter. As such, a direct parallel between bishop and synod can be drawn in 16 out of 30 cases. While this represents only slightly more than 50 percent, the number of cases in which there was a direct conflict between bishop and synod was much smaller. In two dioceses the synods voted against the position of their bishops and voted in favour of the ordination of women. In one diocese the synod voted against the direction of its bishop and opposed the ordination of women. The cases of direct opposition comprise only 10 percent of the total. There were three dioceses which made a decision (one pro and one con) when no clear episcopal leadership was given. This represents another 10 percent of the total.

The grey area consists of those dioceses with a bishop who made his opinion known but did not invite the synod to comment. This involved six dioceses or 20 percent of the cases. The fact that no one in these dioceses ventured to raise the issue of their own initiative lends further credibility to our basic premise about the significance of episcopal leadership. 20 percent of the church's population by diocese was content to let episcopal leadership decide of its own volition what course would be taken on the matter, without offering any comment one way or another.

Church historians have traditionally explained the decisions and directions of ecclesiastical life in terms of leadership. There was some hope that in this case there would be evidence of a groundswell movement of support for the issue, as in the American church. That was simply not the case. Although episcopal decisions ultimately require the support of diocesan constituents at least in theory, this was predominantly a top-down decision-making process.

The Ecclesiastical Province of British Columbia

The province is comprised of the dioceses of British Columbia, Caledonia, Cariboo, Kootenay, New Westminster and the Yukon.

• *British Columbia*

The diocese of British Columbia can be characterized as largely inactive on the subject of women's ordination to the priesthood until 1978. That is not to say that the subject was never mentioned in a formal setting. After the General Synod of 1973 the diocese responded to the Synod's request to study the question. It did not, however, formally express an opinion on the issue. Under the leadership of Bishop Hugh Gartrell the diocese addressed this issue in its diocesan synod, 24–26 April 1975. At that point, British Columbia considered the approval in principle of the ordination of women which occurred at the General Synod of 1973. A Canon T. Page of the diocese and the Reverend John Baycroft of Ottawa presented the arguments both pro and con, and questions and comments then ensued. This session was purely educational. The diocese did not vote on the issue and did not mention it again during the time of this study. Even in the context of preparing for and reporting on Lambeth 1978 there is no mention of the ordination of women. From this one might assume that there was opposition to the issue by default. It simply was not considered important enough to discuss at any length. 24 clergymen from this diocese signed the *Manifesto on the Ordination of Women to the Priesthood*. Gartrell never mentioned this issue in his charges to any of the diocesan synods over which he presided. If one were to categorize his 'churchmanship', his comments and views on other subjects tend to demonstrate an inclination toward the Anglo-Catholic worldview.[1]

• *Diocese of Cariboo*

The issue of women's ordination to the priesthood was first mentioned in the Diocese of Cariboo in 1974, following the request of the General Synod to study the matter. Bishop John Snowden raised the issue in his charge and spoke favourably of it. The Synod then discussed the issue and passed a resolution which affirmed the decision of the General Synod of 1973 to support the ordination of women.[2] No further mention of the issue was made formally in the diocesan synods. Cariboo simply became one of the first dioceses to receive the ministry of a woman ordained to the priesthood after 30 November 1976.

The Reverend Patricia Reed offered some comment on her experiences with the diocese. She herself was originally from the diocese of New Westminster and therefore was unfamiliar with the diocese and knew nothing of the process by which it reached a decision to ordain women. Unlike many other western dioceses, Cariboo had had very little exposure to the ministry of ordained women, and indeed it did not ordain another woman to the priesthood for another seven years after Reed. It would appear that her ordination was largely a matter which was between herself and the diocesan bishop who was supportive of the move to ordain women.

Reed first felt a call to the priesthood when she felt called to church work. She pursued church work by studying for the Master of Divinity Degree at the Vancouver School of Theology beginning in 1973, after working as a social worker for 22 years. She was ordained deacon while in the third year of her studies. In January, 1976, she was still being told by her bishop that women could not be ordained to the priesthood. Later in 1976, however, Snowden came to visit her in Caribou and said with great excitement, "Pat, I'm going to be able to ordain you." Reed commented that her bishop was a relatively new bishop who was pleased to be able to be one of the first to ordain women. Two out of the 14 priests in the diocese of Cariboo wrote to Reed beforehand saying that they were opposed to her upcoming ordination. Three priests from this diocese signed the *Manifesto*. The rest offered support. It is interesting to note that Patricia did not see herself as a feminist, and that women's issues had nothing to do with her decision to accept Holy Orders. Rather, "it was a matter of vocation."[3]

• *Diocese of Caledonia*

The Diocese of Caledonia formally mentioned the ordination of women to the priesthood for the first time in 1974. At the 35th regular session of its diocesan synod Caledonia heard of this issue in the report from its delegates to General Synod. Some discussion of the issue followed in the context of the proposal for Church Union.[4] This was an interesting occurrence as the issue was not raised in the Bishop's Charge. It was raised by the General Synod delegates. Bishop Douglas Hambidge declared himself a supporter of the ordination of women early in the church's deliberations on the matter, but did not himself raise it at that diocesan synod.

At the diocesan synod the following year this issue was formally on the agenda. The members of synod received a paper by the Very Reverend Gary Patterson on the matter beforehand, and at synod held a discussion of the pros and cons of the issue. This paper made the synod aware of the struggles of the Swedish church. The synod then passed the following motion:

> THAT this Synod of Caledonia approves the ordination of women to the priesthood and requests the Bishops to proceed cautiously towards implementation in this diocese. The voting on this motion was as follows: in the House of Clergy 34 in favour, and 5 opposed with 2 abstentions and in the House of Laity 14 in favour, and 2 opposed with 1 abstention.[5]

The ordination of women to the priesthood was not mentioned again in the diocesan synod until 1977 when Hambidge identified Dorothy Daly as the first woman ordained priest in the diocese.[6]

The Reverend Dorothy Daly had a long history of work in the church both in England and in Canada when she was ordained to the priesthood in January, 1977. Unlike some of her counterparts she had felt a vocation to priesthood for at least six years prior to her actual ordination. Working as parish and church worker in both the Church of England and in Canada she knew the frustration of hearing confessions without being able to absolve, and of living as a spiritual leader in a community without being able to celebrate the eucharist. Although Daly felt a clear vocation to the priesthood and identified herself a feminist, she was not overtly involved in the process by which a decision was made to ordain women to the priesthood in the Canadian church. In fact she contemplated leaving church work but was assured by Primate Scott in 1974 that the motion to ordain women to the priesthood would pass at the next General Synod. After the machinery of church government had cleared the way, Daly was one of the first women to be ordained. Hambidge ordained Daly in Chetwynd at the Elk's Hall as there was no church large enough to hold the nearly 400 people who attended despite a terrible snowstorm. Of the 20 priests in the diocese 4 attended.

Reflecting on what she knew of the process, Daly stressed that she felt that in her diocese and in the larger church there had been due process surrounding this issue. She stated that in Caledonia some people were opposed to the ordination of women because of old sexual taboos. How could a woman be pregnant or menstruate at the altar? Others were resistant to changing the way that things had always been done, but most people simply did not think about the issue. Interestingly no clergymen in this diocese signed the *Manifesto*. In assessing why the synod agreed to support the ordination of women she stressed that in her view the positive attitude of the episcopal leadership had had the most to do with a positive affirmation of the principle at synod. Hambidge declared his support for the ordination of women early on in the debate.[7]

• *Diocese of Kootenay*

When the issue was first raised in the Canadian church, Edward Scott was the diocesan bishop of Kootenay. He was replaced after his election to the primacy by Bishop Fraser Berry. Scott did not raise the issue in his diocese during the years of his episcopacy. As the leading proponent of the ordination of women in the Canadian church, he did not take up this issue overtly until after Lambeth 1968. As with all other dioceses and aspects of church life, Scott did not raise the issue until the larger church asked that it be done. That is not to say that he was unaware of the issue. Indeed discussions with him reveal quite the opposite; however, it was not formally an issue for the church until after 1968.

Women's ordination to the priesthood was first raised in the diocesan synod of Kootenay in 1977, seven months after the first ordinations had taken place. At that time the synod did not discuss the issue and made no relevant motions. Berry simply stated in his charge that it was, "a really hot issue that General Synod has resolved for us but as a province we were not able to make our voice felt because we have no united voice." Berry went on to say that he hoped all could agree to disagree, letting each diocese, "do its own thing and go its own way."[8] Clearly Berry disagreed with the ordination of women or he would have felt that his voice had been heard on the subject at General Synod. One clergyman from this diocese signed the *Manifesto*.

• **Diocese of New Westminster**
It was in response to the request of General Synod in 1973 to consider the issue that the diocesan synod of New Westminster first considered women's ordination. At this 68th session of the synod a single motion which read as follows was passed:

> THAT this Synod urge the House of Bishops of the Anglican Church of Canada to provide the Church before the end of 1974 with information concerning the ordination of women to the priesthood, as was agreed at General Synod 1973 so that we can move steadily as a church toward a clear and responsible and biblical policy on this question.[9]

The diocesan synod was not prepared to make a decision on this issue without further information. Effectively this meant that the diocesan synod never did make a decision. There is no record of further discussion of this issue at the level of the diocesan synod. The diocesan bishop was in favour of such ordinations as he himself ordained two women on 30 November 1976.

Archbishop David Somerville identified himself as one of three in the House of Bishops who were "really for" the ordination of women, along with Scott and John Bothwell of Niagara. It was his contention that a theology of sexuality which taught that only males could represent God was out of touch with the reality of our world. Reflecting on interactions in the House of Bishops, Somerville stated that discussions on the subject were not bitter. He remembered a lot of teasing and the fact that many who were uncertain were swayed by the force and direction of the debates. Stressing that "churchmanship allies" did not exist as clearly in the House of Bishops as they did in General Synod, he stated that bishops of the church gave the lead in General Synod and the Committee on Ministry. He himself was the chair of the Ministry Committee in the House of Bishops which had dealt with the ordination issue.

Somerville's recollections of the actual General Synod debates led him to comment that the House of Bishops had been generally in favour, the laity had been largely supportive, but the clergy had had more opposition within its ranks. He attributed this to them wanting to protect themselves, and not wanting to work alongside women. Somerville argued that the clergy were moved to change their minds in large part when they saw that the laity clearly wanted women priests. Strategic planning led the Commission on Women to have a lay person (Miss Ruth Scott, principal of the AWTC) make the motion while he himself served as seconder. In voting in General Synod the Commission made sure that it was voted on by the laity first. The small size of the Canadian church was key in enabling the motions to pass in his view. The formidable lobby groups simply did not exist.

Acknowledging that there never was a vote on the issue in his own diocese, Archbishop Somerville stressed that the issue had been discussed in deaneries and parishes in a formalized way through discussion groups led by individuals trained in conflict management. He remembered only five or six clergy being opposed to the idea, and that even those said they would not leave the church over the issue. As such he proceeded to act according to his heart and conscience, ordaining the first two women in his diocese.[10]

The Reverend Elspeth Alley had felt a vocation to serve in the church since she was twelve years old. "If I had been a man I would have been a priest." After marrying and having a family Alley pursued some theological training in 1964 at the Anglican Theological College in Vancouver (later part of the Vancouver School of Theology) but only lasted one term due to persecution by her fellow all male students. She returned and completed her theological degree in 1972.

It was in 1970 that Alley went to talk to Somerville after having a revelation. She saw footsteps on the water, a path that led to ordination. This meeting with Somerville pre-dated the church's talk of ordaining women to the priesthood but was parallel to the decision to ordain women to the diaconate. In 1972 Alley was ordained a deacon by Somerville. Between 1970 and 1975 she remembered others gathering in small groups to discuss women's ordination to the priesthood but she herself avoided such discussions as they seemed, "so negative." She stressed that she had no anger and no animosity, remembering that effective positive leadership came from the episcopacy with regard to this issue and that most of the clergy in her diocese were supportive, as were the laity she worked with.

Alley did remember, however, that her life was literally threatened by a fellow clergyman. When she was ordained to the diaconate she was told, "If you ever seek the priesthood I will kill you," and was then assaulted by the priest. Twelve clergymen from this diocese signed the *Manifesto*.

Alley did not and does not consider herself a feminist and did not understand those women around her who were angry at the church. Somerville told her that he would ordain her when he could and that was good enough for her. In her reflections she emphasized that the leadership of the bishops was determinative in this issue.[11]

• *Diocese of the Yukon*

The diocese of the Yukon did not discuss nor pass any resolution on this matter of women's ordination to the priesthood during the period now under discussion. The bishop of the diocese throughout this time was Bishop John Frame, and he declared himself opposed to the ordination of women both in his diocese and in the House of Bishops. At the 20th session of the Yukon's diocesan synod he referred to the ordination of women in his charge. He stated that the church should be concerned with the larger problems of lay ministry. Further to this he stated, "I believe it is impossible to ordain a woman as a priest, not, that is, a priest as I understand the office and order to be."[12] No further mention of this issue was made during Frame's tenure in office. Two clergymen from this diocese signed the *Manifesto*. It was not until after the election of Ron Ferris as Bishop of the Yukon in 1981 that a woman priest first served in the Yukon.

Within the Ecclesiastical Province of British Columbia, dioceses took diverse positions on this issue. Some bishops opposed the ordination of women, and their dioceses were never invited to discuss the issue. Some bishops supported the ordination of women, and their dioceses openly supported the ordination of women as well, and other dioceses did not make a decision one way or another. What one does not find is a diocese which was in direct opposition to the position taken by its bishop.

Ecclesiastical Province of Rupert's Land

The province is comprised of the dioceses of the Arctic, Athabasca, Brandon, Calgary, Edmonton, Keewatin, Qu'Appelle, Saskatoon, Saskatchewan, and Rupert's Land.

- *Diocese of the Arctic*

The Arctic became a diocese after the issue of the ordination of women to the priesthood had been first raised in the Canadian church. Between 1968 and 1978 the synod met 3 times — 1972, 1975, 1978. At the first and third of these synods the issue was not raised. It was at its second session in 1975 that the diocese responded to the matter.

This small and newborn diocese gave more attention to educating its synod around this matter than many of the dioceses of larger constituency and longer history. It was also the last diocese to eventually ordain a woman as priest in 1991. At the recommendation of its president, Bishop Donald Marsh, the synod studied two documents, one pro and one con which had been prepared as a vehicle for education and discussion in the diocese. These two documents outlined the arguments from Scripture, tradition and theology which were standard in every part of the church. The *pro* argument prepared by the Reverend Laurie Dexter concluded:

> If a woman feels she is called by God to minister, then there seems to be little in the Bible to suggest she may be mistaken, and there is much to suggest that she must heed that call and seek to study and follow her call to its conclusion, and if that conclusion is the priesthood, no one should try to stand in the way.[13]

The *con* argument prepared by the Reverend Canon Gardener was not an overtly negative document. It presented a chronology of events related to this issue, conveying the idea that there was no precedent at all for accepting the ordination of women to the priesthood. It concluded by inviting people to choose saying:

> There is a line (invisible) running from this Synod, around our parishes through Provincial and General Synods over to Lambeth and the rest of the Anglican Communion.... The whole answer to the question depends on not only which side of the

line each of us is on as individuals, but also upon the rest of the people around this line and how far we want the line to go.[14]

The diocese did not chose which side of the issue it was on. There was no record of a resolution of this issue. No clergymen from this diocese signed the *Manifesto*.

At the diocesan synod of 1978 there was a report in the synod journal which discussed the role of women in the church. This document prepared by a lay woman acknowledged that there were women priests in other parts of the church and that the church should welcome the important ministry of women whatever form it might take.[15] The diocesan bishop did not articulate his views on the subject, at least not in a formal manner.

• *Diocese of Athabasca*

The Diocese of Athabasca first heard about the ordination of women to the priesthood in a formal setting at its diocesan synod in 1971. In his charge the bishop, Reginald Pierce, as one in a series of questions asked, "Do you think it matters at all whether the priest in your church is a man or a women?"[16] The views of Pierce were not documented at that point, but one is reminded of the comment by twentieth century theologian Bernard Lonergan: when you make something a subject you promote it.

It was at the next session of the diocesan synod that the members of synod actually discussed and voted on this issue. This was relatively early as it followed immediately upon the heels of the Regina General Synod of 1973. The bishop wasted no time in complying with the request for diocesan response to this issue. In his charge to the diocesan synod he related what had happened at the General Synod. Pierce did not declare his position. Rather he talked about the long and distinguished service that women had given in the diocese of Athabasca. He concluded by saying:

The Church in Athabasca has been well served by women; now it is time to consider whether or not we think it right that they should be invited to serve through the order of priesthood. Can you make up your minds and tell me what you think I should say and do about this at the fall meeting of the House of Bishops?[17]

In its response to his charge, the committee on the bishop's charge recommended that the synod discuss and debate the question of the ordination of women to the priesthood, and that a vote be taken immediately following the discussion.[18] This recommendation was acted upon and after discussion the synod voted to approve in principle the ordination of women to the priesthood. The motion was carried with 58 people voting in favour and 12 voting against.[19]

By the next regular session of the synod a new diocesan bishop had been elected, Fredrick Hugh Wright Crabb. In his charge Crabb conveyed the decisions of the 1975 General Synod and acknowledged that the church was divided on the issue. He promised that he would ordain no one who had not been properly selected and prepared, and that he would not ordain a woman without consultation with the people and parishes affected.[20] No clergymen from this diocese signed the *Manifesto.*

In his next synodical address in 1977 Crabb mentioned that he had ordained two women to the priesthood in the preceeding year—Enid Longwell and Phyllis Lock.[21] The matter was *fait accompli* in the Diocese of Athabasca bringing a long history of women's ministry to both a culmination and a new beginning.

• *Diocese of Brandon*
The diocese of Brandon was unique in its relationship to and treatment of this issue. As noted earlier the diocese of Brandon had a long tradition of women's ministry particularly through the efforts of the Bishop's Messengers. Bishop John Conlin was one of the first bishops to ordain women to the priesthood and indeed for the first couple of years after 1976 the diocese of Brandon had the largest number of women priests of any of the dioceses — four. Conlin himself acknowledged that he would have ordained the four women on the first night possible, if not for the fact that the Synod of the Ecclesiastical Province of Rupert's Land had to clear the way first. It did this when it met five days before the first ordinations.

Conlin then proceeded to ordain the four women at the earliest possible time which was Epiphany, 1977. The diocesan synods did not discuss the issue at any point. No motions were made; however, Conlin discussed the issue at length in his charge at the Synod of 1976. In that address he stressed the fact that there was still disagreement over the matter but that he believed that no one could irremediably harm the church. "If it is truly the will of God at this historic point in time, then to delay is to reject the will of God for the ministry of his church."[22] Conlin stressed that if there was a practical argument for the ordination of women anywhere in the Anglican Communion it existed in Brandon. The long history of women ministers among its people was identified as determinative. His characterization of these women was also fascinating:

> They can hardly be described as a lunatic fringe, or as being in the forefront of the women's liberation movement, and we are sure there is little wish on their part for notoriety or sensationalism. Instead from within the very life of the church itself, they are reckoning with a strong call to the priesthood. If this be so, then what right have we to deny this call.[23]

Apparently the ministry of women had been so much a part of the diocese that no discussion was necessary. Rather there was a simple affirmation of ministries which already existed. The Reverend Marjorie Kennon confirmed this when she stated, "I felt it was the fulfilment of the ministry we were already engaged in."[24]

That was not to say that in the fulfilment there was a total vanquishing of all opposition and difficulty for the women ordained. In a letter to the Primate in February, 1977 another woman priest discussed the pain of the conscience clause and its attendant implications were acknowledged. She wrote:

> The loving support that has been given us is fantastic and because of that I feel more conscious of the pain and sorrow of those who are unable to accept the ordination of women. I'm really not frustrated or resentful, however, over the canonical limitations for myself but pray that younger women and those who will be entering the priesthood will be patient and understanding.[25]

These words are largely characteristic of the sentiments expressed repeatedly by the first women ordinands. They were women of humility and obvious patience. Three clergymen in this diocese signed the *Manifesto*.

• *Diocese of Calgary*

The story of the diocese of Calgary during this period can be told in a few sentences. Throughout the period under examination Calgary did nothing about this issue. During the episcopacy of Bishop M. L. Goodman, the ordination of women to the priesthood was not mentioned in diocesan synods at all. His charges to the synod indicate that he was of an evangelical inclination on other issues. With regard to women's ordination he was simply silent. If it is true that making something a topic promotes it, the idea was certainly not promoted in anyway during his incumbency. As such, this diocese did not report back to General Synod on the issue as it had not discussed it. Interestingly, none of the clergy in that diocese signed the *Manifesto*.

• *Diocese of Edmonton*

The diocese of Edmonton also had little recorded activity on this issue. The diocesan synod first mentioned the ordination of the women to the priesthood in 1977. At that time notice of motion was given that a motion would be brought to the floor of synod which endorsed the acts of the General and the Provincial Synods concerning the ordination of women to the priesthood. It was explicitly agreed that there would be no debate on this motion. According to the minutes, it passed "out of respect for, and based on the discretion of the General and Provincial Synods which had already passed the motions".[26] Obviously there was little enthusiastic support for the idea. There was no educational process of study and discussion at work in the diocese at that time; however, no clergy from this district signed the *Manifesto*.

• *Diocese of Keewatin*

The diocese of Keewatin is another diocese which did not deal with the question of women's ordination up to 1978. During the incumbency of Bishop H. V. Stiff (1969-1973) there was no mention of it at all. In the relevant synod journals until 1980 there was only one mention of it. Newly elected Bishop H. J. P. Allen, elected in 1974, stated in his charge to the session of the synod in 1975 that the church "must deal with women's ordination". This one statement was his only comment and no recorded discussion ensued on the issue. How Bishop Allen felt the church should deal with the issue cannot be discerned from any available diocesan documents. One clergyman from this diocese signed the *Manifesto*.

• *Diocese of Qu'Appelle*

It was in 1973 that the diocese of Qu'Appelle raised the issue of women's ordination to the priesthood for formal discussion. It was only in 1969 that there was a woman delegate to their diocesan synod for the first time. In his charge to the synod Archbishop George Jackson referred to the issue and presented his perception of the key aspects of the negative side of the argument. Jackson stated that the Swedish experience had been a disaster, that tradition and Scripture gave no precedent for such ordinations and finally that men and women were different and as such their roles were not interchangeable. He wrote:

> Sexuality or gender is a reality that transcends the biological. God is male towards his creation...the ordained priest must act officially in the person of Christ and maleness is therefore required for a priest to act in this way.[27]

Although the diocesan bishop was clearly opposed, the synod passed a motion after lengthy discussion in small groups and a plenary session to affirm the 1973 decision of the General Synod. This motion also acknowledged the need for a cautious approach and for a larger educational process before implementation was realized.[28] No record of the numbers of the vote or the content of the debate was recorded. This division between the opinion of the bishop and a majority of the members of synod was atypical in the Canadian situation. Even though the diocesan synod voted to affirm the ordination of women to the priesthood in principle, such ordinations did not happen as long as the diocesan bishop then incumbent was in office. Seventeen clergy also signed the *Manifesto*. By 1976, 2 women had been made deacons with the distinct understanding that they would not be made priest.[29]

In 1977, Michael Peers was elected as the new diocesan bishop of Qu'Appelle. At the first diocesan synod which he presided over, Peers asked the opinion of the synod as to how they felt about implementation at that time. He stressed that he did not require an act of synod to act himself; he simply wanted to know the mind of his people. As he made his request for input, he made it clear that he would not act unilaterally. While he himself favoured the ordination of women to the priesthood, he would not divide the diocese over the issue.[30] The synod voted 138 to 60 that the ordination of women and licensing of women on the same basis as men was appropriate at that time in the diocese.[31] Peers ordained the first woman to the priesthood in the diocese of Qu'Appelle later that same year.

• *Diocese of Saskatoon*

Prior to 1971 the diocese of Saskatoon was led by a bishop who openly opposed the ordination of women to the priesthood.[32] In 1971 the diocese elected a bishop with a different perspective, Bishop Douglas Ford. At its 53rd session in 1975, the synod of the diocese of Saskatoon voted to approve the ordination of women to the priesthood in principle after the bishop stated in his charge that he wanted it discussed. There is no record of his views on the matter at that point. The motion of affirmation passed by a narrow margin in the House of Clergy, 16 in favour and 15 against (note that one affirmative vote was cast by a United Church minister). In the House of Laity the motion passed by a much larger margin with 35 votes for and 16 votes against the motion.[33] The next diocesan synod voted on the issue in order that those delegates to provincial synod who would be asked to vote on the issue would know the mind of Saskatoon. A motion affirming such ordinations was carried.

In 1978 Ford made some revealing comments on the ordination of women in his charge to the 55th session of the synod. He honoured the Reverend Canon Ina Caton whom he had ordained to the priesthood in 1977, after she had served almost thirty years in that diocese. He praised the virtues of the women ordinands who have, "kept a low profile and have emphasized their desire to serve and exercise a ministry rather than create problems for the unconvinced." Ford went on to say that the issue had not divided the church because of the cautious and careful handling it had received in the General Synod.[34] Many Canadian Anglicans valued caution and 'keeping a low profile' as the most appropriate form of behaviour on this issue.

• *Diocese of Saskatchewan*

The diocese of Saskatchewan first heard of the ordination of women to the priesthood in a formal setting through the bishop's charge at the 52nd session of its synod. In that charge, Bishop H. V. R. Short acknowledged that this was a potentially divisive issue for the church in the immediate future. While he seemed to be open to the possibility of such ordinations in theory, he questioned their feasibility, "Let me conclude by saying that the fact that something will not work is often a good reason for not doing it; but this does not rule out the contention that it ought to work and would work if all were as it ought to be."[35] A motion was put to the synod that it affirm the 1973 decision of the General Synod. This motion was lost in the House of Clergy.[36] The matter was then raised again at the diocesan synod of 1975 by the committee which responded to the bishop's charge. In his charge Short stressed the "Gamaliel" principle: if it is of God nothing can stop it and if it is not it will fail of its own accord. The committee picked up this point and presented a motion in favour of the ordination of women to the priesthood. The motion was lost once again in the House of Clergy.[37]

The interactions within this particular diocese were interesting. There was clearly a division of opinion on this issue. The laity's persistence in attempting to pass the affirmation of it was paralleled by the clergy's insistence that the principle not be affirmed. Only one clergyman signed the *Manifesto*. The bishop, while open to the idea, did not actively promote women's ordination.

• *Diocese of Rupert's Land*

The diocese of Rupert's Land was guided by the episcopal leadership of Bishop Barry Valentine during the years in which the national church debated women's ordination to the priesthood. He himself was actively involved in the House of Bishops' committees which worked with this issue from 1973 to 1978. Given that involvement at the national level one would have thought that there would be a fair amount going on in his home diocese with this issue. Such was not the case. However, that is not to say that the issue was never mentioned.

At the diocesan synod of 1973, Valentine raised the issue. It was clear that he was still internally debating it. Following his charge a motion was put to affirm the ordination of women to the priesthood in principle, and the synod demonstrated itself, "overwhelmingly in favour" of the motion. The numbers in the House of Laity were 137 for, 15 against and 27 undecided, and in the House of Clergy 47 voted for the motion, 8 against it and 6 were undecided.[38] No clergy from this diocese signed the *Manifesto*.

The subject did not come up again on the diocesan agenda until the synod of 1977. At that time, Valentine stated that he believed the ordination of women to be intrinsically right, and announced that he would implement it on or before All Saints Day, 1978.[39] Valentine was waiting until the matter had been discussed at the Lambeth Conference, 1978. He was one of the bishops in the House who felt strongly that the Canadian church should wait until the conclusion of Lambeth before it took any unilateral action on the matter.

Ecclesiastical Province of Ontario

This province is comprised of the dioceses of Algoma, Huron, Moosonee, Niagara, Ontario, Ottawa, Toronto

• *Diocese of Algoma*

In his charge to the 26th session of the Algoma Synod in 1973, Archbishop William Wright introduced his diocese to the issue of women's ordination to the priesthood. Giving a historical synopsis of events surrounding the issue, he informed them that he had voted against the motion at General Synod because he did not want to pre-judge the issue. He was unwilling to act in support of the ordination of women until the synod of Algoma had had a chance to express its mind on the subject.[40] Later in his episcopacy Wright announced that he would take no action on the ordination of women until after the Lambeth Conference of 1978. A new diocesan bishop was in place before that and the action was no longer his to take. Three clergy in this diocese signed the *Manifesto*. Bishop Les Peterson assumed the office of the episcopate in 1976. In 1978, the diocesan synod discussed the issue and passed a motion in support of the implementation of the ordination of women to the priesthood.[41]

• *Diocese of Huron*

The Diocese of Huron discussed the ordination of women to the priesthood at its diocesan synod in 1973. Under the direction of Bishop Carman Queen the synod considered the decisions of the preceeding Lambeth Conference and of its own General Synod that year. Queen provided the synod with an overview of what had happened in the church on this issue to date in his charge to the synod. He concluded with the comment that he had no reservations concerning the ordination of women to the priesthood, "providing our clergy and laity representing the parishes are prepared and willing to accept women as priests in the Church." He then emphasized his hope that no bishop would take unilateral action on the matter before the Anglican Church of Canada had reached a decision together.[42]

In the middle of all of this, however, Queen died and David Ragg, his suffragan, replaced him. Bishop David Ragg had not articulated his position on the matter up to that point. Ragg, who declared himself to be of the broadstream in terms of his churchmanship, was elected as diocesan bishop in 1974. Previous to that he had been the Suffragan Bishop of Huron and had not worried about his position on this issue. He said he would vote as his diocesan bishop directed him to vote. When Queen died suddenly, Ragg was abruptly called upon to decide what stand he would take on this issue. He was greatly troubled and could not sleep because of his internal struggles over it. One evening late at night, with this debate heavy on his mind, he arose from his bed to get a glass of milk . As he descended the staircase to the kitchen he heard God say, "I wouldn't call them if I didn't want them." That was it. Ragg's mind was decided on the issue. He felt that he had no right to stand in the way of those whom God had called to do God's work.[43] From that point on he became a supporter of the ordination of women to the priesthood, and was one of the first bishops to ordain a woman on 30 November 1976.

The diocese of Huron did more than many other dioceses in its attempts to study this issue. In the fall of 1973, the diocese published a study report to aid in the educational process of the deaneries and parishes as it dealt with this issue. This report was prepared by the then Reverend Canon Jack Peck, now Bishop Peck. This report was so well received that it was adopted by the House of Bishops for national dissemination. It became the official study guide for the Canadian church on this subject. The study report gave a brief historical background on the issue, raised areas for further consideration, identified arguments both pro and con from Scripture and tradition, reflected theologically on "Man-Woman" relationships, looked at practical considerations such as education and employment, ecumenism and vocations and marriage.[44] The tone of the document was intentionally middle of the road, attempting to weigh both sides of the argument objectively. Apparently the diocese of Huron used this study guide in several deaneries and parishes to discuss the matter before it voted on the issue at its diocesan synod in 1975. In 1975, 29 clergy of that diocese signed the *Manifesto*.

In 1975 the 116th session of the synod of the diocese of Huron passed a motion affirming the ordination of women to the priesthood.[45] No record of the discussion was kept. On 30 November 1976, Ragg ordained the Reverend Mary Mills to the priesthood. This issue did not come up again on the agenda of the diocesan synods.

Mills had worked in the diocese for over 10 years and had been the first woman ordained deacon in the Anglican Church of Canada in 1969 by Bishop Luxton. Ragg appointed her deacon in charge of Kirkton. Throughout that period Mills felt a vocation to the priesthood but never participated in promoting women's ordination in any way. She did not see herself as a feminist but rather as a woman with a vocation to serve, a job to be done. In her words, "The people gave me my ministry." As the issue became openly discussed after 1973, her parishioners at Kirkton and her friends at her home parish in Glencoe affirmed her priestly ministry and encouraged the church to acknowledge what was already happening. When Queen asked Mills' parishioners their opinion they were ready with an affirmative answer. When the procedural changes had been made, Ragg approached Mary and asked her if she would like to be ordained priest. She said yes.[46]

• **Diocese of Moosonee**
Archbishop James Watton was president of the Synod of the diocese of Moosonee during the years when the question of women's ordination to the priesthood occupied the attention of the Canadian church. He himself did not support the ordination of women during those years and his diocese largely followed his example. After discussions in June of 1973 the synod of Moosonee passed a motion which said, "Since General Synod has accepted the principle of women priests, be it resolved that Canadian House of Bishops should approach this whole matter with extreme caution."[47] It felt that it could not affirm women's ordination in principle or implementation. Apparently issues involving male headship and the need for a male icon of Christ were determinative in the formulation of this view; the strong opinion of many members of native groups within the diocese was also influential.

Four clergymen from the diocese of Moosonee signed the *Manifesto*. Although their diocesan bishop was himself opposed, he was vocal in chastising those members of his diocese who had signed the *Manifesto*. He stated that although much of the document fairly represented important arguments against the ordination of women, he felt that the comments about the clergy's inability to obtain other employment made a mockery of the priestly vocation. He also accused the signers of attempting to blackmail the church and said that he could not accept that from any priest in his diocese.[48] There is no record of how those who signed the *Manifesto* responded to their irate bishop.

- *Diocese of Niagara*

Under the leadership of Bishop Walter Bagnall the question of women's ordination to the priesthood did not arise. This in large part must reflect the years of his incumbency which ended in 1973. By the 99th session of the diocesan synod in 1973, Bishop John Bothwell had been elected diocesan bishop. In his first charge to the synod he identified the struggle over women in orders and made it clear that he supported the idea of women in the priesthood.[49] The synod itself did not discuss the issue until two years later in 1975. 1974 was taken up in planning for the diocese's 100th Anniversary in 1975.

At the 100th session of its synod, Niagara heard a charge from Bothwell which stressed that arguments against the ordination of women had something to do, in part, with "hang ups" about the changing role of women, and that the church must experience a female priesthood in order that it might test the call of God to such ministry fully.[50] The diocese of Niagara handled this issue somewhat differently than other dioceses. It did not pass a motion supporting the ordination of women; it was clear that its diocesan bishop was going to ordain women when the time came. It did, however, pass a motion which contained a conscience clause which paralleled the conscience clause passed by the General Synod that year. The wording of the clause was the same as the wording of the national clause with the exception of a specific reference to the diocese of Niagara.[51] Some clergy and laity in the diocese felt the need to protect themselves from the actions of their progressive bishop. 11 clergymen from the diocese signed the *Manifesto.*

Bothwell readily identified himself, and was quickly identified by his peers as one of the members of the House of Bishops who actively sought the introduction of women into Holy Orders in the Canadian Church. When asked why he sought this change, he said simply that he believed it was right and just. He believed it was what the Holy Spirit was calling the church to, and in that belief was able to articulate a clear theology of sexuality which talked about the redemption of all of humanity. Some of his fellows in the House identified him as a radical, as they had his fellow bishop, David Somerville. This, however, was not a label with which he was uncomfortable. Bothwell remembered the debates over this issue in the House as having a great deal of sensitivity and very little heat. The bishops listened to each other, agreed to differ and were able to move together in a positive spirit toward the future. He actively pursued the course toward the ordination of women and on 30

November 1976, he ordained two women in Grace Church, St. Catharines.

The two women that Bothwell ordained as the first women priests in the diocese represented two different dimensions of women working and living in the church. The Reverend Beverley Shanley was a worker of long standing in the church, formerly a deaconess who did not identify herself with feminism. The Reverend Mary Lucas was a younger woman who articulated a feminist vision for the church; she did not remain in parish ministry. Shanley remembered that although she had an interest in being ordained to the priesthood, she did not actively seek it. It was Bothwell who came to her and invited her to become a priest of the church.[52]

• *Diocese of Ontario*

Bishop J. B. Creegan introduced the matter of women in Holy Orders to his diocese in his charge to the 107th session of the diocesan synod in 1973. He noted that the General Synod had decided to affirm the ordination of women to the priesthood, but that he had voted against the motion, and refused to implement it in his diocese. He observed that he had had four priests say to him that they would leave the Anglican Church if it ordained women. He was unwilling to support such a potentially divisive action. He felt that the General Synod decision contravened the leading of the Holy Spirit, "I regret that we did not pray for the guidance of the Holy Spirit before a vote was taken."[53] The diocese of Ontario did not pass any motion on this subject up to 1978. In 1974, the diocese did hold a "congress" on the matter, at which both sides of the issue were considered and debated. No clear consensus was reached. The congress highlighted the fact that there was considerable division. Creegan advised all members of the diocesan synod in 1974 to avail themselves of the study materials and to keep praying.[54]

A new diocesan bishop was elected in 1975. Bishop Henry Hill, who was of Anglo-Catholic orientation, noted that the "thorny problem" of women's ordination continued to plague the church. He stated that this issue should not be confused with the issue of women's liberation, and that whether the ordination of women was right or wrong, it should not be undertaken for the sake of ecumenism. He then noted that violent protest from either side would not reveal the working of the Holy Spirit.[55] After the Lambeth Conference of 1978, Hill reflected on women in Holy Orders and seemed to have moved toward a greater openness to the prospect. "It is my view that the Church as a whole will eventually come to a richer and deeper acceptance of the priesthood of men and women." However, he concluded, "we have no alternative but to attend steadfastly to the will of our Lord and await his answer."[56]

• **Diocese of Ottawa**

The diocese of Ottawa struggled at length over whether or not women should be admitted to the presbyterate. Throughout the 1970s Ottawa had a bishop, William Robinson, who was vocally opposed to the ordination of women. There was, however, some openness to it within his diocese. At the diocesan synod of 1973 both the bishop and the delegates from General Synod reported on the motions on the ordination of women which had passed at General Synod. The bishop noted that he had voted against the motions, and that he did not support the ordination of women; the delegates offered no comment one way or the other.[57]

In October of 1973, a special session of synod was held for the purpose of discussing women and Holy Orders. A lengthy discussion ensued, after which a motion was presented which contradicted the motions of General Synod. It read: *We move that this synod urge General Synod and the House of Bishops to reconsider the above motion* (i.e., the General Synod motion re. the ordination of women to the priesthood). Members of the special synod voted by orders, and by secret ballot yielding the following results: 43 clergy for and 39 against, and 69 lay people for and 109 against.[58] This was the only motion produced on the subject and it was defeated.

At the 86th session of the synod in 1977, Robinson stated that he was still in disagreement with the ordination of women and that he was not prepared to ordain women in the diocese of Ottawa. Women ordained elsewhere were welcome to visit in the diocese.[59] After the Lambeth Conference of 1978, Robinson reported the relevant resolution to his synod and then stated that he was now prepared to ordain women to the priesthood in his diocese. Apparently Robinson felt that the Holy Spirit must have somehow been at work in the deliberations of the church. Further, Lambeth 1978 had demonstrated that the Canadian church's actions would not precipitate an irrevocable break. As such, he was prepared to proceed.

• *Diocese of Toronto*

Presiding over the synod of the diocese of Toronto during the years of debate over the admission of women to priesthood was Archbishop Lewis Garnsworthy. From 1973 to 1976, the issue of the ordination of women to the priesthood was on the table at each diocesan synod. In 1973, Garnsworthy raised the matter in his charge to the synod. He told members of his diocese that the bishops of Toronto had voted to affirm the principle of the ordination of women because they could find no reason to refuse the principle. He stipulated that the ordination of women without the conviction that the church would accept their ministry would be wrong.[60] A motion was made which demonstrated strong disagreement with the decision of General Synod:

> THAT mindful of the doctrine and practice of the Book of Common Prayer of the Solemn Declaration of General Synod, and of the Anglican commitment to Scripture, Creeds, Sacraments and the Apostolic ministry and believing that too frequently General Synods have promoted resolutions and changes affecting the life and teaching of the Church without first justifying the same with reference to effect upon our internal unity and possible damaging effect upon our relations with several major Christian Communions; the Synod of Toronto deplores the decision of General Synod approving in principle the ordination of women to the priesthood; and respectfully asks our Diocesan to convey to the House of Bishops its wish that there be a deeper study and wider consultation on this subject not only within the Anglican Church of Canada but also within the Anglican Communion; that there be a genuine seeking for a real consensus of the faithful; and that there by no corporate or individual attempt by our Canadian Bishops to admit women to the priesthood until such time as the whole church may assent.[61]

This motion contained a more strident opposition to the General Synod motion than is found articulated in any other diocese of the Canadian church. The above motion was not voted on at the 1973 synod; it was tabled for further study by the Doctrine and Worship Committee and parishes in the diocese.

At the synod of 1974, the Doctrine and Worship Committee reported that it had spent several meetings examining the questions of principle and practice in the ordination of women to the priesthood, and presented a brief summary of its findings, which included arguments both *pro* and *con*. The motion from the 1973 synod was not voted on. Rather the Committee gave three new notices of motions which said that the synod supported the General Synod's decision and would appoint priests without regard for race, sex or colour.[62]

In Garnsworthy's charges to the synods of 1975 and 1976, he acknowledged that the House of Bishops had decided to proceed with the ordination of women, and although he continued to be deeply troubled by the issue, particularly with reference to the relationship with Rome and the Orthodox church, he would not ignore it. By 1976, he was saying that he would take the choice of the church seriously and work to provide equal employment opportunities within the diocese of Toronto.[63] One has the sense from his words that he was acting almost under duress, but certainly out of respect for the choices of the larger church. In 1977 Garnsworthy and Suffragan Bishop Allan Reed ordained the first women priests in the diocese.

When Sister Rosemary Anne Benwell, SSJD, was ordained to the priesthood in 1977, she was fulfilling a vocation she had felt since she was 15 years old, "If I had been a boy I would have been seeking priesthood." She remembered that even as late as January of 1977, Garnsworthy was not willing to ordain women. One month later she read a newspaper article which said that he had changed his mind and was going to ordain Margery Pezzack. In her view, the question of whether or not women were fully human was paramount in the diocesan debates on this issue. 30 clergymen from the diocese of Toronto signed the *Manifesto*. During the actual ordination of Benwell there was an objection from a clergyman during which, "Some cried, some dropped to their knees and prayed, held each other—it was a very tense moment."[64] Even the actual event of ordination reflected the tension of a diocese which was still divided on the issue.

Ecclesiastical Province of Canada

This province is comprised of the dioceses of Fredericton, Montreal, Newfoundland, Nova Scotia, and Quebec.

• *Diocese of Fredericton*

This diocese was the home of the Reverend R. B. Stockall, founding member of the St. James Group which wrote the *Manifesto on the Ordi-*

nation of Women to the Priesthood. This fact is representative of what happened in the diocese of Fredericton with regard to women and Holy Orders. The only recorded discussion on this matter revolved around the person of Stockall. Stockall was a delegate to General Synod in 1973. He returned from that experience to his own diocesan synod where he made a presentation on what had transpired in Regina. He was extremely disillusioned by the affirmation in principle of the ordination of women to the priesthood and in fact warned his synod that the decision would contribute to the continuing downslide of the Anglican Church of Canada. "I am one who believes that there are theological reasons against women priests, though I make no claim to be a theologian." Rather than expounding on these reasons, Stockall went on to say that such action would needlessly divide the Anglican Church from the rest of Christendom.[65] Stockall also made a motion which the synod passed and later sent as the report of the diocese of Fredericton on this issue to the General Synod of the church. The motion read:

> Be it resolved that the 100th session of the diocesan synod of Fredericton express its deep regret and disapproval to the action of General Synod 1971 in accepting the principle of the ordination of women to the priesthood, and further that this resolution be sent to the General Secretary of the House of Bishops.[66]

Primate Scott was present at that synod during its deliberations and appears to have played a diplomatic role rather than lobbying on the side of the ordination of women. He said, "I would like to thank Reverend Stockall and others for raising this issue. Sometimes people do not bring forward issues which are on their heart, and I am grateful that this has been done."[67]

The diocesan Bishop, Harold Lee Nutter appears to have played only a minor role in the deliberations. There was no record of him having spoken either for or against the motion or the issue. When the question was put it was carried by a close vote, 67 in favour and 64 opposed.[68] The discussion surrounding the passage of this motion was the only recorded interaction on this matter in the diocese of Fredericton during the time covered by this study.

• *Diocese of Montreal*

In 1974 Bishop Kenneth Macguire suggested to his synod that the diocesan theme for a Lenten study in the upcoming year should be the ordination of women to the priesthood. He informed the synod that the General Synod had affirmed such ordinations in principle the preceeding year and that Montreal should study the questions so that it would be well prepared to vote on the issue at the next session of the diocesan synod.[69] By the next session of the synod a new bishop had been elected, Reginald Hollis, and he felt that it would not be appropriate for the synod to vote on the issue. Hollis invited all members of the synod to fill out a questionnaire relating their views on the subject, so that delegates to General Synod would know how the members felt.[70] This action effectively stopped any formal discussion of the issue in the diocese.

It was in 1978 that this issue was mentioned in the diocese again. Hollis raised it as he discussed the upcoming agenda of the Lambeth Conference. He mentioned that he had been informed that there had been 113 ordinations of women as priests in North America up to that point (18 of these would have been Canadian) and that there had been agreement in nine of the provinces. Hollis made it clear that he was still struggling with the issue. There was a female deacon in the diocese who wanted to become a priest. He stated that he would not make up his mind until after Lambeth.[71] By the following session of synod he had ordained the Reverend Lettie James to the priesthood (1 October 1978). Hollis noted that he was concerned over the secession of some Anglicans with the formation of the Anglican Catholic Church over this issue and that he hoped time would heal the division.[72] The diocese did not discuss or make a decision on this issue. It was in the hands of its diocesan bishop.

• *Diocese of Newfoundland*

In his charge to the synod of 1973, Bishop Robert Seaborn listed women's ordination to the priesthood as one of three concerns facing the larger church, along with Christian Initiation and the Church Union dialogue then ongoing with the United Church of Canada. He noted that the ordination of women to the presbyterate had been affirmed in principle and had been sent to the House of Bishops for further consideration.[73] Again in 1975, Seaborn reported what had happened in the larger church. Women's ordination was not identified at any point as something which needed the attention of the diocesan synod. It was presented as a matter 'out there' which was being dealt with by the national decision-making bodies of the church.

In 1975 the diocese of Newfoundland was divided into three dioceses. Seaborn presided over what became the diocese of Eastern Newfoundland and Labrador. He did not refer to the ordination of women to the priesthood again, even when reporting on the events of the 1978 Lambeth Conference. In the new diocese of Central Newfoundland Bishop Mark Genge raised the matter of women in Holy Orders at the second session of the synod in 1977. He asked the synod to give its attention to the matter. The synod journal reported that there was a discussion and that a large majority were in favour, but no vote or numbers were recorded.[74] In the diocese of Western Newfoundland William Legge assumed the office of diocesan bishop. He did not mention the matter of women's ordination to the priesthood during the time of his incumbency, which was only two years. When a new diocesan was elected and presided over the diocesan synod in 1978 he also did not mention the issue.[75]

How one interprets the silence of bishops on this issue is a matter for debate. Their silence might have indicated opposition or it might have been that they simply did not think it was an important issue for the church.

• *Diocese of Nova Scotia*

At its annual synod in 1973, the diocese of Nova Scotia heard about the ordination of women to the priesthood from its bishop, the Most Reverend William Davis. He raised the issue in his charge with language that seemed open to the idea. At that same synod two members, one a lay person and the other clergy, put a motion which read as follows:

> That this diocese request the House of Bishops not implement the principle of the ordination of women to the priesthood until 1. every diocese in the province of Canada has expressed itself in accordance with the wishes of General Synod and the Primate, and 2. the principle has been approved by at least 3/4 of the dioceses in Canada.[76]

This motion was essentially an 'anti' ordination of women motion; it was defeated. A lay woman, Nancy Morrison, then gave notice of another motion affirming the ordination of women, agreeing to present the motion at the next session of the diocesan synod.[77]

When the synod of 1974 arrived, Davis talked about the division in the church on this issue, but in so doing demonstrated his support for the admission of women into Holy Orders saying, "We can't escape responsibility for a decision that involves the continued exclusion from ordered ministry of persons who meet all of the requirements but sex."[78] The motion by Morrison was then put forward, and after a vote by a secret ballot the motion affirming the ordination of women was passed, 157 for and 91 against with 17 abstentions.[79]

Davis retired and a new diocesan, George Feversham, was elected in 1976. In his first two addresses to the synod he did not mention the issue. In 1978 he noted what happened at the Lambeth Conference on the subject. Observing and acknowledging that he had had reservations, Feversham said that Nova Scotia, "might anticipate the action which has the approval of our national church."[80]

• Diocese of Quebec

It was at its annual session of synod in 1974 that the diocese of Quebec first debated the ordination of women to the priesthood under the presidency of Bishop Timothy Matthews. As an item on the agenda a formal debate on the matter was held, with the Reverend John Baycroft presenting the 'pro' side and Brother Nevil Cheesman, SSJE, presenting the 'con' side of the argument. After several hours of "heated debate," the motion was put. It asked that the Anglican Church of Canada proceed with the ordination of women to the priesthood. The motion was passed in the House of the Laity with 34 in favour and 20 against, but lost in the House of Clergy with nine in favour and 14 against.[81] The clergy defeated the motion.

It was not until the following session of the synod that the views of the diocesan bishop were clearly articulated on this matter. In his address Matthews talked about his desire to ordain a woman to the priesthood, "It would be the fulfilment of my episcopate if in due course I have occasion to perform this rite." He encouraged his fellow bishops to move in the direction of opening their arms to the women in the threefold order of ministry:

To deny priest's orders to a woman seems to me to question the validity of her calling and of God's wisdom in extending it. I don't feel that any of us has that right.... I am sorry, yes ashamed that the church or that part of it to which I belong should be so divided and feel so threatened about what seems to me a very simple straightforward issue-allowing God to call whom he will to render him service in such ways as He may please, be they male or female.[82]

Matthews ordained the Reverend Ruth Matthews in 1977.

CONCLUDING OBSERVATIONS

The diversity present in diocesan decision-making processes is evident. Each process was unique. Ultimately, most bishops supported the ordination of women, as did most clergy and laity. Most dioceses affirmed the ordination of women to the priesthood by 1978. Their sentiments, for the most part, were shared by the General Synod and House of Bishops.

Endnotes

1. This comment made after an examination of Bishop Gartrell's charges to the synod between 1968 and 1980.
2. B.C. Synod, *Journal of Proceedings*, 72nd session, 1975, p. Bp5.
3. Oral History Interview with the Reverend Patricia Reed, 29 July 1991.
4. Caledonia, *Journal of Proceedings*, 35th session, 1974, section 64.
5. Caledonia, *Journal of Proceedings*, 36th session, 1975, Motion 11.
6. Caledonia, *Journal of Proceedings*, 38th session, 1977, Bishop's Charge.
7. Oral History Interview with the Reverend Canon Dorothy Daly, 19 August, 1991.
8. Kootenay, *Journal of Proceedings*, 45th session, 1977, p. A16C.
9. New Westminster, *Journal of Proceedings*, 68th session, 1974.
10. Oral History Interview with Archbishop David Somerville, 20 July 1991.
11. Oral History Interview with the Reverend Elspeth Alley, 29 July 1991.
12. Yukon, *Journal of Proceedings*, 20th session, 1974, pp. 23–24.
13. Arctic, *Journal of Proceedings*, 2nd session, 1975, p. 76.
14. Arctic, *Journal of Proceedings*, 1975, p. 74.
15. Arctic, *Journal of Proceedings*, 3rd session, 1978, Appendix XII.
16. Athabasca, *Journal of Proceedings*, 35th session, 1971, p. 14.
17. Athabasca, *Journal of Proceedings*, 36th session, 1973, Appendix A.
18. Athabasca, 1973, Appendix B.
19. Athabasca, 1973, Appendix B, p. 7.
20. Athabasca, *Journal of Proceedings*, 38th session, 1975, p. 18.
21. Athabasca, *Journal of Proceedings*, 39th session, 1977, p. 17.
22. Brandon, *Journal of Proceedings*, 1976, Bishop's Charge, p. 2.
23. Brandon, *Journal of Proceedings*, 1976, p. 2.
24. Letter from the Reverend M. Kennon to W. Fletcher, May, 1991.

25. Letter to the Primate, February 1977, Scott Papers, (M101).
26. Edmonton, *Journal of Proceedings*, 37th session, 1977, p. 12.
27. Qu'Appelle, *Journal of Proceedings*, 53rd session, 1973, Bishop's Charge, p. 2.
28. Qu'Appelle, *Journal of Proceedings*, 1973, p. 32.
29. Letter to the Primate, 1976, Scott Papers, (M101).
30. Qu'Appelle, *Journal of Proceedings*, 56th session, 1978, p. 4.
31. Qu'Appelle, *Journal of Proceedings*, 1978, p. M.25.
32. Letter from Bishop S. C. Steer to W. Fletcher, May, 1991.
33. Saskatoon, *Journal of Proceedings*, 55th session, 1975, p. 12.
34. Saskatoon, *Journal of Proceedings*, 55th session, 1975, Bishop's Charge, p. 3.
35. Saskatchewan, *Journal of Proceedings*, 1973, p. 30.
36. Saskatchewan, *Journal of Proceedings*, 53rd Session, 1973, Bishop's Charge, p. 12.
37. Saskatchewan, *Journal of Proceedings*, 1975, p. 10.
38. Rupert's Land, *Journal of Proceedings*, 77th session, 1973, Bishop's Charge, p. 2.
39. Rupert's Land, *Journal of Proceedings*, 81st session, 1977, p. SP8.
40. Algoma, *Journal of Proceedings*, 26th session, 1973, p. 57.
41. Algoma, *Journal of Proceedings*, 28th session, 1978, pp. 211–213.
42. Huron, *Journal of Proceedings*, 114th session, 1973, p. 60.
43. Oral History Interview with Bishop David Ragg, 20 July 1991.
44. *Study Report on the Ordination of Women to the Priesthood*, Fall, 1973, by the Rev. Canon Jack Peck.
45. Huron, *Journal of Proceedings*, 116th session, 1975, Motion 3.40.
46. Oral History Interview with the Reverend Mary Mills, 15 October 1991.
47. Moosonee, *Journal of Proceedings*, 1973.
48. Letter from Archbishop James Watton to clergy in his diocese who had signed the *Manifesto*, October 16, 1975 (G.S. 81-1, Box 2).
49. Niagara, *Journal of Proceedings*, 99th session, 1973, p. J19.
50. Niagara, *Journal of Proceedings*, 100th session, 1975, p. H6.
51. Niagara, 1975, p. D12.
52. Interview with Archbishop John Bothwell, 3 October 1990.
53. Ontario, *Journal of Proceedings*, 107th session, 1973, p. 31.
54. Ontario, *Journal of Proceedings*, 108th session, 1974, p. 33.
55. Ontario, *Journal of Proceedings*, 109th session, 1975, p. 35.
56. Ontario, *Journal of Proceedings*, Special Session, October, 1978, Appendix A.
57. Ottawa, *Journal of Proceedings*, 81st session, 1973, pp. 47–51.
58. Ottawa, *Journal of Proceedings*, 82nd session, 1973, pp. 5–31.
59. Ottawa, *Journal of Proceedings*, 86th session, 1976, p. 62.
60. Toronto, *Journal of Proceedings*, 1973, p. 6
61. Toronto, *Journal of Proceedings*, 1973, pp. 150–151.
62. Toronto, *Journal of Proceedings*, 1975, pp. 168–171, 207.
63. Toronto, *Journal of Proceedings*, 1976, pp. 235, 241.
64. Oral History Interview with the Reverend Sr. Rosemary Anne Benwell, SSJD, 30 July, 1991.
65. Presentation to the Synod of Fredericton by R. B. Stockall, 1973, Scott Papers, (M101).
66. Fredericton, *Journal of Proceedings*, 100th Session, 1973, pp. 62, 74–76.
67. Fredericton, *Journal of Proceedings*, 1973, p. 76.
68. Fredericton, *Journal of Proceedings*, 1973, p. 76.
69. Montreal, *Journal of Proceedings*, 115th session, 1974, p. 24.
70. Montreal, *Journal of Proceedings*, 116th session, 1975, p. 42.
71. Montreal, *Journal of Proceedings*, 119th session, 1978, Bishop's charge.

72. Montreal, *Journal of Proceedings*, 120th Session, 1979, p. 24.
73. Newfoundland, *Journal of Proceedings*, 50th session, 1973, p. 55.
74. Central Newfoundland, *Journal of Proceedings*, 2nd session, 1977, p. 7–9.
75. Western Newfoundland, *Journal of Proceedings*, Sessions 1–3, 1975–78.
76. Nova Scotia, *Journal of Proceedings*, 101st Session, 1973, p. 76.
77. Nova Scotia, *Journal of Proceedings*, 1973, p. 78.
78. Nova Scotia, *Journal of Proceedings*, 102nd session, 1974. p. 55.
79. Nova Scotia, *Journal of Proceedings*, 1974, p. 21.
80. Nova Scotia, *Journal of Proceedings*, 108th Session, 1978, p. 55.
81. Quebec, *Journal of Proceedings*, 61st session. pp. 20–21.
82. Quebec, *Journal of Proceedings*, 62nd Session, 1975, Bishop's Charge, pp. 45–56.

Messengers' cottage at Rorketon. Diocese of Brandon, 1935.

Photo courtesy of:
General Synod Archives.

Bishop's Messenger,
Helene Hannah
(*below*), presents new
curriculum, 1944.

Photo courtesy of:
General Synod Archives.

Bishop's Messenger travels frozen river. Diocese of Caledonia, 1940.

Photo courtesy of: General Synod Archives.

Miss Hasell's Caravan Mission, Diocese of Athabasca, 1965.

Photo courtesy of:
G. P. Lebans

A Manifesto

on the Ordination of Women to the Priesthood

from concerned clergy of the Anglican Church of Canada

This document, after limited circulation among clergy, has, of early September, been subscribed to by the following:

The *Manifesto* occupied one full page in the Canadian Churchman, a page clearly marked as "advertisement," along with a signature coupon soliciting tax-deductible donations to aid in defraying costs. This advertisement also included the names of many of the clergy who subscribed to the *Manifesto*.

Courtesy of Canadian Churchman, October, 1975 (General Synod Archives).

Bishop's Messenger, St. Faiths in the Diocese of Brandon, 1969.
Photo courtesy of: General Synod Archives.

Archbishop Edward W. Scott.
Photo courtesy of: General Synod Archives.

Ordination of the Rev. Patricia Reed,
Diocese of Cariboo, 1976.
Photo courtesy of: General Synod Archives.

Ordination of Mary Mills,
Diocese of Huron, 1977.
Photo courtesy of:
General Synod Archives.

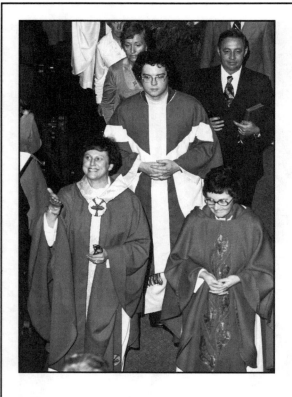

The ordination of
Elspeth Alley and
Virginia Bryant,
Diocese of New
Westminster, 1976.

Photo courtesy of:
General Synod Archives.

The ordination
of Mary Lucas and
Beverley Shanley,
Diocese of
Niagara, 1976.

Photo courtesy of:
General Synod Archives.

PART THREE
REVOLUTION FAILS
IN ENGLAND

5

Change and Resistance

The decision not to ordain women to the priest-hood made at the Church of England's General Synod in July, 1978 was preceded by a lengthy and passionate history. Unlike the situation in the Canadian church, the Church of England was actively aware of the issue of women's ordination before the Lambeth Conference, 1968. In keeping with its 'Mother Church' status, England began to explore this issue of its own volition; that is not to say that the issue was considered an important one by the Church's decision-making bodies. As we saw in the Canadian case, the actual process by which the church made a formal decision began only after the Lambeth Conference of 1968.

THE ORDINATION OF WOMEN AND THE POPULAR MIND OF THE CHURCH OF ENGLAND, 1920–1967

Between 1920 and 1967, the question of the ordination of women to the priesthood was a recognized issue by many in ecclesiastical circles; however, central Church authorities and many women workers and deaconesses viewed the issue as peripheral, involving only a fringe of the church population. Specific interest groups and individuals promoted this issue but much of the general populus of the church was largely unaware of it until the 1970's.

Prior to Lambeth 1920

Although 1920 signalled the official starting point of discussions on women in Holy Orders in the Anglican Communion, there were people in the Church of England who discussed women in the priesthood prior to that point. The hierarchy of the Church of England was aware of the issue before Lambeth 1920 but did not give it serious or intensive consideration until after Lambeth 1968.

A report from as early as 1916 comments on the question of women and the priesthood. In 1916, a layperson in the Church of England attempted to organize a conference to discuss the issue of women's ordination to the priesthood. Toward that end he circulated a letter looking for interested parties. His report on this issue was a record of the responses of individuals to his request. He divided the responses into five distinct categories: unfavourable, interested but not convinced, favourable but will take no action, favourable but not a churchperson, favourable and involved in the church. This individual recorded 30 favourable responses, apparently an insufficient number to conduct the conference at that time;[1] however, the Archbishop of Canterbury as the titular head of the Anglican Communion was aware of this as an issue from as early as 1916.

GRASSROOTS ORGANIZATIONS

That layperson in 1916 was not alone in his interest in this question. Indeed, it would have been difficult for the ecclesiastical structures of any tradition in England at that time to have been totally unaware of this as a possibility. Gramsci's theory of revolution suggests that a transition to a new historic bloc cannot be successfully affected without leadership which is supported by the grassroots of an institution or social structure. We will see that between 1920 and 1978 (particularly after 1968), there is evidence of significant support for the ordination of women at the grassroots, but no positive leadership initiative, thus making a move to a new form of ministry a virtual impossibility at that time.

Between 1909 and 1919, an active and vocal organization named the Church League for Women's Suffrage consistently lobbied for the enfranchisement of women in society. Many Anglicans were actively involved in the leadership of this movement, most notably Maude Royden. At that point in history, the close connection between secular and ecclesiastical feminism is indisputable. The leaders of the secular feminist movement were the feminist leaders in their own denominational traditions. The origins of a feminist voice in the church grew parallel to the feminist movement in secular society. The causes and issues were related, but the period of direct overlap lasted only as long as the issue of women's suffrage. After that, secular and ecclesiastical feminists had their own trails to blaze.

While the Church League for Women's Suffrage was not specifically concerned with the issue of women's ordination it was significant in that it served as the precursor of the first formalized lobby for such ordinations. When the vote was granted to women in English society, the League for Women's Suffrage disbanded. Many of those who had been involved in lobbying for the vote realized that there were many other issues which needed attention. As such, although the group formally disbanded, it would be more accurate to say that it took on a new form, with a new agenda, and with a largely unchanged membership. In 1920, the group became the League of the Church Militant, and actively campaigned for the vote for women on equal terms with men inside the church. Through prayer and education, it also addressed issues such as the use of the word "obey" in marriage ceremonies, the right of women to speak in church, and by 1925, advocated the admission of women to the priesthood. By 1930, the League had disbanded and in its place the Interdenominational Society for the Equal Ministry of Men and Women was formed. The strength of Anglican involvement in those organizations was demonstrated by the move also in 1930 to form a specifically Anglican group to lobby for women's ordination. This group became known as the Anglican Group for the Ordination of Women to the Historic Ministry of the Church (AGOW). The AGOW continued its work of public education on the issue of women's ordination until the mid-1970s.

The specific work of this group was carried out in conjunction with a broader lobby for the equality of women in Christian churches in English society. Small groups of committed church people, male and female, ordained and lay actively advocated women's ordination to the full three orders of the church from 1919 onward. Individuals such as Royden, herself an Anglican who was not allowed to preach from an Anglican pulpit but who regularly preached from the pulpits of other ecclesiastical traditions, worked to bring the issue to the attention of the general church population through the distribution of such materials as the 1921 pamphlet entitled *Women Priests and Deaconesses, and Women and the Church of England*.[2]

In works such as these, the logic of excluding women from a full participation in the ministry of the church was argued. Royden highlighted the sexist attitudes of traditional church policy and promoted the value of empowering women to preach, teach and preside. Public meetings were occasionally organized to address and debate the issue. The response of the average person in the pew to these attempts at public education is difficult to document. While membership in such lobby groups continued to grow, the groups remained small in number representing only a very narrow group of the church's population; however, the materials and activities of these groups demonstrate that ecclesiastical structures were aware of a grassroots movement on this issue throughout the period under discussion. The inability of church structures to hear and to work with this small but growing voice characterized its position throughout this early period.

The AGOW is the organization which was most significant in the Anglican situation. The group, held its first annual meeting on Thursday, 23 March 1933, in St. George's Church, Bloomsbury. The group had actually begun two years previously but there was no formal annual meeting until 1933; the first available record of minutes and policy exist from the fourth annual meeting held on Saturday, 23 May 1934. At the meeting for which the first actual written record exists the group changed its name from the original title of "The Anglican Group for the Ordination of Women to the Historic Orders of the Church's Ministry," to the name by which it was known for most of its history, "The Anglican Group for the Ordination of Women to the Historic Ministry of the Church." At the fourth annual meeting it was noted that there were, "forty-two members and friends", present. Apologies from 15 additional members were recorded.[3]

The secretary did not record the full list of members, but the minutes indicate that the membership included lay people, particularly women, some deaconesses and some practising clergy. The Deaconess Order as a whole was generally not supportive of the work of the organization at that time. This lack of support was predicated on the perception, held at least by the members of the AGOW, that the Deaconess Order as a whole seemed ready to accept the idea that deaconesses were a fourth or supplementary order rather than an integral part of the threefold order of the church.[4] This acceptance was at odds with the primary views of the AGOW, as outlined below. Individual deaconesses, however, did choose to support the work of the group.

At its fourth general meeting, members noted that membership in the AGOW was increasing. In light of this, they appointed a sub-committee to draw up a constitution for submission to a general meeting of members, which would define the criteria for membership and the purpose of the group. In anticipation of a formal constitution some discussion of the general aims of the group ensued. The AGOW agreed that the primary purpose of the group was to "uphold the principle of spiritual equality between men and women." This was to be achieved by first drawing attention to the growing need for the admission of women to the threefold order of the church's ministry, and secondly by bringing together and supporting those women who believed themselves to be called to Holy Orders.[5] At this stage in the AGOW's life, membership was open to all baptised persons over the age of eighteen in the Anglican Communion.[6] That definition underwent several slight adjustments as the years progressed.

At the fourth annual meeting, the AGOW considered the issue of the diaconate and women's exclusion from it. The group agreed that the recommendation of the Archbishop's Commission on the Ministry of Women from 1934-5 that the order of deaconesses should be regarded as a Holy Order which was, "not exactly parallel to any of the three orders open to men," was a serious breach of Catholic principle and practice. In other words, the AGOW considered the orders of the deaconess to be the same as the diaconal orders of male deacons of the church. The group further stipulated that a right development of the ministry of women in the future world would depend on the recognition of the diaconate as being equally open to men and women. It was observed that if such recognition existed many more women would be willing to enter the ministry of the Church.[7]

Between annual meetings, the AGOW arranged public gatherings to discuss important considerations related to the primary purpose of the group which was the promotion of the spiritual equality of men and women within ecclesiastical structures. At one such meeting, it was argued that women priests were needed for the spiritual health of the nation.[8] This opinion was reflective of an AGOW position which was primary during the 1930s and 1940s. The AGOW argued that women's methods of doing things were different from those of men. As such, the full co-operation of men and women in the ministry of the church would enrich it at a time when the church was struggling to survive in an increasingly secular society. From its earliest days, the

AGOW demonstrated a sensitivity to the crisis of the church which was characterized by lagging membership and questionable legitimacy within society and connected this crisis at least in part to the exclusion of women from full participation in the church's life. In short, it realized that the ministry of the church was such an arduous task, that it demanded "the full resources of humanity be available for its fulfilment."[9]

By its annual meeting on 23 May 1936, the AGOW had not completed the task of drawing up its constitution. It did reiterate the principles it articulated in 1934, making a small change in the basis for membership. While previously the wording allowed all baptized members of the Anglican Communion to participate, in 1936 members added a second clause. From 1936, membership was open to any communicant of the Anglican church who "believes that it is reasonable and desirable that women should be ordained."[10] Obviously this had previously been an assumed criteria for participation, but in 1936 they clearly spelled it out. Members adopted the first existing copy of a formal constitution for the AGOW at the group's annual meeting on 22 March 1958. At that point, members spelled out all aspects of the group's life and work from membership, objectives, and meetings, to finance, management and trust deeds. They retained the name of the group as it was established in 1934, but in all other areas they made some slight changes.

The objectives of the group fell into four areas. Firstly, they agreed that the first object of the group was to secure the ordination of women to all orders of the historic ministry of the Church of England. Secondly, the group was designed to promote equality between men and women in the offices and affairs of the Church of England. Thirdly, the AGOW committed itself to assisting women engaged in theological studies and fourthly it agreed that it would do all "such other lawful things as are incidental to or conducive to the attainment of the above objects or any of them."[11] Ordination was only one of the issues of spiritual equality. At this point in the history of the Church of England, women were not allowed to preach and had not been fully enfranchised as equal lay members of the church. As such, the AGOW realized that ordination was essential to full spiritual equality; in a real sense it was the pinnacle of the group's aims. Many other areas and aspects of spiritual equality were implicit in the struggle for women's ordination. The AGOW did keep itself firmly centred in its primary objective of women's admission to the threefold orders of the church. It did not, however, ignore the other issues along the way.

From the mid-1950s onward the AGOW organized and carefully orchestrated a public education campaign for women's ordination to all three orders of ministry. Its activities took several forms, all of which were aimed at public education on the issue and support of women engaged in theological pursuits. Increasingly, the group carried out its work in conjunction with other societies which held the same purpose in a cross-denominational perspective. Most significantly the AGOW worked in active co-operation with the SWMC (the Society for the Ministry of Women and Men in the Church). In fact in 1957, the AGOW offered honourary membership to all Anglican members of the SWMC. Twenty SWMC members accepted the offer.[12]

Throughout the 1950s and the 1960s, the AGOW actively and creatively promoted women's ordination and general spiritual equality among all dimensions of the church's population. They sent letters to individuals who might be interested in supporting the work of the group. Pamphlets were prepared, one for the "educated" and one for the "homely," in a question-and-answer format which provided information about the status of women in the church on the issue of ordination in a cross-denominational perspective. On a regular basis, the group placed advertisements in publications such as the *Church Times*, the *Church of England Newspaper*, parish magazines, *Illustrated Everybodies*, the *Picture Post*, and the *Radio Times*. They asked members of the groups to write letters to, or articles for, the secular press. The group also had representation on the National Council of Women from 1955, and commissioned the compilation of a "propaganda book" in that same year. This book collected the various other aspects of the group's literary campaign into one place. The AGOW paired this publicity in the form of the written word with the ongoing organization of public meetings and debates on relevant issues.[13]

The actual number of Anglican people involved in these groups was not recorded. As such it is difficult to assess the overall visibility and impact of the AGOW's work. It is reasonable to assume that the group was dealing with fairly small numbers; the number of new members for the year did not exceed ten people at any one time. The AGOW stated that as of 5 April 1945, it had 200 members, comprised of Anglican communicants of all "shades of churchmanship."[14] Obviously this movement was committed and determined, but in relation to the size of the general church population it was not large. Throughout this period the AGOW continued to be viewed by the church's hierarchy as a nuisance fringe group which was not representative of the interests of many church goers.

DOROTHEA BELFIELD

A deaconess by the name of Dorothea Belfield was prominent in the AGOW in its earliest years. Throughout the 1930s she actively promoted the group's work. As an individual she was no stranger to the Archbishop of Canterbury. Deaconess Belfield was active in promoting the cause of women from issues such as ordination to others such as the opening of the lay readership to women in the Church of England. She wore male clerical attire and referred to herself as "The Reverend," while requesting a license to preach. Although ridiculed for her actions, she apparently had been given the permission of her bishop, the Bishop of Salisbury to present herself as a cleric.[15] When Belfield found herself without work, she asked the Archbishop of Canterbury to help her find a diocese that could use her services. While there was a fair amount of discussion about the possibility of such a job, the tone was not enthusiastic on the part of Canterbury.[16] Deaconess Belfield was viewed as a problem. The AGOW referred to Deaconess Belfield with respect and appreciation for her contribution to an important work. When episcopal offices, including Canterbury, dealt with her, it was with resignation, suspicion and dis-ease. Her views and her person were considered bizarre. She was associated with a "radical fringe" issue in the eyes of the church's administration.[17]

THE AGOW AND THE ARCHBISHOP OF CANTERBURY

The Archbishop of Canterbury did have contact with the AGOW during its earliest years. The group solicited a meeting with him to discuss women's ordination to the priesthood. At that meeting on 2 May 1931, representatives of the AGOW asked that the subject of the admission of women to the priesthood be brought before the next Lambeth Conference. This did not happen until seventeen years later when Lambeth finally occurred. In the meantime, the group made several reports which stated that there were women in the Church of England who had vocations to the priesthood and who would offer themselves as deaconesses if there was any hope that they might be ordained to the priesthood eventually.[18] According to the AGOW there were women as early as 1931, and earlier, who felt they had a vocation to the priesthood.

The response of the Archbishop of Canterbury to groups such as the AGOW who actively lobbied for women's admission to the threefold orders of the Church was not significantly different in subsequent decades. During his short tenure as Archbishop of Canterbury, William Temple received several letters from women who expressed a sense of vocation to the priesthood. In 1943, the daughter of a Church of England Canon, wrote to Temple saying that she hoped that the ordination of women would soon be a possibility in the Anglican Church, as she wanted to study for a theological degree and enter the ministry. Temple's response was a firm, 'Forget it.' He stated that this would not be an option which she could pursue in her lifetime.[19] Obviously, he was right!

In November 1943, a deaconess wrote to Temple telling him that educated women would not tolerate the discrimination of the church for much longer. Would it not be nice, she suggested, if the church could lead in the women's movement instead of attempting to repress it? "The women's movement is like a great tide which nothing can stop because it has the Holy Spirit behind it."[20] Temple answered this letter on 26 November 1943. The letter was actually a supportive letter which was gentle in its tone:

> The wind (of the Holy Spirit) blows first as a rule in certain small groups and sections; the main body always takes a long time to move.... No doubt the Christian Church ought to be permanently under the influence of such a wind of the Spirit but unhappily it is not, and for a long time past has not been except at rare moments.[21]

The resignation expressed with those words says something about ecclesiastical leadership. Even a strong and progressive theologian such as William Temple did not have visionary expectations for ecclesiastical structures, at least with reference to women.

When the AGOW requested a deputation from Archbishop of Canterbury Fisher in April, 1945 to discuss whether the time had not come for the admission of women to the ministry, the request was denied. Fisher responded to the initiative by stressing that this was not an immediate issue for the church. Furthermore, his time was taken up with much more immediate concerns. He stated that there would have to be a very great change in the general opinion of the church before such action could be taken. A change would take many years, and as such the group's request, along with the issue itself was not urgent.[22]

Fisher obviously did not change his mind about this issue significantly during his time in office. In January of 1959, he received a letter from the Bishop of St. Edmoundsbury and Ipswich. In his response to the bishop of that diocese, Fisher stated that there was still a very great need to convert the clergy to the recognition that women had a very real and important ministry to fulfil in the diocese, in the centre of the church, and in parish. He wrote:

> All along, one end of the Church has resisted it because they thought that it was the thin edge of the wedge for women priests. They ought by now to recognize that no responsible people in the Church of England have the slightest desire to take up the question of women priests. That is out, as I have said in convocation with the utmost emphasis.[23]

One cannot say that the Archbishop was unsupportive of women's contribution in ministry. He seemed to affirm it; however, the issue of women's ordination as an extension of that affirmation was simply out of the question. Perhaps most striking in this text is the blatant dismissal of everyone connected with the issue on the affirmative side. Many clergy, some bishops, some deaconesses and active lay women supported the issue; yet in Fisher's eyes, no responsible people were involved with it. His opinion of the credibility of groups such as the AGOW is clear.

One cannot help but be impressed by the persistence which members of the AGOW demonstrated in their continuing efforts to make their views known and their position understood. Undaunted by the attitude of Archbishop Fisher, the executive committee of the group prepared a statement for the Lambeth Conference of 1958. This statement was designed to promote the cause of spiritual equality in the church's ministry by arguing in favour of women's ordination to the priesthood. The AGOW distributed the statement to both the visiting bishops of Lambeth and their wives but no action was taken by the bishops on this issue at the 1958 conference.[24]

That is not to say that the work of the AGOW and other such groups was without any impact at all. Indeed, as early as that first meeting of the

AGOW with Canterbury in 1931, some effect was noticeable. Members of the AGOW felt that the 1931 meeting had been instrumental in encouraging the appointment of an Archbishop's Commission on the Ministry of Women, which produced its report in 1935.

The Archbishop's Commission on the Ministry of Women, 1932–1935

An Archbishop's Commission on Women's Ministry had produced a report in 1919, but at that time the issue of women's ordination to the priesthood was not addressed. Following the Lambeth Conference of 1930, another Archbishop's Commission on the Ministry of Women was formed in response to a request of the Lambeth Committee on Ministry for a theological statement on the ordination of women. The Commission held its first meeting on 3 February 1932 and worked on the report for the next three years. Its overall task was to report on the general work of women in the church. Its more specific task was to address the issue of women's ordination to the diaconate and priesthood.

The framers of the report noted that the question of women's ordination to the priesthood was the most difficult and controversial that the predominantly male Commission had had to deal with. Some consideration of the report's findings will provide a fair reflection of the attitude of ecclesiastical structures to the issue at that time. The Commission spent time studying the arguments for and against the ordination of women to the priesthood in its attempt to answer the following question: Is the office of priesthood one that it is impossible for a women to fill; or, without decision on the possibility of a woman exercising a valid priesthood, is there any binding principle of a theological nature on the basis of which it is right to continue the exclusion of women from the priesthood?[25]

Ultimately, it stated that while it desired to see the office of deaconess developed fully as the one existing Holy Order for women, the Commission concluded that it was unable to recommend the ordination of women, in light of divine revelation as revealed in the teaching of Scripture and tradition. Of particular consequence was the Commission's view that there was no precedent in the New Testament for the exercise of a priestly function by women, and that the continuous tradition of the church was actualized in a male priesthood.[26] The Commission did not accept arguments against women's ordination based on psychological and physiological considerations. It classed arguments that women were too emotional, particularly during their time of menstruation (previously highly popular arguments) as irrelevant. It did accept the sociological argument that the work of a priest could not satisfactorily be combined with the responsibilities of a wife and mother. While the possibility of requiring women to remain celibate was considered, it was eventually agreed that such a demand was unacceptably inconsistent with church policy regarding male priests.[27]

In addressing psychological, physiological and sociological arguments against women's ordination, the Commission responded to the climate of the society. There had been many in the church who had assumed that women must be precluded from orders based on centuries old Christian myths about the nature of the female person. From the church's earliest centuries, some Christian theologians argued that woman was simply an imperfect man. Her nature was defined by emotion and irrationality. Her capacity to function was severally limited by her menstrual flow and her subsequently diminished intellectual abilities. This view was still being propagated in the 1930s. Dr. Letitia Youmans, an English medical doctor, ardently refuted popular notions that women were inferior to men because of their physical and psychological limitations, in a public debate in London in 1932.[28] Popular opinion about women as a gender had yet to be informed by modern thought and research.

It is noteworthy that the Archbishop's Commission was sufficiently enlightened that it rejected arguments against the ordination of women on such grounds. The Commission argued that women would be capable of meeting the physical demands which pastoral work would make on them; women were already engaged in pastoral work. Indeed, in the view of the framers of the report, women's lesser physical strength was augmented by her "greater powers of endurance."[29] Likewise, they argued that there was no evidence that women were less intelligent than men. Their mental capacities would be sufficient for the task of ministry![30]

The report stated that psychology did not offer any evidence whatsoever on the question of women's admission to Holy Orders. In and of itself, psychology was not seen as a sufficient basis for dismissing women. The report did find that the existing system of church order had satisfied certain psychological needs for centuries. As such, the Commission stressed that it would need far more evidence of the need for change before it could possibly recommend the disturbance of "an established arrangement resting on long-standing, powerful and sometimes unconscious motives; the loss might well be greater than the gain."[31] The assumptions behind this statement are fascinating. The Commission felt that the church was working as it was, and therefore, there was no need to change it. Critical analysis of bias, prejudice or error was not necessary as long as the machine was operating.

The Commission claimed that it did not find many women in full-time church work who wanted to have parochial or priestly responsibilities.[32] The key word here is "many." There were women who felt a vocation to the priesthood; however, the number of women was small and not worthy of causing a larger change in the eyes of church administrators. The fact that the numbers of women who expressed a vocation to ordained ministry gradually grew throughout the twentieth century is one of the most interesting aspects of the issue. During the 1930s the consciousness of a majority of women in the church, including deaconesses and church workers, did not incline toward priesthood. A majority modelled the prevailing gender expectations of the time; they did not ask for recognition outside of their traditional sphere of accepted labour. The assumption that many women must assert a vocation before the law of the church could be changed makes an interesting comment on the nature of church leadership.

The relationship between ordination for women as an issue of "right" or of "vocation" is significant. Many who have argued against the admission of women to Holy Orders from the 1920s onward stressed that the issue was simply an outgrowth of the secular feminist movement, and that vocation cannot be decided by right as it is a gift of grace. For many the issue has been clearly divided into either right or vocation.

During the period under discussion, groups such as the AGOW talked about both rights and vocation. They claimed that the spiritual equality of men and women was a right to which the church's people were entitled. The AGOW also argued, however, that the spiritual equality which was a right was also the prerequisite for the church to fulfil its vocation in the world: "We exist not to vindicate solely the rights of women but we believe that the Church of England needs the fullest service that women as well as men can give. Right understanding of the contribution of laywomen cannot be reached as long as the possibility of ordination to the historic ministry is denied by that church to those women who believe they are so called."[33] In other words, the issue of right versus vocation is a non-issue. For groups such as the AGOW what was right in this sense was essential to the full realization of the church's ministry in the world.

Throughout both stages of the discussion on the matter of women in the priesthood in England, those who opposed the ordination of women contended that those who promoted it were 'corrupted' by the feminist influence in society, and were leading the church down a road which led away from the God of the Judaeo-Christian tradition. Even many of those who supported the ordination of women were afraid of linking the ordination issue to anything with a feminist label. Clearly, many deaconesses did not identify themselves with feminism as such. Given this, some examination of the relationship between feminism as thought and movement and the ordination of women is necessary.

Those who opposed the ordination of women repeatedly argued that some were pressuring the church to accommodate a societal whim. They said the church was being led away from its tradition. This interpretation of tradition regarding the relationship between men and women held that "feminists" were synonymous with evil. Among those who supported the ordination of women, two perspectives were articulated. Members of groups such as the AGOW and the SWMC had no difficulty linking themselves to the word, the philosophy and the movement of feminism. More 'conservative' church people, however, rejected this label. In other words most bishops and deaconesses in this camp rejected the word 'feminist' and stressed that it was a desire to serve rather than to engage in a lobby for a justice issue which led them to support the ordination of women as priests.

What then is an accurate picture of the relationship between secular feminism and the ordination of women to the priesthood? A feminist position is grounded in a belief in the fundamental equality of women and men. Feminism exists both as a philosophy or world view and as a social movement for change, change which facilitates the creation of more just structures within societies and institutions. In keeping with this definition, it can be concluded that there is a relationship between feminism and the ordination of women in the Church of England. Secular feminism and the ordination issue in England have a relationship of considerable length. The movement for women's suffrage spawned the first groups to ask for the admission of women to the priesthood in the Anglican Church. When women's suffrage was won in 1918, those women who had worked for this secular end under a church umbrella, redirected their energy into ecclesiastical matters.

The movement for women's suffrage and the ordination movement were intimately related. They shared the same mother, if you will, but after the vote was won, the sisters went in separate directions to pursue different life objectives. Theirs was a blood relationship, but with the exit of the mother, the sisters saw each other only occasionally. From the birth of the League of the Church Militant, the SWMC and finally the AGOW, there was a place in the Church of England where individuals could discuss and educate others from a feminist perspective. These groups were small and always located on the periphery of church life. They were a gadfly to ecclesiastical structures. They promoted equal access for women to all places and jobs occupied by men. They argued repeatedly that the criteria for ordination should be vocation rather than genitalia. Those small, marginalized groups did not feel that there was any conflict in arguing for gender equality on the basis of vocation. They, unlike their colleagues in the hierarchy of the church, did not see vocation and justice as mutually exclusive.

Ultimately, the Commission of 1935 concluded that the ministry of women was a "problem" which the church had to address. It suggested that the "right solution to the whole problem of the ministry of women in the Church", was to be found in the development of the status and functions of the deaconess, and in the further extension of the various opportunities open to lay women workers, rather than in an assimilation of the functions of women in those of men.[34] The Commission stressed that if its proposals were to be carried into effect, deaconesses and lay workers would have to hold a position different from the one they had previously known. In other words, women should be welcomed with a more definite status in the church.[35]

With these last observations, the Commission identified something of a crisis in women's work in the church, which had been present since 1862 when women had first been able to serve in the Church of England as deaconesses. From that point, women's work was plagued with problems and difficulties. From the 1860s the nature of women's work in the church branched out in two different directions. Up to that point women's labour was primarily voluntary at the parish and diocesan level. From the 1860s women could serve their church either as volunteers or as paid labour.

Even to the present day, the vast majority of church women support the church's ministry though their voluntary, usually part-time, efforts. Table 8 documents the numbers of women in voluntary and paid labour from 1920 to 1939. Clearly most women were volunteers. Table 9 demonstrates the numbers of paid women workers between 1960 and 1978. The question of women's ordination to the threefold order of ministry is most closely related to the area of full-time paid labour for women, rather than to volunteer labour. It is in the context of the issues surrounding the paid women's work that the ordination question is most often found.

The Archbishop's Commission of 1935, as with all other commissions on the question of women's ministry in the Church of England primarily dealt with those issues which involved women who had chosen church work as a profession. Some of these individuals served part-time, but during the period under discussion most were full-time workers. These women were almost always single, as the prevailing view of the time was not unlike that in other parts of society; married women should remain in the home as their primary workplace. Women workers could choose to serve the church in one of several capacities: as a deaconess, as a lay worker which included parish workers, social workers and diocesan workers, as a church army sister or as a sister in a religious community. It is the category of deaconess which is particularly relevant to the issue of women's ordination to the priesthood. Although the ordination of women to the priesthood was always distinct from the issue of women's ordination as deaconesses, it is crucial that one understand the deaconess dilemma if one is to fully appreciate the scope of the priesthood question. Until many of the issues of spiritual equality around the work of deaconesses were solved, the question of women and the priesthood could not be answered.

DEACONESSES

As the Church of England was one of the earliest to revive the Order of Deaconesses, their place in the life and work of the church was an issue which received a fair amount of attention from its earliest days. The first ordination in the revival of the Deaconess Order in the Church of England was that of Elizabeth Ferard in 1862, by the Bishop of London, Archibald Tait. In the previous year Ferard had founded the Community of St. Andrew, which after 1862, became the Deaconess Community of St. Andrew. Members of this community were both professed sisters and ordained deaconesses. As of 1995, the community still exists although in dwindling numbers, with the Mother House located in Westbourne Park, London. Gradually the number of deaconesses who served the church outside of the Community of St. Andrew's grew. A majority of deaconesses were not also religious sisters as is the case with the members of the St. Andrew's community.

The nature of the work of the deaconess from the late nineteenth century onward was varied. Many deaconesses worked on the staff of different types of parishes. Others served the church as chaplain's assistants, lecturers in theological education programs, social outreach and overseas missionary work.[36] For much of its history the work of the deaconess was confined primarily to work among women and children, but this did change as the twentieth century progressed.[37] The number of deaconesses was always significantly smaller than the numbers of paid lay workers or of religious sisters. Apparently, with its sacrament of ordination it was viewed as a very specific and unique vocation. It was after the commencement of the twentieth century, that questions about the role and responsibilities of the deaconess became more pronounced. By 1920, there were a number of women presenting themselves for that office in the Church of England; however, their function and authority were not clearly defined. In the report of the Commission of 1935 the particularly problematic issues noted revolved around the nature of the deaconess's orders, and the standardization of her commissioning.

At the Lambeth Conference of 1920 resolutions 46 through 54 established the parameters within which the Church of England defined its Order of Deaconesses. Considering itself sequels to the Lambeth Conference the Convocation of Canterbury meeting in 1923 and the Convocation of York meeting in 1925 passed resolutions which were reminiscent of those adopted at Lambeth. The highlighted portions included here reflect a significantly different wording. The resolutions said something in addition to what Lambeth was saying:

> That the order of deaconesses is an apostolic order of ministry of the Church of God; that the women admitted thereto are episcopally ordained with prayer and the laying on of hands; **that it corresponds closely to the Order of Deacons under its primitive rather than its modern conditions;** and that it is for women the one and only order of the ministry which, in the judgement of this House, the Church of England as a branch of the Catholic church can recognize and use.[38]

The convocations also affirmed that the deaconess vocation was a life-long commitment. As was the case with male clerics, no vow of celibacy was required or implied by her ordination. Those who wanted to commit themselves to a life of celibacy might do so. The interesting thing with regard to this resolution is that virtually all deaconesses who actually served in the church were single women. When and if she married, the deaconess no longer continued to function in her ecclesiastical office.[39] This was the case until the 1970s.

In their third resolution, the Convocations of Canterbury and York affirmed that the office of the deaconess was primarily a ministry of bodily and spiritual succour to the whole church, but especially to women. Throughout the Communion, the ministry of women was seen primarily as a ministry with and to women.

In its fourth resolution the Church of England outlined the functions of the deaconess. These were parallel to those identified at the Lambeth Conference of 1920, and included such things as preparing candidates for baptism and confirmation, teaching the faith, and assisting at baptisms; in the case of private baptism when no minister was present, she herself would be considered the administrant by virtue of her office. The deaconess was also expected to carry out church work among women and children, and to pray with and give counsel to women in distress. The Church of England also added the responsibility of organizing and carrying out social work, and working with women in educational settings including universities.[40]

Perhaps the most interesting shift between Lambeth 1920 and the wording of the resolutions of the Convocation, was in the area of liturgical participation. As noted, the Lambeth Conference of 1920 stated that with the approval of the bishop and the parish priest, the deaconess could read morning and evening prayer and the litany in church, except the portions assigned to the priest, and secondly could lead in prayer and instruct or exhort the congregation, by license of the bishop—in other words, preach. The Convocations defined the liturgical participation of the deaconess with less clarity. It was stated that with the approval of the bishop and the incumbent the deaconess, "under such conditions as from time to time be laid down by the bishop," might speak and pray in consecrated buildings, "on occasions other than the regular and appointed services of the church, and normally for congregations of women and children."[41]

This last section reflects a significant shift away from the comparative openness articulated by Lambeth. Lambeth did not define what speaking and praying entailed. In practice, the Church of England only allowed deaconesses to speak and pray at special services for women and children and explicitly excluded them from verbal liturgical participation in 'regular' church worship. Lambeth allowed women to preach and pray at morning and evening prayer. The Church of England did not sanction that.

In its remaining resolutions the Convocations more specifically elaborated the process and rules whereby a woman might become a deaconess than Lambeth had done. They put an age requirement on the deaconess office; a woman should be at least 25 years old and preferably 30 before her ordination.[42] Before a women was ordained, the bishop was to satisfy himself as to her character, her training and her general fitness, and should examine her theological knowledge. They also agreed that the Archbishop and the bishops should draw up and authorize a "Form and Manner of Making a Deaconess," which would include a prayer by the bishop and the laying on of his hands, a formula giving authority to execute the office of the deaconess, and finally the giving of a New Testament to the candidate by the bishop.[43] A final interesting addition to the Lambeth resolutions was the inclusion of an admonition that deaconesses should wear a distinctive dress approved by the bishop of the diocese in which they were serving.[44] Even dress fell under the direction and supervision of the ecclesiastical structure, at least in theory.

After the Lambeth Conference of 1930 the Convocations of Canterbury and York once again discussed the issue of deaconesses. Both Convocations accepted the resolutions of Lambeth. The only changes were qualifying additions to resolution number 70 which detailed the functions of the deaconess. In the case of the Upper House of the Convocation of Canterbury held on 4 June 1931, the words, "in exceptional circumstances," were added after the words, "to baptize in the church" in Resolution 70. In the case of the Upper House of York the words "in exceptional circumstances" were added before the same phrase.[45]

The Lower House, comprised of the clergy and laity, of both Convocations had considerably more difficulty in the area of the deaconess's functions. In January, 1932, the Lower House of York approved paragraphs (a) and (b), but rejected paragraph (c) and reserved judgement on paragraph (d). On 31 May 1933, the Lower House of Canterbury agreed to defer consideration of the functions of the deaconess until the report of the Commission on the Ministry of Women was released in 1935.[46]

As has been noted, the Commission's report concluded that it could not recommend women's ordination to the priesthood. It did stress that the primary issue around the order of deaconesses should be the question of the nature of their orders. The Commission suggested that if that question were satisfactorily answered, greater clarity could be easily found with regard to issues of function. It was the opinion of the Commission that the deaconess should be considered to be within Holy Orders; however, it was stressed that the order should not be considered to be equivalent to the male order of deacon, but rather should be seen as an order *sui generis*.[47] In short, the Commission was not saying anything that had not already been said at the Lambeth Conference of 1930. Ultimately the Commission advised that deaconesses should be allowed the liturgical functions assigned to them at Lambeth.

The problem with the findings of the Commission was that they opened the door on decades of subsequent confusion and conflict about the role of the deaconess. What the framers of the report gave with one hand they took away with the other. On the one hand they agreed that deaconesses were within Holy Orders, but on the other those orders were inferior to those of their male colleagues. As long as that distinction of inequality was made, there would be confusion about the actual nature and function of the deaconess. Who was the deaconess anyway? Was she clergy? Well sort of, but not really. As long as that kind of ambiguity persisted, there would inevitably be a lack of clarity and consistency with regard to the place and person of the deaconess, and often times an accompanying lack of respect for their place and work in the Church.

Many deaconesses stated that they simply assumed that their orders were the same as the men's with whom many of them had been ordained to the diaconate. That official church policy stressed that they were not was a peripheral issue, except when their place, function and authority were questioned at various levels within those same church structures.

In March of 1921, the then Archbishop of Canterbury, William Temple, wrote a response to a request for clarification from Head Deaconess Mary Siddall. Apparently Siddall was unclear as to what Lambeth actually said about deaconesses. The Archbishop responded by saying that the net result of Lambeth 1920 was not unsatisfactory. It adopted a resolution formally raising the revival of deaconesses to a canonical status in the church. What that actually meant, however, was something which would be worked out at a later date.[48] The confusion which Siddall identified as early as 1921 was not going to be easily resolved.

In a letter dated 24 September 1933, William Temple wrote to an unnamed deaconess concerning this matter. The letter was obviously a response to a letter sent by this unidentified person, who had apparently asked the Archbishop for clarification about this matter of the nature of a deaconess' orders. In this correspondence, Temple disagreed with a statement previously made by the Head Deaconess at the time, Deaconess Siddall. He stated that he did not agree with Siddall's claim that it would be retrograde to make the distinction of an order of women's ministry on the grounds of sex. Temple felt that such an argument was too reminiscent of the secular feminist argument that women should have the vote because they were the same as men. His view was that women should have the vote because they were so different from men. Similarly he argued that women were so different from men that they should have their own distinct order, or fellowship of women workers with which they might network.[49]

In the letter, Temple reaffirmed the findings of the Convocations that while a vow of celibacy was not required, a married women would not be able to fulfil the demands of the vocation. He stressed that the Order of Deaconesses "must make its way by its own value."[50] He then concluded that he himself would be glad to consider the deaconess as part of the clergy, but that this was not likely to happen "at all quickly." With this statement, however, Temple did not say that the women were the same as the male deacons. Even if they might be considered part of the clergy they would still be in his view, a fourth category. He concluded his letter by saying, "So my advice, for what it is worth—keep the deaconesses distinct—ready to co-operate but from outside."[51]

Obviously a tension existed in the Church of England. The decision-making bodies of the church wanted to affirm the work and ministry of women but did not want women to be included as part of the traditionally male threefold order of ministry. Some women on the other hand, as reflected in the thinking of Siddall, and others as reflected in the work of the AGOW, felt that such a distinction was nonsensical. The result was confusion, conflict, and ongoing problems of deaconesses around their status and authority in the structures of the church. Women continued to remain on the "outside."

In March of 1938, the Executive Committee of the Deaconess Chapter made the following statement:

The majority of deaconesses today were ordained in the belief that they were being admitted to the third order. The new view of the order taken by the committee of the Lambeth Conference of 1930 as an order *sui generis* came as a surprise and a matter of deep concern to a great number of deaconesses and laywomen. Some still feel that to make a separate order sui generis for women would be a retrograde step and would be creating a fourth order within the ministry for which the Church of England has no authority.[52]

Those who were responsible for overseeing the work of deaconesses in the church were not in agreement with the decisions of the church's councils. The committee noted that there were others in the Deaconess Order for whom the new conception had, "increasingly commended itself as holding more promise of development than an Order precisely parallel with the male diaconate."[53] The position of the majority as it is defined here was not necessarily the position of the whole.

WOMEN'S WORK AND THE COUNCILS OF THE CHURCH

From 1920 onward, there were committees and councils in place in the Church of England which dealt with the issues and problems which arose in connection with women's work and ministry, particularly women's paid labour as a part of the church's work force. In 1930, it was agreed that these various groups should be streamlined into a more centralized authority. As such, the Central Council for Women's Church Work (CCWCW) was formed from three other organizations — the Central Committee for Women's Work, the Inter-Diocesan Council for Women's Work and the Advisory Council for Women's Work. In 1934 the Council for the Order of Deaconesses united the various provincial councils for deaconesses, which had administered the work of deaconesses between 1925 and 1933. Then in 1960, the CCWCW joined with the Council for the Order of Deaconesses to become the Council for Women's Ministry in the Church (CWMC). It was not until 1972, that the category of women's ministry was included in the general category of the ministry of the church; at that time the CWMC became a part of the Advisory Committee on the Church's Ministry (ACCM), which is the committee which previously and as of 1995, deals with matters such as candidates for ordination and so on.

Both the Central Council for Women's Church Work and later the Council for Women's Ministry in the Church were untiring advocates for the work of women in the Church of England. As a group, they invariably responded to the various reports which commissions and committees produced dealing with issues affecting the labour of women. In their responses they often raised critical questions about the findings of the various reports, always attempting to address their remarks from the perspective of the concerns of the women themselves.

When the CCWC was formed from three other agencies, it pledged to maintain and extend the standards set up by the Inter-Diocesan Certificate (I.D.C.) (by which women were licensed for paid work), between 1919 and 1930. By 1930, the granting of licenses to women workers, both deaconesses and lay women, was a relatively new phenomenon. The CCWC felt that the granting of a license, and eventually the standardization of the educational and training process which led to that license, was a step forward for paid women's labour in the church. It accelerated the movement of women's work into the category of a profession.

These bodies were appointed by the church structure to monitor and exercise some responsibility for the ongoing enterprise of women's work as a whole within the church. Over the years such issues as standardization of training, salaries, pensions, functions and status for women, both lay and deaconess occupied the energy of the committees. It was with the response of the CCWCW to the Archbishop's Committee's "Report on Women's Work in the Church" in 1943 that the adoption of an advocacy role by the group in relation to women began.

In 1943, a committee appointed by the Archbishop of Canterbury issued a report on the condition of women's work in the Church of England. This lengthy report did not deal directly with the question of women's ordination to the priesthood. It did, however, acknowledge that such ordinations were an issue in the church. Declining to acknowledge it as within the frame of reference of the report, however, the committee made the following statement:

If there should prove to be sound reasons of faith and order for admitting women to the priesthood then the fullest use of women in the church in other ways need not be feared as the "thin edge of the wedge." To make the fullest use of the services of women would be the most effective answer to the suspicion that the

refusal to admit women to the priesthood is really based on social prejudice and professional jealousy.[54]

After having made this statement about women and the priesthood,
the report proceeded to make four central points about the condition of
women's work in the Church of England. The committee said that women
in the church were not being used to their full capacity. Particularly at a
time when a strong "Christian offensive" was needed in society, the report argued that full use should be made of the ministry of women. In
light of this recommendation the report argued that in practice as well as
in theory women should be eligible for any office or duty that was open
to laymen. The framers noted that it would take a considerable amount
of money which was not readily available to train women for this role.
Finally, the report concluded that women workers, including deaconesses, should be fairly paid and should be given the responsibility which
would provide the greatest scope for their gifts.[55]

Shortly after this report was released the Central Council for Wom-
en's Church Work wrote a response to the report, beginning with the
opening line, "What the cynic might ask is there new in the recently
published report on this well-worn theme?"[56] The basic contention of
the response was that the report of 1943 said nothing significantly different from the report of 1935. Paradoxically, the church had yet to do
anything to respond to the concerns raised first in 1935 about poor pay,
and the lack of status and support for women workers. The CCWCW
then challenged the framers of the report to put their money where their
mouth was and to fully support initiatives in women's work.[57]

The CCWCW did not make any comment on the question of wom-
en's ordination or its lack of place in the report. The CCWCW was concerned with the ongoing reality of women's paid labour as it already
existed within the church and not with the larger philosophical issues of
gender, except as they influenced the working conditions of women in
the field. In 1946, the CCWCW completed the plans for an "Inter-Diocesan Certificate of Recognition." The desire to regulate the training and
qualifications of active lay ministry, which ultimately would include deaconesses, led to CCWCW to construct this Inter-Diocesan Certificate
which laid down basic standards which all incoming women were to
adhere to in terms of their training.[58]

The CCWCW itself formulated the Church of England's next report
on women in the church. This report, *Women in the Church*, did not com-

ment directly on ordination of women to the priesthood. After observing that there had been improvements in women's work and voicing a general optimism about the future, it did identify one interesting "hindrance." In its final section the report observed that the one great hindrance to women's work in the church lay with "the failure of authority to come to any clear decision as to the place and function of women in Church Order."[59] It identified the uncertainty in the present situation with regard to women's status and function as deaconess and as lay worker. So little progress had been made in this regard that it "may increasingly have the effect of discouraging women from church membership altogether."[60] In short the framers of the CCWCW viewed the contribution of women to church life as positive and promising. It was the response of ecclesiastical authority structures, on the other hand, which was viewed as problematic.

THE BISHOP OF HONG KONG AND CANTERBURY

As we saw in Chapter 1, one of the most interesting interactions with regard to the question of women's ordination in the Church of England at this point came about as a result of the decision by the Bishop of Hong Kong to ordain one of his deaconesses, Li Tim Oi, to the priesthood during the Second World War. The extent to which the Church of England still influenced, and perhaps even dominated, other parts of the Anglican Communion was evident around this event. Due to a shortage of priests, the Bishop of Hong Kong ordained a well-qualified woman of the church to function as a priest behind enemy lines in the diocese of Hong Kong. The Archbishop of Canterbury responded to this bishop's action.

Canterbury felt the Bishop of Hong Kong, Bishop R. O. Hall, had acted *ultra vires* with the ordination of 1944. It was acknowledged that in England there was a small group that was vocal in its pressing for the ordination of women. In Canterbury's view, the overwhelming opinion of the church was against them. The view was that most agreed that such an action would be so contrary to Catholic precedent that it would be unthinkable. Canterbury went on to say that if Hall's House of Bishops did not repudiate his action it would cause a very difficult situation in England. As an intermediary measure, Canterbury suggested that "the woman" should be forbidden at once from celebrating the Holy Eucharist. He stressed that he was most anxious to avoid any suggestion of interference with the jurisdiction and full autonomy of the Church of China.[61]

In August 1945, Canterbury suggested to Bishop Hall that if he did not suspend "the woman" immediately, he would have to resign after the Chinese House of Bishops made its decision. The rationale was that anything else would have demonstrated a lack of respect for the House of Bishops. If the House happened to approve the action it would cause a great cleavage in the Communion. Canterbury concluded by stating that if the matter were referred to Lambeth, it would certainly be repudiated.[62]

Bishop Hall responded to Canterbury by extending his personal regret that he was unable to accept the Archbishop's advice. Hall stressed that he knew his action was ecclesiastically *ultra vires*, but felt that spiritually it was not. He had had only one reason for ordaining Li Tim Oi, "I acted in obedience to our Lord's commission. I do not believe that he wishes me to undo what I have done. That is my reason." Hall then advised the Archbishop not to be anxious. It was his view that what was wrongly done would perish and what had been truly done could only strengthen Christ's church.[63] Canterbury wrote to Bishop Arnold Scott of South China (Chairman of the House of Bishops of the Chuang Hua Sheng Kung Hui province), and advised him that he should suspend Li Tim Oi.[64] In other words, Fisher went over Hall's head in an attempt to obtain the desired results.

Neither Hall nor Scott were forced to take such an action. In April of 1946, Li Tim Oi offered to resign from priestly functioning in light of the controversy over her orders. Following this offer of resignation the House of Bishops of South China passed a motion regretting the uncanonical action that had been taken and asked the Bishop of Hong Kong to accept the resignation of the "deaconess." Li Tim Oi was never referred to by name or by the office which the Bishop of Hong Kong had conferred on her. Ultimately, Hall accepted her resignation and the controversy was ended.[65] In a letter dated 2 April 1946, Fisher wrote to Scott and stated, "The action you have taken about Bishop Hall's ordination of a woman priest greatly satisfied me and I am thankful that you were led to that conclusion."[66] Florence Li quietly resigned from the exercise of her priestly ministry to save further difficulties for Hall and the church. Li refused to officially resign her orders, however, saying that she never gave up her belief that her ordination was a, "spiritual gift from God which can never be erased."[67]

Li's willingness to step aside in 1946 won her respect in Anglican circles. She disappeared from sight for many years. During the Cultural Revolution, she worked as a labourer in mainland China. During the 1980s she emigrated to Canada where she lived as a retiree and functioning priest in the Diocese of Toronto. After her death in February, 1992, former Archbishop of Canterbury, Robert Runcie, said, "History will judge that her humility and courage played a major part in the acceptance of the ordination of women to the priesthood as part of the Anglican tradition."[68] Not making waves is a valued commodity in the Anglican ethos, but this in no way diminishes the value of Li's place in Anglican history. However unintentionally, Florence Li was a pioneer and model for future generations of women in the church.

In the exchange between the Archbishop of Canterbury and the Church in South China, an ambiguous message was communicated from the office of Canterbury. On the one hand, it was argued that Canterbury had nothing at all to do with the autonomous affairs of the church in China. On the other, Fisher obviously expended considerable effort in attempting to bend the will of the Chinese church to a position which was acceptable to the Church of England. Secondly, the letters sent from the office of the Archbishop of Canterbury revealed his unwillingness to entertain the possibility of such ordinations during that particular period.

During the 1950s, the name of Hall surfaced in the Church of England once again. Hall had been made the Metropolitan of Hong Kong. In the Fisher Papers, there is correspondence about rumours that Hall was planning on ordaining a "priestess."[69] Letters from irate Church of England clergymen scathingly condemned both the possibility of the action and the man who was rumoured to be planning such ordinations. Correspondence from the desk of Canterbury dated 21 October 1957, addressed letters from irate clergy stating categorically that the rumour was simply not true. Hall himself responded to enquiries from Canterbury saying that the rumours were not true. He stated that although he made Jane Hwang a lay reader in charge of a parish, and stated in the diocesan paper that he hoped that her ordination to the priesthood would be possible before long, he would not act without the sympathetic concurrence of Anglicans in other parts of the world.[70]

This exchange revealed an interesting polarization in the Communion. There were parts or at least a part of the Anglican Communion which was open to the ordination of women by that point in history. Such was not the case with the Church of England. While there were factions within it which were supportive of women's orders, the structures, or decision-making bodies adamantly opposed it. Neither the openness of the Communion to such ordinations nor the attitude to sympathizers of the ordination question, changed the opinion of the English church. In 1956, the Archbishop of Canterbury expressed the view in the National and English Review that, "Whatever the rights and wrongs may be the possibility of the ordination of women to the priesthood is not a live issue in the Church at all, apart from a pretty tiny group of advocates of it." He concluded by saying, "There is all but universal agreement that whatever be the rights and wrongs of it, it would only cause disruption to the work of the Church if it were discussed now."[71]

The titular head of the Church of England considered the issue to be largely irrelevant or more trouble than it was worth, irrespective of right or wrong. A response to the Archbishop's comments printed in the same paper on 18 June 1956, attacked him for his lack of commitment to ethics. The writer stated, "You seem more concerned with maintaining a smooth unruffled Church organization that with major questions of right and wrong." The writer stressed that this was not an unimportant question. The fact that people in the pew were not bothered by it was simply an indication of their "myopia" and lack of vision. The writer concluded by stressing that the Archbishop had not hesitated previously to cause a controversy over premium bonds. He inquired, "Where are your values placed?"[72]

THE ECUMENICAL SITUATION

On the ecumenical scene, it was clear by the late 1950s that the issue of women's ordination was on the discussion tables of most mainline Protestant denominations in England and beyond. In 1957, the office of the Archbishop of Canterbury requested information from other Protestant churches with regard to their position on this question. On 11 January 1957, the Methodist Church in England responded to the request, stating that at its General Conference of 1948 it had decided that no women would be eligible to be ordained in the Methodist Church of Great Britain. The response concluded by saying that the matter should be carefully watched by "those of us" who were interested in a closer relationship between the two churches.[73] The Methodist Church in America reported that it had ordained one woman at that point.

The Congregational Union of England and Wales reported that it had ordained its first woman in 1917. As of January, 1957, they had 43 women ministers ordained, 29 of whom were in full pastoral charge of a congregation. The union also stressed that the principle of the ordination of women was universally upheld by it, although some prejudice against women ministers still existed. The Presbyterian Church of England reported that it had accepted the principle of the ordination of women for over 20 years, but the first woman had not actually been ordained until the preceding year, 1956. The Presbyterians stressed that the one women had been a exceptional candidate and that there were "not likely to be many such cases." The response concluded by noting that over 400 women had served in their church as ordained elders. The Baptist Union reported that 30 or 40 years previously it had declared that it saw no objection to women's ordination, but that, in practice, churches had not generally acted on this declaration. There were only four cases of Baptist women ministers, and they were all unusual or exceptional cases; however, since the first world war there had been an increase in the number of women deaconesses in that tradition.[74] By 1958, there had also been ordinations of women in the Lutheran Church of Sweden. The Church of England was aware of this, but was not supportive. Canterbury stated that the Church of England could not take any notice of the Swedish actions whatsoever. It was felt that the church could not send a bishop to the subsequent consecrations of bishops there, because it might imply some approval of women's ordination.[75]

The highest offices in the church knew about the ordinations in other traditions, but there is little evidence to suggest that this awareness had filtered into the general population of the church. For example, it was not until Christian Howard's report on the ordination of women to General Synod in the early 1970s that any detailed examination or attention was given to the ordinations in Sweden. Groups such as the AGOW continued to attempt public education with regard to ecumenical happenings. At that juncture, ecumenical events, while noted, seem to have had little impact on those who framed the policies which shaped the life of the church, at least from the perspective of those who supported women's ordination.

In 1957, the BBC broadcast a cross-denominational debate on the ordination of women. All speakers in the broadcast were supportive of such action, including those who represented the Church of England.

Apparently the speakers were not representative of all opinion in the church. The broadcast received a significant amount of newspaper coverage and sparked an angry response from many clergy and lay people of the Anglican Church.

This angry response to the BBC broadcast culminated in a discussion which was held in the Church of England's Church Assembly in 1960. After much heated comment about the inappropriate nature of the BBC debate the following resolution was carried:

> That this House deprecates the action of the BBC in presenting as though it were a balanced discussion on the controversial issue of the ordination of women, a program in which in fact all speakers appeared in principle on one side.[76]

Apparently the issue for those who framed and supported the motion was that only those who supported women's ordination were asked to sit on the panel. Some argued that the discussion was not about the Church of England alone, but rather addressed the topic of women's ordination generally. A majority of the assembly took this broadcast as a challenge to the traditions of the established church.

The BBC broadcast which took place in 1957 was not an isolated media event. From the late 1950s onward there was an acceleration in the volume of newspaper coverage of this whole question in English society. The burgeoning interest paralleled a gradual acceleration of interest in church life with regard to this question. During the decade of the 1960s, two crucial reports were produced which in some way addressed the question of women's ordination.

GENDER AND MINISTRY REPORT, 1962

In 1959, the church decided to set up a new Central Advisory Council for Ministry. At the same time, it was suggested that the new Council should examine the question of the recruitment and use of women for full-time service in the church and advise the bishops with regard to whom to ordain. Apparently the primary concern of the committee was to encourage the church as a whole to recognize how little use they were making of various forms of ministry for women in the church. The relevance of this in light of the clergy shortage in England at that time was also stressed.

The result was the formulation of a report to be presented to the Church Assembly of 1962 entitled *Gender and Ministry Report.* This report did not specifically deal with the debate over women's ordination. Like so many of the reports before it, it was designed to assess and comment on an already existing situation. It did, however, acknowledge that the debate over such ordinations existed and suggested that it should be addressed.

The *Gender and Ministry Report* discussed the theology and sociological reality of women workers in the church. It noted that there had been great changes in the "traditionally feminine" pattern of life. Changes such as limited pregnancies through the use of contraception, the eradication of superstition with regard to menstruation, electricity and the resulting decrease in women's "domestic drudgery" and national health services are cited in this report as having contributed to the expansion of women's choices.[77] Social changes which had expanded the role of women were also cited as the means by which a man had "lost a good deal of [their] traditional status as the inevitable representative of the family or social group in his community."[78]

The report argued that the real question at stake was not a question of the respective status of men and women, but a question of the nature of ministry, be it sacred or secular. The framers of the report noted that there were women who "with a strong masculine protest want to be ordained on the argument — anything you can do I can do better."[79] Conversely, it was noted that there were men who found in ordination a strong refuge from competition with other men in secular work, "a compensation for their own sense of inadequacy as males, or a satisfaction of their desire for protected status."[80] All of this led to the conclusion that the nature of vocation was a complex phenomenon about which there was much confusion at that point in the church's history.

One's opinion about what women should be and do in the church is in large part dependent upon one's understanding of the role and function of the laity. Making a distinction between a priesthood of all believers and the vocation to a specific sacramental function as priest, the report stated that the church needed the "representative ministry of women" just as it needed the "representative priesthood of men."[81] Lay ministry was for women and a sacramental ministry was the sole preserve of men.

While inviting women to a full lay ministry may not seem progressive in retrospect, at that point in history, women were not allowed to administer the chalice and few were servers except in girls' schools and colleges. The report observed that in the Church of England women also were not ordained priests, did not celebrate the eucharist, and did not bless congregations. This did not mean that functionally they could not perform these acts as members of the priestly body which was the church, but that the Church of England together with the "overwhelming majority" of Christendom did not call its women members to minister sacramentally.[82] The report highlighted the hopeless confusion of the church with regard to deaconesses and women workers as an area of great concern.

The Church Assembly received the *Gender and Ministry Report* in 1962, and passed five resolutions related to it. The motions asked the church in its various aspects to study the situation of women workers at the diocesan and Convocation levels and to implement such actions as were necessary to ameliorate disparities in salary, job opportunities and work as lay readers. In its final motion, the Assembly agreed to study the various reasons for withholding ordination to the priesthood from women.[83] This final motion led to the formulation of the report *Women and Holy Orders*, which was released in 1966.

WORLD COUNCIL OF CHURCHES REPORT, 1964

While the Archbishop's Commission was preparing *Women and Holy Orders*, an interesting piece of information was collected on the ecumenical scene by the World Council of Churches. In 1964, the WCC released a study of the ordination of women which was cross-denominational and global in its outlook. The Archbishop's Commission had this information at their disposal as they framed their own report. The WCC gathered the information for the report in the year 1958. In 1958, out of 168 member churches of the WCC, 48 reported that they admitted women to "full ministry," nine to partial or occasional ministry, 90 churches did not admit them at all, and 21 churches did not answer the WCC's enquiry.

The WCC had found that in Switzerland, a majority of churches admitted women to full ministry. According to the report this was not a matter of "pure theological principle...but as a coincidence of the campaign to secure equality for women in all things civil, social and political."[84] The Lutheran tradition admitted a variety of practices and doctrine. Women had been ordained for some years in Denmark and Norway. In Sweden, women had recently been ordained. In that situation it was argued that the impetus came from the government. Apparently the Archbishop of Canterbury warned the Archbishop of Uppsala in Sweden, before the first ordinations, that such ordinations would introduce a "cause of embarrassment and dispute between the two churches."[85]

There was an obvious difference of attitude between the Protestant and the Roman/Eastern churches in their view and approach to this question. The Roman Catholic Church and the Orthodox Church then as now remained categorically opposed to the ordination of women to the priesthood. The Protestant traditions at least in theory demonstrated a greater openness to the concept.

The WCC report also considered the Anglican Communion, that *via media* which as always lived in tension between the Protestant and the Roman Catholic streams. The report made note of the 1944 ordination and subsequent retraction in Hong Kong, as well as the subsequent proposal from Hong Kong for a twenty year experiment in women's ordination. It also noted the action of a bishop in the Protestant Episcopal Church in the United States who proposed to ordain a deaconess as a deacon. This proposal had been referred to the American House of Bishops who decided against it and expressly stated that deaconesses should not be permitted to administer the elements at Holy Communion.[86]

WOMEN AND HOLY ORDERS REPORT, 1966

The terms of reference for the Commission which produced the 1966 report *Women and Holy Orders* were direct and to the point, "to examine the question of women and Holy Orders."[87] The specific frame of reference of the Commission was the question of whether or not women should be ordained to the priesthood, rather than the wider question of their admission to other forms of ordained ministry. The church had not asked the Commission to make a recommendation in response to the question of their primary mandate. They were asked to study and report on the various aspects of the question. The framers of the report acknowledged that they could not make a recommendation on the issue in any case, as the opinion of the Commission was divided. The method of research utilized a public forum where each side expressed their views. The Commission did not attempt to provide a representative analysis of the opinion of the church.

The report of the Commission identified four functional or practical issues which necessitated the opening up of the questions of women's ordination to the priesthood at that point in history. These four reasons included, the emancipation of women, the new insights gained by the spirit of the times (for example with regard to the place and role of women which had traditionally categorized women as inferior), the failure of the church to provide an adequate ministry for women (as reflected in the ongoing marginalization of women's work in the church) and finally the shortage of clergy which existed in England at the time of the study.[88]

The report collected and summarized the biblical and historical evidence with regard to women's ordination to the priesthood. In the final analysis the report found that there was no biblical material which prohibited the ordination of women. This finding reflected a fairly current and critical approach to biblical scholarship which understood comments like those of Paul that women should not speak in church in the larger context of Scripture, with a keen awareness of the socio-historical context in which such comments were made. For example, the report stressed that St. Paul did believe women were subordinate to men. The social context of that belief was also noted; Paul was a product of a male oriented Jewish culture in which the subordination of women was commonplace. Conversely the report also noted that there was no significant biblical evidence that women should be ordained either.[89] In its examination of tradition the report argued that the case was clear cut. It argued that there was no precedent for the ordination of women to the priesthood in Christendom; to ordain women would be a radical break with tradition.

The *Women and Holy Orders* report attempted to deal with the psychological aspects of the ordination issue. It noted that there were significant differences between the sexes with regard to perception, thought, feeling and social behaviour. It concluded that there was no psychological quality which was peculiar to one sex, and that there was a wide variation in individual aptitude. As such, neither men nor women could be said to have innate characteristics which prohibited the exercise of an ordained ministry.[90]

The most significant psychological issue cited was prejudice. While it is true that sexual stereotypes had been changing over the course of the twentieth century, those who compiled the report questioned the ease with which church goers might accept changes in the symbolism and traditional expression of authority embodied in the male priesthood. "Those who advocate the admission of women to the priesthood must be aware of the difficulty in predicting and controlling the behaviour which is prompted by deep-seated emotional attitudes."[91]

The study assessed ecumenical considerations, summarizing the findings of the WCC report of 1964. After reviewing this and supplementary information the Commission found that the division between churches which would accept and those which would reject women ministers no longer corresponded to the division between episcopal and non-episcopal churches. It found that resistance to the ordination of women, however, did correspond to a 'high' doctrine of the church, ministry and sacraments. It concluded that this was one reason why the issue would be divisive within the Church of England itself. Externally, the admission of women would strain relations with the Roman Catholic and particularly with the Orthodox church. A sharper consciousness about doctrinal issues would make the introduction of women ministers a more difficult and divisive issue than a generation earlier.[92]

The case against the ordination of women to the priesthood, as commonly expressed in the Church of England was clearly laid out. Ten specific reasons were offered against women's ordination to the priesthood.

1. It would be contrary to the tradition of the apostles.
2. The belief in the male priesthood was supported by the inclusion by Christ of women in the larger priesthood of the church.
3. Christianity was a revolutionary religion. Therefore, it could not be argued that conservatism was a basis for the male priesthood.
4. All theistic religions have a male priesthood. Female priesthoods belong to the nature religions.
5. The assertion that the ordination of women was the logical outcome of a steadily growing recognition of women's full humanity was fallacious.
6. Women should not try to become like men. The two sexes are complementary.
7. No power short of an ecumenical council could, "dare to assume the responsibility of modifying or altering a practice founded on so august an authority." (p. 27)
8. A female priesthood would present practical difficulties.
9. The professional opportunities open to women by the 1960s

rendered the question of women's admission to the priest-hood obsolete.

10. Women have their own kind of ministry to offer which could be lost if they were drawn into the ordained ministry.

The case for the ordination of women was presented. With a certain sense of symmetry ten reasons in favour were also given.

1. There was an urgent need for renewal in the church and for adapting the ministry of the church to the requirements of the day.

2. Differences between men and women do not constitute grounds for denying women ordination.

3. The argument against the ordination of women carried a latent implication that women are inferior to men.

4. Parental metaphors in God imagery cannot be held to be decisive in establishing the proposition that the priestly function was exclusively male.

5. Both the feminist movement and a revived sense of mission in the church had sparked the call for ordination at that point in history.

6. The shortage of clergy accentuated the need for more priests.

7. The church should reflect the changing outlook on the relationship between the sexes in the priesthood.

8. In the past the priesthood was seen largely in terms of leadership and authority. By 1966, priesthood was seen as a ministry of service.

9. Women were neither more nor less equipped than men for the task of priesthood.

10. The biblical evidence provided no reason to justify the exclusion of women from the priesthood. The priesthood could never be fully representative until both men and women were permitted to take their place equally.[93]

The fairly equal balance between the pro and the con argument was somewhat upset by a final chapter which purported to present a third view but which simply argued against women's ordination from another perspective. It stressed that while no conclusive theological reasons could be found for the view that women should not be ordained, there were powerful reasons why they should not be. In other words, aspects of the ten negative arguments were reiterated. The four rationale were based on arguments from tradition. Tradition should not be broken. The Church of England could not break it unilaterally. Needless controversy would be caused and finally the whole issue diverted away from more urgent questions, such as the ministry of the whole church.[94]

The report also talked about forms of ministry for women other than the priesthood. With particular reference to the work of deaconesses, the report noted that there was general confusion with regard to the role and status of women in the church. The report encouraged the church to clarify this confusion by taking some concrete measures to define the work of deaconesses and their relationship to the church structure.[95]

This report moved from looking at both sides to finishing up with a third side which seemed to reiterate the most key aspects of the negative argument and a final chapter which dealt with another whole dimension of women's work.

CHURCH ASSEMBLY, 1967

It was the Church Assembly of 1967 that discussed and debated the report "Women and Holy Orders." At the February session of the Assembly various arguments on both sides of the question were put forward. Many were opposed to the ordination of women because of prejudice and personal preference. No strenuous argument was made that there were significant theological objections to such ordinations. For the most part, those who expressed opposing opinions, were willing to grant that there were no theological objections to women's ordination, but they were unwilling to accept it as viable for the Church of England at that time.

In keeping with this general feeling, the Reverend Professor Gregory Lampe, a man who became a key figure in the debates of General Synod, posed a motion which reflected this view. Be it resolved:

That this Assembly, believing there are no conclusive theological reasons why women should not be ordained to the priesthood, but recognize at the same time that it would not be wise to take unilateral action at this time, would welcome further consideration of this matter by representatives of the Church of Eng-

land and the Methodist Church, in accordance with the request
made by the Methodist Conference in July, 1966.[96]

Ultimately this resolution was deferred until the July session of the Church
Assembly. At that time, Lampe withdrew the motion and presented another one which re-worked the second part of the resolution. He suggested that further consideration of the matter be carried out by a working party to be set up by ACCM and the CWMC and a joint committee of
representatives of the Church of England and the Methodist Church, in
consultation with any other churches which might be willing to enter
into such a dialogue.

This motion was seen as a progressive motion which left the door
open, at least for dialogue on women's ordination. The motion was ultimately defeated. The pattern of the voting for this defeated motion was
the first in a succession of such defeats with a similar pattern. The vote
was passed in the House of Bishops, passed in the House of Laity and
defeated in the House of Clergy.[97] The resistance in the House of Clergy
reflected by this vote was to be seen repeatedly in the relevant voting of
later General Synods on this issue.

After the clergy defeated this comparatively middle-of-the-road motion, a lay woman presented another motion which was far more 'radical' by implication than the one which was framed by Lampe. Victoria
Pitt of the Diocese of Southwark moved that individual women who felt
called to exercise the office and work of a priest in the church should
henceforth be considered on the same basis as individual men, as candidates for Holy Orders. This motion, which reflected the sentiments of
the wing of the church which was most progressive on this issue was
defeated in all three Houses.[98] In each of the three Houses, there were a
significant number of abstentions.

Although Lampe's motion was defeated, the Assembly struck a working party after the 1967 debates to give further consideration to the proper
role for women in the church. Representatives from both ACCM and the
CWMC formed the party and discussed such things as the status and
function of deaconesses, women's ordination and the nature and use of
the diaconate. In their final analysis, they concluded that the church
must determine its policy in three key areas: the ordination of women to
the priesthood, the nature of the diaconate and the status and work of
deaconesses. The working party was not saying anything that had not
been thought of before.

Most of the recommendations of the working party dealt with the somewhat mundane but important details of church work such as salaries, pensions and lay accreditation. They also suggested that deaconesses should be permitted to fulfil all the functions then open to deacons, with the possible exception of the solemnization of marriages because of civil complications.[99] This was the first time that a Church of England official report actually suggested that the diaconal orders of the male were the same as the diaconal orders of the women. The report recommended that the functions of both should be the same. One might infer from that then that their orders were the same; however, the framers of the report did not themselves made such a claim. Opening up the possibility of sameness in function meant that it opened the door for future deliberations on the sameness of ordination or ontology.

Between 1920 and 1967 the issue of the ordination of women to the priesthood was alive and well in the Church of England. Active promotion of the possibility was pursued by grassroots organizations and resisted by those within ecclesiastical structures who had the power to formulate and implement policy. It was this configuration of activity and resistance which set the stage for the Lambeth Conference of 1968.

Endnotes

1. Minutes of AGOW 4th Annual Meeting, 23 May 1934, p. 1.
2. These pamphlets can be found in the AGOW Papers, ORE/AGOW/B2.
3. Minutes of meeting of AGOW, 23 May 1934, p. 5.
4. Minutes of AGOW, 1934, p. 3.
5. Minutes of AGOW, 1934, p. 3.
6. Minutes of AGOW, 1934, p. 4.
7. Minutes of AGOW, 1934, p. 4.
8. Public Meeting of the Upper House of the Convocation of Canterbury, as recorded in the minutes of the AGOW annual meeting, 23 May 1936, p. 2.
9. Minutes of AGOW, 1936, p. 2. This statement was made by a priest, The Very Rev. W. R. Matthews, D.D.
10. Minutes of AGOW, 1936, p. 3.
11. AGOW Constitution and Rules, Adopted 22 March 1958, p. 1 (S/AGW/A2/1)
12. Minutes of AGOW Annual Meeting, 1 June 1958, p. 1.
13. Minutes of AGOW Annual Meetings, 1955–67.
14. Fisher Papers, v.1, p. 132. (LPL)
15. Lang Papers, v. 93, pp. 18–21. (LPL)
16. Lang Papers, v. 94, pp. 181–190.
17. Lang Papers, v. 94, p. 179.
18. Lang Papers, v. 93, pp. 19–26, p. 78.
19. Temple Papers, v. 36, pp. 228–9. (LPL)
20. Temple Papers, v. 36., pp. 230–231.
21. Temple Papers, v. 36, pp. 231–33.

22. Fisher Papers, v. 1, p. 133.
23. Fisher Papers, v. 232, pp. 178–198.
24. Minutes of AGOW Annual Meeting, June, 1958, p. 2.
25. Archbishop's Commission, 1935, p. 8.
26. Archbishop's Commission, 1935, p. 9.
27. Archbishop's Commission, 1935, p. 10.
28. Letitia Youmans, "Beyond our Sex." ORE/AEOW/A, B2.
29. Archbishop's Commission, 1935, p. 35.
30. Archbishop's Commission, 1935, p. 32.
31. Archbishop's Commission, 1935, p. 34.
32. Archbishop's Commission, 1935, p. 10.
33. AGOW Annual Report, 1955–56, p. 5.
34. Archbishop's Commission, 1935, p. 6.
35. Archbishop's Commission, 1935, p. 12, pp. 36–64.
36. *Church Times*, July, 1962. (CWMC/ACPH/P6)
37. For further information, see "The English Deaconess Movement," by Catherine Prebriger in *Religion in the Lives of English Women*, Gail Malmgren, ed.
38. Archbishop's Commission on the Ministry of Women, 1935, p. 38.
39. The Lambeth Committee on Ministry commented in 1930 that while there was no provision against marriage for the deaconess, if she chose to marry she would have to struggle with the question, "Can I be both wife and deaconess?"
40. Archbishop's Commission, 1935, pp. 37–39.
41. Archbishop's Commission, 1935, p. 39.
42. Archbishop's Commission, 1935, p. 39.
43. Archbishop's Commission, 1935, p. 40.
44. Archbishop's Commission, 1935, p. 41.
45. Archbishop's Commission, 1935, pp. 42–43.
46. Archbishop's Commission, 1935, p. 43.
47. Archbishop's Commission, 1935, pp. 6–7.
48. CWMC/HIST/II, Letter from Archbishop of Canterbury to Dss. Siddall, 2 March 1921.
49. CWMC/CDH/DSS/3 Letter from Archbishop of York, William Temple to an unnamed deaconess, 24 September 1933.
50. CWMC/CDH/DSS/3, p. 5.
51. CWMC/CDH/DSS.3, p. 6. The underlining is for emphasis.
52. CWMC/CDH/DSS/3, Memorandum from the Executive Committee of the Deaconess Chapter, 1 March 1938.
53. CWMC/CDH/DSS/3, p. 3.
54. Archbishop's Committee Report on *Women's Work in the Church*, 1943, p. 6.
55. *Women's Work in the Church*, 1943, p. 6.
56. CWMC/HIST/11, Response from CCWCW to the Archbishop's Report, 1943, p. 1.
57. CWMC/HIST/11, pp. 2–3.
58. CWMC/CDH/DSS/2, Inter-Diocesan Certificate of Recognition.
59. Church of England Report on *Women in the Church*, 1948, p. 12.
60. Report on *Women in the Church*, 1948, p. 3.
61. Fisher Papers, 1946, v. 11, pp. 67–68.
62. Fisher Papers, v. 11, p. 70.
63. Fisher Papers, v. 11, pp. 101–102.
64. Fisher Papers, v. 11, pp. 104–105.
65. Fisher Papers, v. 11, pp. 118–120.

66. Fisher Papers, v. 11, pp. 124–125.
67. Oral History interview with the Reverend Li Tim Oi, 8 October, 1990.
68. *Anglican Journal*, 188, 4 (April, 1992), p. 1.
69. Fisher Papers, 1957, v. 188, p. 116.
70. Fisher Papers, v. 188, pp. 118–121.
71. Fisher Papers, 1956, v. 177, pp. 297–198.
72. Fisher Papers, v. 177, p. 300.
73. Fisher Papers, 1957, v. 190, p. 232.
74. Fisher Papers, v. 190, pp. 233–240.
75. Fisher Papers, 1958, v. 202, p. 105.
76. Church Assembly, *Report of Proceedings*, v. 90, 1960, pp. 458–159.
77. *Gender and Ministry Report*, 1962, pp. 5–8.
78. *Gender and Ministry Report*, p. 9.
79. *Gender and Ministry Report*, p. 10.
80. *Gender and Ministry Report*, p. 10.
81. *Gender and Ministry Report*, p. 17.
82. *Gender and Ministry Report*, p. 20.
83. Church Assembly, *Report of Proceedings*, v. 42, 1962, pp. 681–714.
84. World Council of Churches Report 1964, p. 20.
85. World Council of Churches Report, 1964, p. 21.
86. World Council of Churches Report, p. 23.
87. Report of the Archbishop's Commission, *Women and Holy Orders*, 1966, p. 2.
88. *Women and Holy Orders*, Ch. 1, pp. 4–5.
89. *Women and Holy Orders*, pp. 13–14.
90. *Women and Holy Orders*, p. 18.
91. *Women and Holy Orders*, p. 19.
92. *Women and Holy Orders*, pp. 22–24.
93. *Women and Holy Orders*, pp. 25–29.
94. *Women and Holy Orders*, pp. 30–31.
95. *Women and Holy Orders*, pp. 32–34.
96. Church Assembly *Report of Proceedings*, 1967, v. 47, pp. 190–220.
97. Church Assembly *Report of Proceedings*, July Session, 1967, V. 47, pp. 278–323.
98. Church Assembly, *Report of Proceedings*, 1967, p. 318. The actual vote was:

	For	Against	Abstention
House of Bishops	1	8	8
House of Clergy	14	96	20
House of Laity	45	103	32

99. Report on *Women's Ministry*, 1967, p. 15.

6

A Transitory Failure

The Lambeth Conference of 1968, was a turning point for the Church of England. As we know, Lambeth 1968 asked all provinces in the Anglican Communion to communicate their opinions about the ordination of women to the priesthood to the meeting of the Anglican Consultative Council in 1971. That request set the wheels in motion for the process that led to the General Synod's decision not to ordain women to the priesthood in 1978. In the preceding stage, the institutional hierarchy of the church did not ask its synods to make a decision on this issue, despite the lobby of aforementioned groups. After Lambeth 1968, it did.

THE CHURCH OF ENGLAND'S DECISION-MAKING PROCESS 1968 – 1978: A FAILED REVOLUTION

In 1968, the ecumenical office of the Church of England produced a report which summarized the conclusions of the English Methodist-Anglican Commission on Women and the Ordained Ministry. The Commission was part of ongoing discussions between the two churches regarding possible union. In that report, the Church of England stated that while it would not declare that women would never be ordained in the future of the christendom, it was not an immediate possibility for that church.[1] This language was a shift from even ten years earlier, when the Archbishop of Canterbury referred to those who supported the ordination of women as the lunatic fringe of the church. The language also demonstrates that up to the Lambeth Conference of 1968, the official organs of the Church of England were not anticipating, or even seriously considering the ordination of women to the priesthood.

GRASSROOTS ORGANIZATIONS

One of the most interesting and determinative phenomena which occurred during this period of decision-making was the relative inactivity of organized women's groups on this issue. Apparently it was assumed by those who had promoted this issue since 1920 that much of their work had been accomplished. They struggled for years to put this item on the agenda of the church's primary decision-making bodies. This was realized after the Lambeth Conference of 1968. Particularly after the General Synod decision of 1975, as discussed below, members of the AGOW stated that they felt that the question would be decided in the affirmative by 1978 and that as such, waiting was the only necessary task. Unfortunately, the pressure in favour diminished as the lobby against accelerated.

THE HOWARD REPORT

The Anglican Consultative Council met in 1971 and it was in an attempt to respond to its reiteration of the request of Lambeth 1968 for input that the Church of England began to examine the question in an in-depth manner, asking its General Synod to make a decision on the issue. In response to that request, the Advisory Committee on the Church's Ministry (ACCM) commissioned Dame Christian Howard, an active lay theologian and member of General Synod, to compile a crucial report on the issue of women's ordination to the priesthood in the early 1970s. Working with three ordained consultants (all male clergy), Howard produced the report which established the container within which the church carried on its debate up to 1978. Identified by its number, GS104, this document which was released in 1972, was a pivotal point of discussion and reference for several General Synods. Howard presented GS104 entitled, "The Ordination of Women to the Priesthood: A Consultative Document," to the Advisory Council for the Church's Ministry before it was discussed in the General Synod. ACCM had defined Dame Christian's original task by the following parameter, to discern the pulse of the

Church of England on the matter through a well-researched and presented study. One report by one woman could serve as a frame of reference for the church's deliberations; it would not in and of itself tell the
world what the Church of England thought about the issue, and indeed
it was never designed to do that.

Although she herself was strongly in favour of the ordination of
women, Howard made no absolute conclusion or recommendation on
the issue in GS104. In writing the report, she stressed the importance of
the manner in which the debate would be conducted. She felt that the
manner in which the church held the debate was as important to the life
of the church as the conclusion which it ultimately reached.

The fundamental disagreement that existed in the church on this
issue caused debate in the preparation of the Howard Report over what
could legitimately be used as evidence. Assuming that extensive debate
on this issue would be needed in light of existing prejudice, Howard
proceeded to analyze the Church of England situation in the context of
thirteen separate categories. These included an historical preface, a statement of intention with regard to the task by way of introduction, an
overview of some preliminary considerations, a survey of relevant biblical evidence, an overview of the tradition of the church, a consideration
of the theological questions raised by the issue, and an assessment of the
current situation. Howard partnered all of this with some discussion of
social considerations, the state of the wider Anglican Communion, the
ecumenical situation, women and ministry as a broader category, legal
aspects of the question and finally reflections on the manner in which
the debate might be held.

GENERAL SYNOD, 1972

The General Synod of 1972 received the Howard Report and discussed it
at length; however, no motions were produced from those discussions
which moved the debate in one particular direction or the other. In interview, Howard made the comment that the most explosive question in
the 1970s as she prepared that report was the gender question. She stressed
that the dual assumptions with regard to male and female are deeply
engrained in people and that human beings do not give up their assumptions easily. The problem then became, how do you address and transform assumptions which people experience as absolute truth?

CANTERBURY AND YORK

After the General Synod of 1972, the ordination of women to the priesthood was debated in the Convocations of both Canterbury and York. Of
the two Convocations, Canterbury was more inclined to support the
matter. At Canterbury the Bishop of Derby proposed the following motion "that this Convocation sees no sufficient theological objection to
the ordination of women." He then pleaded for the banishment of prejudice and emotion, arguing that the motion had nothing to do with "Wom-
en's Lib." He stressed that the ordination of women, "would express the
fullness of the stature that Christ gave to women as well as to men." A
priest by the name of Canon Michael Cartwright then supported the
Bishop of Derby, who said that there were no theological objections, and
that the "defenders of the *status quo* have been driven to strange arguments, many of them deeply wounding to women, to prove their case."[2]

The Convocation heard arguments on both sides of the question with
the Bishop of Exeter warning that, "the ordination of women would be a
move backward into the darkness of old pagan religions, and I shudder
at the thought." Ultimately, the Convocation passed the proposed motion with the addition of the words, "but there are a number of issues
which have to be taken into consideration before the Church of England
decides its future policy." This addition was proposed by the Bishop of
Winchester, after other amendments failed to pass.[3]

The Convocation of York did not make a decision on the issue. It
passed a motion, by a large majority, commending the Howard Report
for study in the Convocation. The debate over this motion for study was
introduced by the Bishop of Liverpool who argued that he felt there was
no reason for excluding women from ordained ministry, and that the
issue should be seen in the context of the larger issue of the nature of
ministry generally. The Bishop of Chester came out strongly in favour.
He had chaired the committee which had produced the report *Women
and Holy Orders* in 1966 and since then had "come off the fence—There
are many women who could bring a very healthy influence into the whole
concept of priesthood."[4] Arguments from the opposition included the
observations that women were, "naturally obedient and want to be dominated by men."[5]

The Howard Report received an extensive amount of press coverage
in England after its release. Although Howard did not express her personal feelings on the issue in the Report, she did publicly declare her

opinion on the matter when asked by the press. She defended the idea of the ordination of women saying, "The tragedy of discrimination is that it weakens the human race as a whole. The scarcest resource we have is human ability, and discrimination endangers the best use of the ability of some women and thus impoverishes the community."[6]

THE ESCALATION OF OPPOSITION

The extensive amount of press coverage generated by the Report sparked a reaction. Those who were opposed to the ordination of women began to organize and publicize their opposition. The opposition was comprised of clergy, laity and some bishops, but the primary initiative on organization came from the clergy.

Antonio Gramsci's theory of revolution identifies one significant group who may have the influence to effectively halt any movement toward change. He calls this group the "traditional intellectuals". Often in history the clergy have served this function. The traditional intellectual is one who is a member of the intellectual elite of a social structure who has a vested interest in the status quo. In other words, the traditional intellectual is one who resists change in a self-protective desire to preserve the privilege of his or her own position in the old order society.[7] In the Church of England scenario, a small but significant group of clergy served the function of resistance; they facilitated the organization and escalation of opposition.

After the General Synod of 1972, both groups and individuals began to express their views through public forums and the publication of a few tracts which outlined the position against the ordination of women to the priesthood. A clergyman directly refuted the Howard Report in a tract entitled, "The Case Against the Ordination of Women." In this piece the author took issue with Howard's starting point. He argued that she had based her report on the assumption that the issue of the ordination of women was about ability and function, about the capacity of women to do a particular job. This, he argued, missed the central point which was at issue in the matter. It was not that women could not perform a particular function, it was that they were not created nor called to perform that function. They could do the job, but they could not be a priest. He argued that God the Father, and Christ the Bridegroom of the Church were "irreducible images of faith" that disallowed the participation of women as priests in the church.[8]

The author contended that 'woman' as a category was different from 'man,' and that her place in the universe and in the church was distinct from man's. Using the best language of feminism, he turned the usual arguments in favour of ordination around and stated:

> The ordination of women would be the victory of all those tendencies which have worked to enslave, dominate and inhibit woman. Man has always found it easy to accommodate woman, on his own terms in his own world. Christianity though faces him with the challenge of recognizing the unique charisms of woman and allowing them to develop. Man must learn to let woman be woman.[9]

While ostensibly promoting the liberation of women, his words in fact perpetuated a rigidly defined sphere of activity and endeavour for women. In this tract the writer went on to say that the ordination of women would be the most "bitter fruit of the clericalization of the Church."[10] He felt that by opening the doors of the traditionally male occupation of priest to women, the church would be robbing itself of the unique gifts which women already brought to the church. Rather than admitting women to the priesthood, he argued for a reclamation of the traditional women's role which had been lost in modern society. He expressed a longing for the salvation of the church by women, through ensuring that they remained "untainted" by the clerical structures which had corrupted men. Using the classic Anglican language of "unity in diversity," he stressed that man and woman were different and, as such, their functions should be different.[11] This writer felt that if the church adopted the ordination of women it would simply have been co-opted into a popular societal trend:

> Despite the clear warnings about the repercussions of women's ordination (relations with Rome and the Orthodox) the Church of England moves inexorably toward it, morally and theologically bankrupt, bereft of real spirituality, blindly conformed to the decadent values and moribund structures of this present evil age.[12]

He argued that the teaching of Scripture reinforced the idea that men and women were different and as such should assume a different place in the Christian community. Given all of this, it was his conclusion that the Howard Report had simply sold out the church to the "women's lib movement" which demanded equal rights and opportunity.[13] The emphasis on the difference between men and women, and ecumenical considerations were the predominant motifs of the argument of the opposition during the 1970s in the Church of England.

The Church Literature Association printed a tract written by the Reverend E. L. Mascall in 1972 and again in 1973 which posed the question, "Women Priests?" Mascall went on to answer this question in the negative. Interestingly, he justified his position through direct quotes from the report on *Women and Holy Orders* which had been produced for the Church of England in 1966. Mascall argued that feminism was the mother of this issue in the church, and that the mother, as with all women, was illogical. Discussing the essential differences between the sexes, Mascall refuted the basic aims of the "women's lib" movement. He stated that "women's lib and equality" demanded the same function for men as well as women. In his view, this demand proved the superiority of men: "the women want to be like us."[14] If women were therefore inferior, why should they be given equal status and employment? Mascall cited Scripture to justify his view that the Father, Son and Holy Ghost of the Trinity were a divinely inspired revelation. As the masculine imagery of Christianity was divinely inspired it could not simply be discarded by the hands of "men." Mascall went on to articulate the classic evangelical argument of the opposition in this issue by drawing on Scripture to defend the idea that, "God reaches men by Christ, and women by men."[15]

The Church Literature Association also produced another pamphlet entitled, "Women in the Priesthood?" This tract, published in 1973 was composed by "a group of theologians" who remained anonymous. Although it was clear from the language that the group included clergy, no names were given. The framers of this piece were self-declared Anglo-Catholics, and they opposed the ordination of women on largely ecumenical grounds. The validity of excluding women from the priesthood on ecumenical grounds was reinforced by the argument that sexual difference was evidenced in Scripture and was therefore a valid criteria for excluding women from the priesthood.

As in the other cases considered, these writers attempted to refute the philosophical assumptions of feminism, which they viewed as undergirding the movement toward the ordination of women. They referred to Dr. Una Kroll, founding member of the Christian Parity Group, who had argued for women in the priesthood by saying that true mutuality and complementarity was impossible in the church as long as opportunities were denied to women because of their sex. The writers of this anonymous tract refuted that argument by questioning the relationship between sameness of function and mutuality. Using the model of a married couple, they commented that true mutuality would be impossible until men were able to have babies.[16]

Issues of sexuality and sexual and biological difference were key for those who wrote this tract. They went on to refute the position that there were masculine and feminine elements present in everyone. Using the example of X and Y chromosomes they argued that the above contention was simply not true: the Y chromosome which determines masculinity is present in men but not in women, while the X chromosome is present in men and women alike. This might therefore provide some sort of argument for the exercise of female functions by men, but none whatever for the exercise of male functions by women.[17] Obviously, the framers of the report were caught up in some form of bizarre biological determinism.

This report concluded by stressing that ecumenical considerations were primary. In their words, although the American church might be able to minimize ecumenical considerations, England could not follow that example.[18] This ecumenical argument was tacked on to the end of a much longer argument from biology for the exclusion of women (women could not be ordained because of their physical form as women), which they supported with their interpretation of Christian Scripture.

Opposition to the ordination of women between 1920 and 1978 was preoccupied with sexuality. In the mind of those opposed, the category of 'woman' was sufficient to disqualify vocation to priesthood. In the documents of virtually every debate, in every available article dealing with opposition to women as priests, this 'fact' is a leading argument. This opposition was in large part grounded in the acceptance of a traditional framework of theology which identifies women as inferior to men. Such a position argues from ontology saying that there is a primary and determinative difference between men and women. Drawing on Scripture and history, the argument is made that women are simply different than men and therefore cannot be priests; they argue from ontology to make a claim about function.

Something is missing in the logic of an argument grounded in biological determinism. Thinkers such as the first mentioned clergyman argued that women were different from men and therefore should fill a different function in the church. He argued that the purity and goodness of women must remain untainted by the corruptness of the male hierarchy in order to save the church. While at first glance such theology may appear to elevate women, in actuality it demeans them. Feminism argued for the equality of women. That was a position unacceptable to the opposition because for them difference actually meant inferiority. While the opposition in the 1970s may not have dared to alienate their predominantly female congregations by stating this directly, it is implied. Christ represents God. If a woman cannot represent Christ she cannot represent God. Her image cannot be a reflection of the divine. The feminine cannot reflect the ultimate.

General unspoken assumptions about the uncleanness and profanity of woman's sexuality are implicit in church practises which prohibit women from the sanctuary of the church. For centuries the Christian tradition has accepted the teaching that women are unclean at the very least during certain periods of their reproductive cycle. Such teaching has become part of the mind of the church, part of its unconscious archetype of women. How can evil Eve become a priest?

The Church of England formally disposed of such objections to women in the priesthood in 1935. In interview, however, many stated the belief that those clergy who were opposed to the ordination of women did not want their sanctuaries defiled by unclean women. The extent to which these unconscious assumptions still affected the minds and attitudes of those who opposed women in the priesthood cannot be empirically measured, but the opposition tracts speak for themselves. Howard, writer of GS104, said:

> The idea of women becoming priests arouses in some an antagonism almost a sense of indecency, for the very possibility shocks them at a deep and probably nonrational level of consciousness.[19]

Between the release of the Howard Report in 1972 and the General Synod vote in 1978, the opposition to the ordination of women gradually gathered force. The process of the consolidation began with the publication of tracts such as the ones discussed above. Newspaper reports document the gradual consolidation of the opposition around already existing societies within the Church of England. Both Evangelical Societies and Anglo-Catholic Societies agreed to oppose the ordination of women to the priesthood.

Churchmanship, or ecclesiological orientation has traditionally affected many aspects of life in the Church of England. The ordination of women is no exception. The differing attitudes which the three branches brought to decisions in the church were well known. For example, when delegates to General Synod in 1970 were being elected, a group organized that named itself the "middle ground" or broad stream to serve candidates for the Synod, as they were afraid that the interests of the less politicized and previously unorganized broad stream would be lost.[20] The Anglo-Catholics and the Evangelicals had a much longer history of organization. Each of the two extremes had organizations of affiliation already in place at the grassroots level of the church. As the church prepared for the 1978 debate in the General Synod, newspaper articles asked, "It was the Anglo-Catholic wing...combining with the Evangelical wing which brought to nought Anglican-Methodist reunion. Will these two groups within the church line up together again?"[21] The answer to that question as far as it can be determined is yes. Although their rationales were different, their willingness to join together to defeat the ordination of women was clearly stated.[22]

Before the General Synod vote in 1978, newspapers reported that fifteen Anglo-Catholic societies representing nearly 500,000 "High Church" Anglicans had unanimously decided to oppose the admission of women to the presbyterate. This decision was an unprecedented action of solidarity between those societies. Those societies included groups such as the group for Church Union, the Society of Mary, Ecclesia, the Catholic League, the Confraternity of the Blessed Sacrament, and the Guild of the Servants of the Sanctuary.[23] This decision to form a united opposition by Anglo-Catholic societies was all the more influential as some of the societies were over one hundred years in age, and had a considerable number of followers at the parish level.

Before the 1978 General Synod, there were attempts in various parts of the country to secretly gather the signatures of those clergy who opposed the ordination of women to the priesthood. In 1977, it was reported that a North Humberside curate was drawing up a secret list of clergymen who were ready to leave the Church of England over the ordination of women issue. A curate at Howden claimed to have collected the names of more than 40 clergy in Britain who were strongly opposed and who would leave the church if such action was ever taken.[24]

Eventually a group of more than one hundred clergymen in the Church of England signed statements committing themselves to leave the church if women were ordained to the priesthood. This group of signatures was collected at the initiative of one of the Anglo-Catholic societies mentioned above, Ecclesia. Ecclesia worded the declaration as follows:

> I, the undersigned, being a member of the Church of England and in major orders of the One, Holy, Catholic, and Apostolic Church, do hereby assert our belief, in accordance with the Lord's example and the Catholic tradition, that the orders of the apostolic ministry can be conferred only on men; and I further declare that I will not and cannot in conscience remain in communion with any bishop who attempts to admit women to the order of bishop, priest, or deacon.[25]

Ecclesia prepared and presented this declaration to the House of Bishops before the November debate by the General Synod in 1978. It was the only sizable list of signatures collected in opposition prior to 1978.

The years between 1972 and 1978 were years during which those who opposed the ordination of women gathered force. Prior to that point, they had not felt that there was any likelihood that the issue would actually be taken seriously by the church. After the Howard Report, the potential threat of such action appeared more immediate.

GENERAL SYNOD, 1973

In 1973 the General Synod met again. At the 1973 Synod, members made two specific motions which were then referred back to the dioceses. Firstly, the Synod made a motion that there were no fundamental objections to the ordination of women to the priesthood. This motion differed significantly from the motion that was passed at the Lambeth Conference in 1968, as the Synod deleted the word "theological" from before the word "objections." The scope of the motion at the Synod was much broader as it encompassed all possible objections, for example, sociological, theological, psychological, and so on.

All acknowledged that there was extensive dissent on the issue. Fourteen people spoke to the issue of women's ordination and of these, one person who spoke to the Synod was undecided, three spoke against wom-

en's ordination to the priesthood and ten individuals, clergy, lay and episcopal, spoke strongly in favour of women's ordination.[26] One can only
wonder what the results would have been if a vote had been taken on the
issue at that point. Of those who spoke against women's ordination the
primary areas of concern were that the Church of England would be
jumping on the bandwagon of popular sentiment with regard to wom-
en's equality, male headship of the family, *kephale*, and the inability of
women to represent the male icon of Christ. Interestingly, ecumenical
relations with the Roman and Orthodox churches did not come up at
that juncture.

Of those who spoke in favour of women's ordination the prevailing
sentiments were diverse. Some argued that there were neither theological objections nor scriptural justifications for excluding women. Others
raised questions about the criteria for excluding women. For example,
what was the primary criteria of qualification for priesthood — masculinity, feminist or redeemed humanity? Some argued that women's ordination was simply right, the leading of the Spirit and that women who
felt they had such a vocation had the right to have that vocation tested in
the same way that their male colleagues did. One priest argued that there
was a strong precedent for the exercise of women's leadership in Christianity through the great abbesses of the middle ages, which he defined as
the exercise of episcopal authority.

As it was felt that there was obvious and wide dissent on the motion,
a second motion to refer the first motion to diocesan synods was made
and carried.[27] This decision to refer the issue to the diocesan synods was
an interesting procedural move. Usually the General Synod would take a
stand on a particular issue and then refer it to the dioceses for comment
and response. In this case, however, the Synod decided to take no particular stand, to make no decision on the issue before the dioceses had
offered their opinion on it.

The Synod also referred a subsequent motion to the diocesan synods
because of the "divided nature of the voting." This motion went one step
further than the first motion and proposed that the Church of England
should proceed to remove the legal and other barriers to the ordination
of women.[28] The contentious nature of the content of that motion meant
that it was never voted on at the General Synod.

Constitutional Structure

Some explanation of the constitutional structure of the Church of England as it pertains to the decision-making process at this stage is illuminative. The popular myth that the complex constitutional structure of the Church of England limited the possibility of an affirmative decision being made on this issue is widely held. This myth reflects something but not everything of the actual situation.

Whenever an affirmative decision might have been made regarding the ordination of women, actual ordination would not have happened , and subsequently did not happen, immediately. Any such decision would have been a preliminary decision; this is then followed by a revision stage and then a final approval stage. After final approval by the General Synod it would have been referred again to the dioceses for comment and would have fallen at that stage without the approval of a majority of dioceses. The motion would then be returned to General Synod and if passed by a two-thirds majority it would then be sent to parliament for approval. The parliament in its turn would either recommend Royal Assent or not. If such Assent is given then the legislative changes would be put into effect.

While this is a lengthy and complex process most of it is not relevant to this analysis, as the latter stages were never reached. What is of interest is the extent to which the structure of synodical voting influenced the outcome of the debate. The General Synod was not required by its constitution to refer the matter to the dioceses before it had clarified its intentions. By its decision to refer the issue to the dioceses in 1973 the General Synod voluntarily decided that it would not give direction to the church at large. There was not a pro-active leadership in the Synod. Rather there was a sentiment of caution and delegation of authority. If the General Synod had been able to make a decision in 1973, the motions still would have gone to the dioceses at that point. What would have been different was that the dioceses would have had the affirmative opinions of the members of General Synod in front of them during their deliberations. The General Synod would have initiated a positive decision. Desiring the input of the grassroots is commendable, it might be said; however, as we will see, the General Synod ultimately did not take the direction of the grassroots to heart.

REFERENCES TO THE DIOCESES, 1973–1975

One does not hear of these motions again at the level of the national church structure until the General Synod of 1975. The interdenominational group, the Society for the Ministry of Women in the Church (SWMC), did record something about what happened in the meantime with this motion at the diocesan level in their newsletters. While it is evident from diocesan synod journals that all the dioceses debated this issue, the newsletter of the SMWC also tells us that many deaneries within dioceses also debated the issue. In its private newsletter to its members in July of 1974, it noted that the voting in deanery synods had been varied. At least 11 deaneries voted in favour of both resolutions. The newsletter commented that voting by houses had been significant in the results of these votes. It stated that the laity voted against the issue in only one deanery. In all other deaneries known to have voted, it was the clergy who were opposed, thus defeating favourable motions. In Northhampton the vote was lost by one clergyman; in a Norfolk deanery the clergy tied 5-5, and the motion was declared lost; in Peterborough, the clergy were tied 8-8 and the rural Dean cast a deciding vote in favour. Apparently the wording of the first motion posed some difficulties in the deaneries, as people were of different opinion as to what constituted a "fundamental objection."[29]

Six months later the SWMC members heard that about 80 deaneries in total had voted on the motions. Out of that 80, 50 were known to have voted in favour of the first motion, but only half of those again voted in favour of both motions. As was the case in dioceses adverse votes almost always came from the clergy; however, not all deaneries voted by Houses and as such, clerical and lay votes were indistinguishable in some cases.[30]

According to the newsletters between 1973 and 1975, the opposition organized and lobbied at deanery and diocesan meetings. In response to that opposition, the SWMC called upon its supporters to be prepared to "get out there" at the meetings and promote the cause of the ordination of women.[31] In 1974 the editor of the newsletter noted that seven members had been out promoting the issue at deaneries and synods, and acknowledged that probably many more were doing this in the situations in which they found themselves.[32] Obviously this issue was fairly politicized at the deanery and diocesan level.

The newsletters noted that the issue was also being discussed by groups and organizations elsewhere in English society. Apparently in Brantham and Suffolk in 1974, the SWMC circulated a questionnaire among the villagers of the area and a large majority of people pronounced themselves in favour of women in the priesthood. Out of 131 replies, 94

(71 per cent) said they would be happy to accept a woman as rector.[33] While these results cannot be said to be representative, they are an interesting indication of attitude at the grassroots level.

GS 252

A document titled GS 252, "The Ordination of Women: Report of the Standing Committee on the Reference to the Dioceses," recorded the results of the 1973 referral. In its summary of the responses, the document noted that with regard to the first motion (no fundamental objection to the ordination of women), 30 dioceses supported the motion, 12 defeated it, and in the case of two other dioceses, the bishops did not record the vote, but it was also defeated.[34] A majority of the dioceses came out in support of the first motion. With regard to the second motion (the implementation of legislation to make such ordinations possible) only 34 of the dioceses proceeded to address it. The other ten felt that there was no point in proceeding to address the second motion after the defeat of the first. Of the 34 who addressed the motion, 15 carried the motion unamended in all three Houses. The dioceses of Lichfield carried it in an amended form. A final 18 dioceses defeated the motion.[35]

The SWMC recorded slightly different results from the diocesan voting. In its newsletter of July 1975, it noted the following results. It found that there were 18 dioceses which had passed both motions. There were 16 dioceses which had passed only motion #1. Nine dioceses defeated Motion #1 by the Bishop in Chichester, by the clergy in Ely, Gloucester, London, Southwell (tied), by the Bishop and clergy in Chester, Blackburn and Peterborough, and by all three houses in Truro. There was an overall majority in favour of the above but the house system of voting defeated it.[36] The above figures differ slightly from the official count found in GS 252 because the Standing Committee of General Synod which presented the report did not count the vote of the diocese of Lincoln because it had not voted by houses, despite a large majority in favour of motion #1. Secondly, the three dioceses where the bishops abstained, Exeter, Norwich and Lichfield were recorded as having 'lost' motion #1, because all three houses had not voted in favour. This appears particularly unrepresentative for the diocese of Norwich which had passed BOTH motions by large majorities of clergy and laity. As such, GS 252 concluded that 30 dioceses had passed motion #1, whereas if the above considerations are

taken into account 34 out of 44 dioceses voted in favour of motion #1.
See Table 21.

What can we say about the support and opposition to this ordination of women as it was revealed by this reference to the diocese? First,
it is undisputable that the laity who comprise a real majority of the
church's population were overwhelmingly in favour of the ordination of
women to the priesthood. The House of the Laity voted in favour of the
first motion in 42 out of 43 dioceses. In other words 97.7 percent of the
dioceses had a majority of lay people in synods in favour of the ordination of women in principle. Only the laity of the Diocese of Truro voted
against the motion. While only 70 percent of the dioceses were in favour of the motion, if the figure represented only the views of the laity it
would have been 97.7 percent.

In 35 out of 43 dioceses, the House of Clergy also voted in favour of
the motion. This represented 81.4 percent of the clergy in synods, in
favour. This is a surprising statistic as we will see that it was the House
of Clergy at General Synod which defeated the movement toward the
ordination of women on more than one occasion. The diocesan bishops
were actually the group which was the least supportive of motion 1, and
they were significantly in favour. The bishops in 34 out of 43 dioceses
(79.6 percent) voted in favour.

Bishops and clergy were more opposed to the ordination of women
than were the laity; in no diocese were the laity solely responsible for
defeating the motion. In the one diocese where they voted against motion 1, the clergy also voted against and as such the motion was defeated
by the laity and clergy together. In two other dioceses (16.7 percent of
the cases) the clergy alone defeated the motion, thus causing it to fail in
the synod. In four dioceses, the negative vote or non-vote of the bishop
alone caused the motion to fail (33 percent of the cases). In five more
dioceses the clergy and bishops were both opposed. As such the motion
was defeated by the bishops and clergy together in 41.7 percent of the
cases.

Motion 2 was voted on in only 34 dioceses (79 percent). The remaining nine had defeated the first motion and as such felt it would be
redundant to raise the second. Of this 34, 15 dioceses carried the
motion in all three houses (53 percent). This marginal majority in
favour looks somewhat different when the statistics by House are
compiled.

In 33 dioceses, the laity voted in favour of the motion (97.1 percent of the cases). In only one case (the diocese of Chelmsford) did the laity vote against moving toward implementation.

In 22 dioceses the clergy voted in favour of the motion, while 12 voted against it. In other words, 64.7 percent of the clergy by diocese voted affirmatively.

In 23 dioceses the bishops voted in favour of Motion 2 (67.6 percent of the cases).

Contrary to popular myth, there was not a direct majority of opposition in any one category. The numbers indicate a majority of support for the idea and then, where applicable, a majority in favour of implementation. The real majority or minority is difficult to assess with complete accuracy given the nature of synodical voting, and the pattern of voting which the synods adopted for this issue. Suffice it to say that while there was opposition it was predominantly among the clergy and bishops, and it was not a majority.

GENERAL SYNOD 1975

It was at General Synod in 1975, that results of the diocesan voting were received in the document GS 252. The Synod heard that 70 percent of the dioceses had voted in favour of Motion 1 and only 34.9 percent had voted in favour of motion 2.

The reception of that report meant that the General Synod could proceed to vote on the two original motions itself. The first motion, that there were no objections to the ordination of women, was voted on in the form presented to the General Synod of July, 1973. Of the 15 individuals who addressed the motion, seven spoke in favour of it and seven spoke against it, while one was undecided. In addressing the motion, issues such as changing conceptions of God and theology of sexuality were raised. The issue of ecumenism on the pro and the con side emerged. Each side argued that the other would damage ecumenical relations. The male nature of Jesus' chosen apostles was raised, as was the "corrupting" influence of the feminist movement. The issues of male headship and traditional biblical exegesis were used to reinforce the position of those who opposed the motion.

It has often been true that those who identify themselves as part of the Anglo-Catholic branch of Anglicanism are opposed to women's ordination. Even as early as this 1975 debate, there were those of the Anglo-Catholic stream who stated clearly that such a categorization was unfair.

In addressing the first motion of the 1975 synod, Sister Irene Benedict stated clearly that she was an Anglo-Catholic who warmly supported the ordination of women:

> I have come to the conclusion that it is right that women should be ordained to the ministry...there is a sphere within which their femininity can be exercised, within which their gifts can be expressed, and that is not, of course, a masculine priesthood. This is exactly what I feel. I do not want a masculine priesthood.[37]

The recorded votes which demonstrate the Synod's support for the idea that there were no fundamental objections to the ordination of women were as follows:

House of Bishops: 28 yes, 10 no, 0 abstentions
House of Clergy: 110 yes, 96 no, 2 abstentions
House of Laity: 117 yes, 74 no, 3 abstentions.[38]

In percentage terms, 74 percent of the House of Bishops was in favour and 26 percent was opposed. The necessary majority in favour was realized. In the House of Clergy, 53 percent were in favour, 46 percent were opposed and one percent abstained from voting. In the House of Laity 60 percent were in favour, 38 percent were opposed and two percent abstained from voting.

The second motion as the original framers presented it to the Synod of 1973 was never voted on. Instead an alternate motion was presented to the Houses of Synod in its place. This motion was the inverse of its predecessor. It declared that, "in light of divided opinion in diocesan voting" the Synod felt that it would not be right at that time to remove the legal and other barriers to the ordination of women. In defending this motion, individuals such as the Dean of Ripon argued that both priesthood and motherhood were primary vocations, and as such were incompatible:

> The fact that motherhood is a primary vocation does not, of course, mean that a mother must be tied to sink and cradle all the time. A part-time job may indeed make her a livelier and better mother. But family must come first. The Church must be seen to be standing for this principle realising how strong are

some of the economic and other pressures the other way. But priesthood is a primary vocation. It is priesthood I am talking about, not ministry…unless you drastically modify the whole theology of priesthood, you cannot be a mother and a priest.[39]

The voting on this motion went as follows:

House of Bishops: 19 yes, 14 no, one abstention
House of Clergy: 127 yes, 74 no, zero abstentions
House of Laity: 80 yes, 96 no, zero abstentions[40]

In percentage terms, 57 percent of the House of Bishops was in favour of the motion, 41 percent was opposed and 3 percent abstained. In the House of Clergy, 63 percent was in favour, 37 percent was opposed, and no one abstained from voting. The House of Laity defeated the motion with 46 percent voting in favour and 54 percent opposing the motion. As such, the requisite majority in each house was not achieved and the motion was lost by the action of the laity.

At first glance one might assume that the failure of this motion meant that the Synod was ready to proceed with removing the barriers to women's ordination. That was not the case. The laity was the only group which seemed to indicate some readiness to that possibility at that point. Some members then put a third motion to the Synod which stated that the Synod felt that the church should then proceed to remove all legal and other barriers to the ordination of women to the priesthood. That motion also failed to pass. It did not achieve a majority among the bishops or the clergy. It did, however, pass in the House of Laity, with 60 percent voting in favour of the motion. In the House of Bishops it was an even split in the voting and in the House of Clergy it failed with 57 percent of the house opposing the motion.[41]

	Pro	Con	Abst.
House of Bishops	15	15	0
House of Clergy	78	108	4
House of Laity	101	64	3

The Synod had arrived at a deadlock. It was unable to agree to proceed and it was unable to agree to stop. In so doing it reached a state of relative paralysis.

Many who attended this Synod thought that the state of paralysis was undone by the fourth motion addressing the issue. Canon Colin Craston moved that the Synod should invite the House of Bishops to bring a proposal to admit women to the priesthood before the Synod when, "They judge the time for action to be right."[42] It was this motion that ultimately carried. This decision to refer the entire matter to episcopal control was a standard Anglican move. A decision resolving the conflict cannot be reached, and so we will defer it. As Anglicans, we respect the authority of our bishops to offer pastoral oversight and direction. On this issue, the episcopacy up to that point had not offered any unified and strong direction of the issue, at least not such that it can be retrieved from available documentation and interviews. The Synod placed great trust in the top level of its hierarchy, but it also abdicated responsibility and gave away its power in the situation, whichever way it might have chosen on the issue.

The significance of concern over ecumenical relations with the Roman Catholic and Orthodox churches was manifest in the next motion presented and carried at the Synod. The Reverend G. Moss of the diocese of Hereford put the following motion:

> That this Synod, not wishing to prejudice improving relations with the Roman Catholic and Orthodox Churches by removing prematurely legal and other barriers to the ordination of women in the Church of England, requests the Presidents (1) inform the appropriate authorities in those churches that there are no fundamental objections to such ordinations and (2) invite those authorities to share in the urgent examination of the theological and other implications of the removal of those barriers by the Church of England.[43]

Of the five people who addressed this motion all spoke in favour of it and it was carried, but in the following amended form. The motion read the same as the above up until (2) where the Synod changed the wording to, "to share in an urgent re-examination of the theological grounds for including women in the order of priesthood, with particular attention to the doctrine of Man and the doctrine of Creation."[44]

In a final motion which was put and lost, the Bishop of Guildford asked for further study of the issue and its "pastoral and practical implications by the House of Bishops and ACCM."[45] At least sufficient progress was made at the 1975 Synod that the issue was not sent back again to the committee study table of the church. The Synod agreed that sufficient work of a high calibre in the area of study and research had been done and that further work along the lines suggested was not necessary at that juncture.

The voting at General Synod 1975, reflects the influence of the voting by diocese, as represented by the 70 percent for Motion 1 and the 34.9 percent for Motion 2. It is apparent that the Synod felt that support for the idea was not overwhelming and as such could not be fully embraced at that time. Support in all three Houses of the General Synod was less than support shown in the voting by diocese.

GENERAL SYNOD 1978

It is the November Session of the General Synod of 1978 that is the momentous culmination of our story. By the time that Synod met the important Lambeth Conference of 1978 had been held. The Church of England had participated in the Lambeth discussions which demonstrated the commitment to unity within the Communion was stronger than the division by attitude and action on this issue. That commitment by the larger Anglican Communion did not influence the outcome of the Church of England decision-making process.

Prior to the November session in 1978, the Standing Committee sent delegates to the General Synod a memorandum which outlined the procedures and implications for dealing with the motion regarding the ordination of women to the priesthood. The memorandum noted that as a result of Section One of the Church of England Provisions Measure 1978, a two-thirds majority would be required in each of the three houses, only if the time came for the Synod to give final approval to a measure which would remove the barriers to the ordination of women. In others words, at the November 1978 session, only a simple majority in each of the three houses was required for the motion to pass. Final approval requiring a two-thirds majority would only be necessary after a majority of diocesan synods gave their approval. The memorandum reminded General Synod that an affirmative decision did not in and of itself remove the legal barriers to the ordination of women. An affirmative decision at that point would only begin the process by which legislation might eventually change and allow the admission of women to the presbyterate.[46]

GS Misc 87 also addressed the possibility of the failure of the motion. It stated that if the motion was not carried, the Standing Committee strongly advised that a further period of reflection was needed and that no immediate attempt to bring forward further motions on the subject be made.[47]

Participants of that 1978 Synod recall that the climate had changed since 1975. The debates of 1973 and 1975 had been amicable. By the Synod of 1978 a climate of entrenched hostility had emerged. The lines between the two sides were more definitely drawn. The opposition had worked energetically between 1975 and 1978 to ensure that they were represented by delegates in both the House of the Clergy and the House of the Laity. The opposition gathered early on the morning of that Synod debate, filling the front rows of the Synod so that their voice and opinion would be most clearly visible and audible when the time for the debate came.

The House of Bishops presented a motion reminiscent of the 1973 motion in 1978 which asked that the Standing Committee prepare and bring forward legislation which would remove the barriers to the ordination of women to the priesthood and their consecration to the episcopate — note the inclusion of the episcopate which was not present in earlier motions. As stipulated by the Synod of 1975 this motion was presented by the House of Bishops which apparently judged that the time was right to bring the issue back to the Synod, following the Lambeth Conference of 1978.

Several speakers over the course of the debate referred to a sense of "unease" over the whole issue. Those who professed to be undecided were apparently uncomfortable with the implications of a decision on the issue whichever way the debate went.[48] There were several speakers who stressed that they would base their decision on the actual debate. Many who voiced opposition appeared concerned over the implications of an affirmative decision for ecumenical dialogue and strongly reiterated the need to be faithful to the tradition of sexuality established by the example of Jesus, an all male apostleship. Those who spoke adamantly in favour attempted to refute these by then familiar arguments against, rather than aggressively promoting an argument in favour.

As mentioned, church law required a majority in each of the three houses for this motion to pass. A majority was achieved only in the House of Bishops and the House of Laity, with 65 percent of the bishops and 53 percent of the laity supporting the motion. The motion was defeated in the House of Clergy which clearly said no to it with 61 percent of the house voting against it. The voting was as follows:

House of Bishops: 32 yes, 17 no
House of Clergy: 94 yes, 149 no
House of Laity: 120 yes, 106 no[49]

The episcopal leadership of the church was more open to this motion than were the other two Houses, although the House of Laity was obviously open to it by a simple majority. The clergy were the most clearly opposed.

The opposition had been successful in its attempts to populate the Synod and to sway opinion. Both the House of Bishops and the House of Laity passed the motion which would have begun the process of removing the legislative barriers which excluded women from the priesthood. It was the 'traditional intellectuals,' the clergy, who soundly defeated the motion. This vote is not surprising in so far as it is generally true that clergy tend to be more opposed to the ordination of women than the other two groups within Anglican structures. The pattern does not tell the whole story, however. It is the voting of the laity which seems most surprising at this juncture; they passed the motion with only 53 percent in favour. As we know, this is radically at odds with lay support as demonstrated by diocesan synod voting.

Explaining the shift in the House of the Laity is no easy task. Clearly the opposition had gathered force and successfully lobbied for the election of opposition people to the General Synod — their numbers do not reflect the larger constituency of the church. As we saw earlier, parallel to the activity of the opposition, lobby groups in favour of the ordination of women, after fifty years of activity were largely inactive. Some contend that attitudes against had hardened during that period through the expenditure of a lot of money and the aggravation of a lot of fear.

The opposition as preponderantly expressed by the clergy was able to succeed because of a relative leadership vacuum at the upper levels of the church structure. The vacuum was in turn reinforced by a relatively quiet and non-aggressive support for the issue at the grassroots. The ecclesiastical and societal container within which this drama was played out was also determinative in so far as it was inhospitable to change.

A LEADERSHIP VACUUM

When we name a leadership vacuum, we are not saying that the episco-pacy was not largely in favour of the ordination of women. After the Lambeth Conference of 1968, there was remarkable positive movement on the subject, but that leadership was not organized or pro-active. At that stage, the members of the House of Bishops were sufficiently di-vided that they could not offer cohesive direction to the rest of the church. Indeed, it was not until 1987 that the House of Bishops produced its first official report on the subject. The relative inactivity of the bishops as a group created the leadership vacuum into which the opposition clergy were eager to step.

At that point in its history the Church of England did have a titular head, the Archbishop of Canterbury, who was in favour of the ordina-tion of women. Archbishop Donald Coggan had reached a decision about the ordination of women long before the General Synod debate of 1978. He stated that this was an issue which could not be argued on the basis of rights, as ordination was purely a matter of grace, "Women should not force the issue, should not seize power, but they must make their voice heard." He placed the onus on women to move the church forward on this issue. It would be their claim to a vocation that would move the ministry of the church in his view, "It is not an issue of rights but of complementarity of ministry." [50]

This focus on the role of the women as key in the decision-making process, in a sense absolves the church's structure from responsible and visionary leadership. The grassroots become the protagonists, the gadfly which provokes change. The intellectual leadership in this scenario be-comes that group which must be persuaded to give up the old ways in which they have a vested interest.

Coggan also commented that most bishops did not want their posi-tion on the issue identified at the General Synod of 1978. While some openly declared their attitudes, most voted quietly. There was some epis-copal unwillingness to openly declare opinions; there was certainly no united leadership in either direction.

THE ECUMENICAL SCENE

During the 1978 debate, the General Synod had a document at its dis-posal entitled GS Misc. 88, "The Ordination of Women—A Supplement to GS 104." The Standing Committee prepared this report as a supplement which updated the church on what had been happening in other parts of the Anglican Communion and in other denominations since 1972. Obviously it reported that the Anglican Church of Canada, the Church of New Zealand and the Episcopal Church in the United States had begun ordaining women to the priesthood.

The fact that the ordination of women was *fait accompli* within the Communion did nothing to change the mind of those who were stalwartly opposed. In fact, there were those who used what they termed the "precipitous actions of the colonies" to justify the responsibility of England as the Mother Church to assert itself as the true guardian of the Catholic faith, as the Anglican tradition had received it.[51] This self-perception by some in the Church of England that its mother-status gave it greater obligation to safeguard the tradition influenced some to resist the ordination of women. This self-designation as the guardian of tradition is also of particular interest in the English case, as the Church of England has a long history as the establishment religion within English society. The extent to which that history and role was determinative cannot be measured but was hinted at in the debates of 1978.

The ecumenical segment of the update in GS Misc 88 presented a pessimistic view of ecumenical concerns. In other words, the report dealt only with summarizing the positions of key churches who remained opposed to the ordination of women. These recorded positions were the product of ongoing bilateral ecumenical dialogue. Particularly, the document recorded the responses of the Roman Catholic, the Eastern Orthodox and the Old Catholic churches to Anglican initiatives in this area.

While affirming that God created humanity in his image as male and female, the Orthodox Church stressed that in their view these gifts were differing and complementary. As such, they stated that it was not possible for women to be admitted to the priesthood. From the Orthodox perspective, if the Church of England proceeded with the ordination of women, ecumenical dialogue would be damaged:

> In the name of our common Lord and Saviour Jesus Christ, we entreat our Anglican brothers not to proceed further with this action which is already dividing the Anglican Communion, and which will constitute a disastrous reverse for all our hopes of unity between Anglicanism and Orthodoxy.[52]

The Roman Catholic Church also rejected the possibility of ordaining women to the priesthood. In its bilateral dialogue with the Church of England, it reiterated its commitment to ongoing ecumenical dialogue:

> While we do not underate the reality of obstacles, we are convinced that our communions ought to maintain that deep trust in each other which has been built up over recent years. We have a grave responsibility to continue and intensify co-operation and dialogue in everything that promotes our growing together towards full unity in Christ.[53]

Finally, the Old Catholic Church was adamant in its opposition to the ordination of women but appreciated the Church of England's desire to discuss the matter ecumenically. The Archbishop of Utrecht wrote to the Archbishop of Canterbury and said:

> That means that only men and not women can be the bearers of this priesthood of Christ, because Jesus Christ was a man and delegated His Work of Redemption to his apostles, who were also men.... I am greatly satisfied with the resolution of your Synod to seek common counsel on this matter with the Old Catholic church.[54]

The collected responses of denominations who opposed the ordination of women to the priesthood were weighty in their opposition. Together they presented a serious obstacle to ecumenical dialogue, if the purpose of such dialogue was re-union, or even inter-communion.

Assessing the actual impact of ecumenical concerns on the outcome of the 1978 debate is difficult. They were referred to many times. What lies at the heart of ecumenical issues, however, might be debated. Christianity has never been a homogenous phenomenon. Even the early Christians were often unable to agree on matters of policy, discipline, doctrine and practice. It took nearly 500 years to establish a creed with which most could live, the Nicene Creed affirmed at the Council of Chalcedon, 451 C.E. Christianity is and always has been a culturally conditioned phenomenon. While unanimity may be desirable, it has never been the Christian norm. The Church of England's life originated in a difference of opinion with its sister, Rome. As such it should appreciate the reality of intimate relationships which sometimes demand that individuals move away from each other as they act according to their own conscience, and in so doing struggle to move closer to the heart of God. Unity in diversity is a most prized Anglican value.

When the motion to proceed to formulate legislation removing barriers to the ordination of women to the priesthood was defeated in 1978, those who supported the ordination of women felt shock and betrayal. After the results of the voting were announced, Dr. Una Knoll stood up in the gallery and with great pain shouted, "We asked for bread and you've given us a stone."

LABOUR SHORTAGE

The full meaning of what was being communicated at the General Synod in 1978 cannot be fully appreciated without knowing the employment context in the Church of England. During the 1970s when this issue was being debated, the Church of England had a clergy labour shortage. In many cases, people in parishes were being deprived of adequate pastoral and sacramental ministry because there simply were not enough priests to meet the demand. All levels of church life were aware of this shortage. Between 1973 and 1980, the number of full-time clergy declined from 13,000 to 11,235, and between 1974 and 1979, the number of men ordained each year dropped from 348 to 303. The church responded to this shortage in two ways. In 1978, the same year as the General Synod decision about the ordination of women, the English bishops issued a call for an increase of men for ordination; a letter was sent to clergy and laity by the bishops asking for renewed efforts in fostering vocations. The bishops also agreed that money and energy needed to be committed to ensure that the existing number of theological colleges for their training be maintained.[55]

At the same time that the church rejected the ordination of women, it was aggressively promoting vocations among men in the face of a severe clerical labour shortage. The message in the rejection of women is all the more clear. The laity who appear to have been very supportive of the ordination of women at the diocesan level are the group most directly affected by the clerical labour shortage. The clergy as a group were most opposed. They had the most too lose if the labour pool became too large and competitive. In interview, several deaconesses commented that they felt that the men were afraid of competition, afraid that their own jobs might be jeopardized if women were granted access to the clergy labour pool.

THE WOMEN THEMSELVES

Who were these women about whom this debate was being waged, and who threatened to change the balance of power in ministry by their presence? As we saw in Chapter 5 women workers and deaconesses had demonstrated their competence in ministry for decades in the Church of England. They had traditionally been a small group of dedicated church workers who, for the most part, perceived themselves to be in diaconal orders. They were part of a numerically declining component in a numerically declining church. Tables 10 through 19 graphically depict this steady decline of deaconesses as a percentage of the church's labour force and of the segment of that labour force comprised of women between 1920 and 1978. By 1970, the Deaconess Order in England had greatly declined. It had closed all but one of its deaconess training centres as it no longer had the vocations or the money to continue to operate several different centres. By 1970, virtually all English theological colleges were open to women and the need for separate theological education and training was not necessary. Ironically those women who sought a theological education were still being prepared for a ghetto of women's employment within the church, a ghetto historically plagued with employment difficulties such as low status, inferior wages, the need for standardized training and a regularized pension plan.

The ghetto image accurately depicts the exclusion of deaconesses and other women workers from full participation in the life and ministry of the church. The ghetto label, however, puts a particular spin on the situation which was not fully reflective of the situation. A former Head Deaconess talked about the ghetto differently. She talked of the secret walled garden of the life and work of the deaconess. She talked of the beauty of the contribution which women made to the life of the church which the church had failed to embrace. This wall enclosed the women in a sphere of their own, clearly marking the limits of their involvement in the life of their church. As much as those limits had inhibited the full participation of women, they had deprived the church itself. With the wall erected, the hierarchy of the church was unable to walk in the garden and see its beauty. It had cut itself off from the richness which women as deaconesses and lay workers brought to ministry.

As a group the deaconesses were uninvolved in the formal decision-making process, which culminated in the General Synod debate of 1978. Uninvolved that is, except in so far as they were doing the work of ministry in parishes where people had a chance to benefit from their gifts and dedication. Although women as deaconesses were not overtly involved in the decision-making process, it is clear that they were watching the actions of the church closely. As Table 16 demonstrates, between 1976 and 1978, the numbers of deaconesses jumped by 48 percent. This was unprecedented in deaconess history. It was thought among deaconess circles that after 1978 the path for deaconesses to make the journey to priesthood would be open and thus vocations to the office grew.

As a group the deaconesses interviewed shared their commitment to the idea that their work of ministry was a vocation; any move to be ordained as priests should and would only happen because of God's call, and not because of equal rights. In other words, as a group the deaconesses were virtually unanimous in their rejection of feminism; their desire was simply to be faithful stewards for God. In this respect then, they resembled their Canadian sisters and were dissimilar to their English lay sisters who lobbied for the ordination of women on their behalf. Individuals connected with groups such as the AGOW readily identified their relationship to feminism as a positive thing.

The deaconesses both acted and were acted upon in this piece of their church's history. Perhaps their lack of pro-active involvement in the decision-making process influenced the outcome of the debate in 1978. The church's hierarchy had stressed for years that it felt no great need to act, because there were not large numbers of women clamouring at their doorstep demanding ordination.

MOW IS BORN

It took a brief time for lobby groups such as the AGOW to recover from the shock of defeat. The virtually inactive AGOW was rejuvenated with a much more focused and even outraged energy after the 1978 defeat. It was from that energy that the Movement for the Ordination of Women (MOW) was born. It was that group which was actively engaged in the full-time work of education and strategizing for the successful realization of women's ordination to the priesthood in the Church of England in 1994.

THE FAILED REVOLUTION

With the rejection of the motion to proceed with implementation of the ordination of women in 1978, the Church of England experienced something of a failed revolution. Through its synodical decision-making process, it failed to hear the cry of its own constituents for change, a cry which had been echoing in some corridors for decades. The cry was not proclaimed aggressively enough to be heard. Through the action of some clergy, the church preserved its role in the social structure as a hegemonic institution aligned with the ruling caste of a patriarchal structure which protected the values of a status quo which had named women as inferior for centuries at any cost, a cost paid by the broken dreams and vocations of women.

Endnotes

1. Report of the Methodist-Anglican Commission on *Women and Holy Orders, Women and the Ordained Ministry*, 1968, pp. 5–10.
2. Canterbury *Chronicle of Convocation*, 1973, p. 5.
3. Canterbury *Chronicle of Convocation*, 1973, p. 6.
4. York *Journal of Convocation*, 1973, p. 7.
5. York *Journal of Convocation*, 1973, p. 8.
6. Evening Post, 30 November 1972.
7. Antonio Gramsci, "Problems of History and Culture- The Intellectuals," in *Selections from the Prison Notebooks*, (New York: 1971) pp. 5–23.
8. John Savard, "Case Against the Ordination of Women," p. 4. (ACCM/PB/120)
9. Savard, p. 12.
10. Savard, p. 12.
11. Savard, p. 15.
12. Savard, p. 18.
13. Savard, p. 15.
14. E. L. Mascall, "Women Priests?" Church Lit. Association, (London: 1972), p. 12.
15. E. L. Mascall, p. 21.
16. "Women in the Priesthood?" Church Literature Association (1973) p. 8.
17. "Women in the Priesthood?" pp. 10–11.
18. "Women in the Priesthood?" p. 13.
19. Guardian, 10.10.72.
20. Paul Welsby, *A History of the Church of England, 1945–1980* (Oxford: 1981), pp. 208–209.
21. Church Times, 14.3.78; Yorkshire Post, 22.5.78.
22 The Anglo–Catholics were predominantly opposed to the ordination of women because of ecumenical issues and because they thought that a woman could not adequately represent the male Christ. The Evangelical opposition was grounded in the *kephale* or headship argument, a women cannot exercise authority over a man. Both Evangelicals and Anglo–Catholics argued against women in the priesthood because of their 'womanness'.
23. Yorkshire Post, 22.5.78.

24. Daily Mail, 17.12.17.
25. British Weekly, 16.2.78.
26. G.S. *Report of Proceedings*, July 1973, pp. 534–550.
27. G.S. *Report of Proceedings*, July 1973, p. 550.
28. G.S. *Report of Proceedings*, July 1973, (motion 2), p. 551.
29. SWMC Newsletter, July 1974.
30. SWMC Newsletter, January, 1975.
31. SWMC Newsletter, January 1975.
32. SWMC Newsletter, July 1974.
33. SWMC Newsletter, January 1975.
34. GS 252, p. 2.
35. GS 252, p. 4.
36. SWMC Newsletter, July 1975.
37. G.S. *Report of Proceedings*, July 1973, p. 556.
38. G.S. *Report of Proceedings*, July, 1975, p. 556.
39. G.S. *Report of Proceedings*, 1975, p. 561.
40. G.S. *Report of Proceedings*, 1975, p. 573.
41. G.S. *Report of Proceedings*, 1975, p. 577.
42. G.S. *Report of Proceedings*, 1975, p. 580.
43. G.S. *Report of Proceedings*, 1975, p. 592.
44. G.S. *Report of Proceedings*, 1975, p. 598.
45. G.S. *Report of Proceedings*, November 1978, p. 1070.
46. GS Misc. 87.
47. GS Misc. 87.
48. For example, the Reverend Broadhurst (London) G.S., *Report of Proceedings*, November 1978, pp. 1044–6.
49. G.S. *Report of Proceedings*, 1978, p. 1081.
50. Oral history interview with Archbishop Donald Coggan, 12 May, 1991.
51. Layman, Dr. Stanley Heatheate, a personal commentary, Daily Telegraph, November 21, 1978.
52. GS Misc. 86—"The Ordination of Women: Report of the Anglican/Orthodox Joint Doctrinal Commission," p. 7.
53. GS Misc. 88.
54. GS Misc. 53.
55 . Paul Welsby, *A History of the Church of England 1945–1980* (Oxford: 1983), pp. 208–9.

PART FOUR
COMPARISON AND
CONCLUSION

7

Autonomy in Relationship

The issue of the ordination of women to the priesthood in both the Anglican Church of Canada and the Church of England was addressed in the context of the larger Anglican Communion, and in its turn the Anglican Communion addressed the question as part of a global multi-denominational religion. All Christian denominations were affected to varying degrees by the women's suffrage movement, changing theology in the modern era and the professionalization of women's labour in the churches. Similarly, virtually all, with the possible exception of the Orthodox and Old Catholic churches, were affected in some measure by the cross-denominational, but unorganized and formally unrelated movement for the equality and ordination of women.

Anglicans as a Communion came to the issue of the ordination of women after most Protestant churches and before most of the episcopal branches of Christianity. This place between Protestant and episcopal traditions is not surprising as Anglicans have historically identified themselves as the *via media* between Protestantism and Roman Catholicism.

Some Protestant denominations have never denied the possibility of women being ordained ministers. At different points in history there have been women of the Baptist, Methodist, Episcopal, Methodist Protestant and Pentecostalist persuasion leading congregations, not to mention the women who preached and led worship among the Quakers. These women were atypical, however, and their activity the result of individual achievements. They were not representative of the usual practice of their denominations. The turning point was the beginning of the twentieth century when the movement for women's suffrage in Western European and North American society, debates over the place and role of women in society, the activity and influence of women in missionary societies and the professionalization of the Christian community generally gave rise to movements for the ordination of women in many Protestant churches.

A common progressive pattern was followed throughout Protestantism. Under different titles all denominations began to develop roles for women in the arena of paid labour. These jobs did not revolutionize women's sphere, but rather adopted and incorporated 'proper' ideas of what women could do at home into the ecclesiastical arena. In 1910 in Kaiserworth, Germany, a Deaconess Conference was held which attracted over 20,000 deaconesses from Protestant denominations. As early as 1919, an Association of Women Preachers was formed in America.[1] Simultaneously paid women workers and ordained women in some denominations became a part of Protestant church life. Before denominations were able to agree to ordain women, most had to struggle with questions of the admissibility of women to all levels of church life. For example, the enfranchisement of women in society was paralleled by the enfranchisement of women in some denominations. Anglicans generally took longer to settle these questions of equality. It is not surprising that in many cases they are taking longer than their Protestant brothers and sisters to settle questions of ordination. In any case, the Anglicans look progressive compared to the Roman Catholic and Orthodox churches as they forge ahead into this disputed territory, although those churches might not use the word progressive to describe Anglican initiatives in this matter. As an episcopal tradition Anglicans have had a greater number of stumbling blocks to overcome on this issue than those of the Protestant tradition. On a sacramental model, the maleness of Christ, and the priest as the icon of Christ has been, and remains problematic for many.

The relationship between Anglicanism and the larger Christian community on this issue is clear. The ordination of women question was affecting all churches from the later nineteenth century onward. The Church of England, as mother of the Anglican Communion was immediately aware of this issue which was affecting so many other churches. The awareness in the Canadian case seems to have come later. Nonetheless the whole question was raised for Anglicans generally because of what was happening in the larger context of Christianity and society across the board.

The Anglican Communion itself was also influential in the timing of the discussion of this issue. In the case of the Anglican Church of Canada, it was directly determinative in so far as the Canadian Church did not raise the issue in its synods until after the Lambeth Conference of 1968 had asked it to form an opinion on the subject. Interestingly, the Lambeth Conference of 1968 was also directly determinative in the Church of England case. It was not until after that event, that the Church of England formally debated the ordination of women to the priesthood as an issue about which it would make a decision. Unlike the Canadian situation, however, the English ecclesiastical structure had been aware of this issue since the 1920s. The Archbishop's Commission on women discussed the matter and formed an opinion on it as early as 1935. What changed after Lambeth 1968 was that the Church of England struggled to make a decision on the issue by due process through its General Synod. The influence of Lambeth pushed the issue onto the agenda of the General Synod as it did in the Canadian case. This was something that the work of small lobby groups and individuals had been unable to do through fifty years of effort.

In both national churches, a decision was made about the ordination of women to the priesthood because of the ecumenical climate of the twentieth century and because of the initiative of the Lambeth Conference in 1968 and subsequent meeting of the Anglican Consultative Council in 1971. The decision-making processes of both groups were influenced by factors which were beyond their own immediate frame of reference.

Over the years those who had opposed the ordination of women to the priesthood have said that to ordain women as priests would be a revolution. Those who said these words were right. The admission of women to the presbyterate is a radical break with the Christian tradition, at least as it was developed as an institution from the second century onward. The ordination of women represents a radical break in the tradition which has denied women their heritage as full human beings made in the image of God. It represents a break in the established tradition of exclusion which Christendom accepted as norm for centuries, and a return to the mutual model of relationship between men and women which was embodied in the life and work of Jesus.

This revolution has been unfolding in Christianity for over a century and has called successive denominations and churches home to a redeeming model of covenant love and ministry. Although the coming of the ordination of women certainly does not represent the full coming of the way of God, in some small measure it reflects the heart of that way and anticipates the renewal of all relationships in its image. On the journey, some churches have rejected it, holding tight to the bulwark of established tradition.

The model of successful and failed revolution is directly applicable to the decision-making processes of the two national churches. The Anglican Church of Canada, however unaware it was at the time, experienced a revolution in the mid-1970s which changed the reality of its structures in a way which only future historians will be able to measure. The Church of England on the other had an attempted revolution, a coup d'état, if you will, but as a revolution it initially failed. The success and failure of these revolutions provide the answer to the WHY questions with which we began.

The Anglican Church of Canada had a revolution, an overturning of a long established order, because all of the conditions requisite for such a revolution were in place. It had in its Primate and many of its bishops, a leadership, an organic intellectual class which had a vision for change that it worked aggressively to promote and to implement, the ordination of women as priests. It was successful in its efforts because its vision was sufficiently rooted in the interests of the grassroots of its constituency that it was accepted, or at very least not opposed, by those who were most affected by the change. Finally, it had adequate support and insufficient opposition to stop its movement toward change. Although there was opposition among bishops, clergy and laity, that opposition was largely unorganized and was not substantial enough to stop the tide of the revolution. The constitutional structure of the church was hospitable to this revolutionary change in so far as it required only a change in attitude rather than a change in legislation at the national level.

The circumstances in the Church of England were such that the attempted revolution failed at the time. There was a large groundswell of support for the ordination of women among the laity in the mid-1970s. Indeed, the laity in small numbers had worked for the promotion of this issue for almost sixty years when the General Synod debate of 1978 was held. Although after 1968 there were a larger number of bishops and clergy who did support the ordination of women, there was no organized or concerted effort on the part of the formal intellectual elite of the church to promote the cause with sufficient force to pass the 1978 motion. There was a leadership vacuum on the affirmative side of this debate. It was well into the 1980s before the House of Bishops began to publicly comment as a group on this issue.

Into the leadership vacuum stepped a strong opposition led largely by some clergy who loudly made their views known and who wanted to maintain the *status quo* of tradition. One sees virtually no comment in the press or in document from those clergy who supported the ordination of women in the 1970s. Some clergy functioned as a traditional intellectual class whose interests were closely allied to the patriarchal tradition of the status quo which it had inherited. These clergy actively promoted the retention of tradition and rejected a theological revolution as detrimental to the health of the church. The opposition was able to make concrete its objections through the due process of the Constitution of the church which demanded a majority in each house at the General Synod. The constitutional structure of the Church of England also reinforced the hesitation of many who were undecided when it demanded that the change regarding the ordination of women be not only a change of attitude but also a change of law, a more intimidating responsibility.

The church maintained its position as a hegemonic institution through the non-action of the episcopacy generally and the aggressive intervention of the opposing clergy. In a sense, the losers in the debate were the laity whose voice was not heard clearly at that point in history. The whole church suffered insofar as it retained its status as a bastion of patriarchal tradition which, at least on this issue, was unwilling to respond to the voice and the needs of the people.

Even though different decisions were reached in the 1970s in the Anglican Church of Canada and the Church of England there were aspects of their decision-making processes which were strikingly similar.

The role played by women who served the church as deaconesses and who in the Canadian case ultimately were ordained to the priesthood, was largely the same in the two cases examined. First, there was a relationship between deaconesses and the priesthood question. In both churches there were a relatively small and declining number of women who served their churches as deaconesses. In both places during the first stage these women worked in a feminine ghetto. The accepted place of women in the domestic sphere, with women and children in a background or supportive role, defined their work, and for their labours they were underpaid, under-recognized and under-appreciated. They suffered from inadequate salaries, pension plans and status. In both national churches there was debate over the nature of their orders and a certain inability to resolve the problems associated with their ghettoization. It is also true that most of the women in both countries, as represented by the oral history sample, did not identify themselves as feminists and were not actively involved in the decision-making process regarding the ordination of women question. Some in both churches were opposed to the idea of women in the priesthood, as demonstrated in the Canadian case by some of those women who chose not to become priests when the opportunity arose. This lack of involvement in ecclesiastical politics for most deaconesses did not mean that these women had no sense of vocation to priesthood. Again, in both churches some did and some did not feel called to the priesthood during the years that the church debated the issue.

In both national churches, the women themselves, the deaconesses, were *acted upon* in so far as the decisions about their lives were made without their direct input or involvement. They were *actors* in so far as they were the tangible reality which would be most personally affected by the decision which each church made. In both cases the life and work of the deaconesses did not directly determine the outcome of the decision-making processes. In the Canadian case, the history of these women and their contributions in the church offered concrete evidence of their vocation. Canadians say that this contribution was valued and opened the door to the acceptance of the ordination of women. But where does such a claim leave the deaconesses in England? They too had served their church faithfully and well, and were denied ordination to the priesthood. What can be said is that the voting figures from the diocesan synods seem to indicate that their contributions were valued by the laity of the church, but in the end did not serve as convincing validation of arguments for the ordination of women among their clergy peers. This had nothing to do with the women, and everything to do with the structures and prejudice of the system in which the women lived.

The point of separation between the two national groups of deaconesses only came with the actual decisions. After the Anglican Church of Canada decided to ordain women, most deaconesses became priests. After the Church of England decided not to ordain women, they remained deaconesses, labouring to serve their church within the context of subordination which was defined for them by the General Synod decision.

A further striking parallel between the two countries are the arguments for and against the ordination of women. In both churches those who argued for the ordination of women had embraced a feminist-based model of incarnational theology which celebrated the redeemed humanity of Jesus rather than the maleness of Jesus as a criteria for priesthood. The opposition in both countries focused on the same issues. Women could not be priests because they were women and, therefore, could not be the icon of Christ, nor could they have authority over men; in a hierarchical system such as the Anglican church, the priest is placed in authority over his/her congregation.

In both national churches, there were individuals who had been influenced by the changing times in society and theology which advocated a new and redeemed place for women. In Canada and England people argued that the place of women in society had changed and that it was time for the church to reflect a new understanding of the person and place of women. There were people in both places who demanded that the traditional sphere of women be opened up so that women might pursue their vocations in ways which did not limit or obstruct the action of God in the world. The difference between the two cases was that in Canada, this view was primarily promoted for a relatively short period of time by the Primate and other people with power, as it is traditionally understood. In the Church of England, the people who primarily promoted this view had been around for a much longer period of time, but they were not those who held official power.

In both national churches there were individuals who claimed the legacy of traditional patriarchal theology, with the attendant subordination of women as its inalienable birth rite. As such, the discussions and reports in the second stage are strikingly similar. What is different is the force of the opposition in England. The structural realities of the church meant that a strong opposition was able to block the change which much of the church was asking for. It organized and acted before the General Synod made a decision. In Canada, the opposition never organized to the same extent, and then only after the fact. The *Manifesto* in Canada was not written until after the motions had passed in the General Synod. By then it was too late for the opposition to have any real effect.

In both churches, the focus of the opposition was the clergy. In the Anglican Church of Canada there was not a clergy shortage and in the Church of England there was. In the Canadian case, women as priests were accepted, and in the English case they were rejected. This says two things. First, accepting the ordination of women as priests was not a stop-gap measure to fill empty altars. Second, in both churches there is some evidence that it was a labour issue in some sense. In Canada, long-term problems with women's paid employment in the church were solved with the ordination of women. In the English church, the force of a clergy who did not want to share the altar with women pre-empted any possibility that such a solution to the women's labour problem be found in England. In short, there were economic factors which may have influenced the two outcomes.

In both churches, the opposition cited ecumenical concerns as a prohibitive factor, a far greater concern in the English case. Indeed, in both churches those who were in favour of the ordination of women considered ecumenical concerns as well. The Anglican Church of Canada had some ecumenical dialogue on this issue, but very quickly decided that acting according to its own conscience was more important than any implications for ecumenical relations. There are some in the Church of England who have not accepted that premise even to this day.

The ordination of women to the priesthood is a twentieth century issue because we live in the twentieth century. Christianity has always lived in the midst of the chaos of the historical reality in which it finds itself. To bury our heads in the sand and fail to respond to the legitimate challenges of the age into which we have been born is the most unfaithful act of apostasy. In keeping with its twentieth century venue, the ordination of women is also a feminist issue. It directly concerns the basic acceptance or rejection of the fundamental equality of men and women. If one accepts that equality, structural barriers which limit and define human activity because of gender are not acceptable. That is not to say that those who have been concerned that the ordination of women would mean the co-option and perversion of women in a patriarchal system are not right. It also does not mean that equality means sameness, *vive la difference*. It does mean that none of those more complex issues and questions can be addressed or resolved until the basic right of a woman to have her vocation tested because of her humanity and not her sex is won.

Opposition to the ordination of women has some relationship to churchmanship in both churches. In the Anglican Church of Canada, it is difficult to measure that relationship except as has been done through interview and some assessment of the thinking of diocesan bishops. The relationship between churchmanship and opposition in the Church of England was much more overt. Ecclesiastical societies based on churchmanship lines openly declared war on the ordination issue. In both churches, Anglo-Catholics and Evangelicals were more generally inclined to oppose the issue than their broadstream counterparts.

The point of separation between the two decision-making processes with regard to churchmanship is in intensity and historicity. The Evangelicals and the Anglo-Catholics were recognized as actual measurable entities in the Church of England. They had a formal structure around which they could gather and act as a group in opposition. In Canada, the churchmanship orientation was a much more ephemeral thing. It was not a structural reality firmly entrenched in existing ecclesiastical life and, therefore, it did not serve as a point around which opposition could organize.

Both churches exist as part of the superstructure of their societies. In both countries the Anglican church has served as a hegemonic institution which reinforces the status quo or the normative values of a pseudo-Christian society. The point of separation on this issue lies in the fact that the influence of the Anglican Church in Canada has declined relative to the existing political power structures of the country. There is no longer a measurable family compact. Anglicanism in Canada is no longer the established religion of the country. As such it has greater freedom to go its own way without any ramifications from the political structure. The Church of England, on the other hand, is an established church which is more directly a pillar of the social order of English society. As patriarchy is the established social norm in both countries, the role of church as guardian of the status quo may have played some part in the unfolding drama. There is not convincing evidence that this establishment or lack of it, as in the Canadian case, had any direct impact on the ordination debates. It is, however, one of those points of difference which might conceivably have influenced the attitudes and values of individuals and as such it needs to be mentioned.

In keeping with a long Anglican tradition, the ordination of women to the priesthood was both a related and an autonomous issue in the Anglican Church of Canada and the Church of England. It was an issue which came to life in relation to changes in the societies and churches of western Christianity in the twentieth century. It came to life vividly in both churches because the larger body of its sister churches asked that it be discussed. The ordination of women to the priesthood was an autonomous event in so far as each national church had to make its own decision about what it wanted for its future. Ultimately internal structural realities were the determinative factor in differing outcomes from similar processes. This finding may serve as a paradigm for the rest of the Anglican Communion or indeed for other denominations as they struggle to resolve this issue for themselves, in relationship to the larger body of Christ. Unity in diversity, and autonomy in relationship—these are the words which best describe the parallel decision-making processes which have been examined here.

Endnotes

1. Sarah Maitland, *A Map of the New Country: Women and Christianity*, London, 1973, p. 86.

Afterword:
Moving toward the Future

While the Lambeth Conference of 1968 did not and could not make a universal decision on the ordination of women to the priesthood, its invitation to study the question opened a door. This door continues to open more and more widely. A gradual movement toward the ordination of women as priests began in 1968, and, one by one, churches have moved to adopt such ordinations, at least in principle. There has been no backward movement. Over the years in various debates individuals referred repeatedly to the Gamaliel principle: if it is not of God, it will fail; if it is of God, nothing can stop it. Nothing has stopped the ordination of women. Rather, province after province in the Anglican Communion has approved and implemented such ordinations.

The Anglican Worldwide Communications office in London, England released a report in June, 1992 which listed those countries which then ordained women to the priesthood and the numbers of women they had ordained to the priesthood (Table 20). As Table 20 demonstrates as, of June, 1992, 14 countries in the Anglican Communion ordained women. The report records a total number of 1,379 women serving the church as priests, 11.5 percent of whom are in Canada. In other words, 51 percent of the Communion had implemented the ordination of women to the priesthood. When the Lambeth Conference met in 1968, the issue had not even been discussed in most of those churches. 24 years later, they are experiencing the hands-on ministry of ordained women.

Five months after the Communications office issued this report, the General Synod of the Church of England passed a motion asking the standing Committee to prepare and bring forward legislation which would allow for the ordination of women to the priesthood. At the end of November that same year, the General Synod of the Anglican Church of Australia also approved legislation allowing women as priests in that church. That legislation passed after a lengthy battle of 15 years, five synods, two civil court actions and a church court decision. Four times since 1985, synods failed to pass legislation allowing women in the priesthood, although it approved women as deacons in 1977.[1]

During that same 24 years, two national churches, including three dioceses, elected women to the episcopacy. Barbara Harris was consecrated suffragan bishop of the diocese of Massachusetts, U.S.A. on 11 February 1989. Penelope Jamieson was consecrated as the diocesan bishop of Dunedin, New Zealand, on 29 June 1990, and Jane Dixon was consecrated suffragan bishop of the diocese of Washington on 19 November 1992. Victoria Matthews was consecrated as suffragan bishop of Toronto on 12 February, 1994.

The question of the ordination of women to the episcopate has been treated as a separate issue from the ordination of women to the priesthood. At the Lambeth Conference of 1978, the motion responding to women in the priesthood included reference to women in the episcopate. Some saw that as an even more potentially divisive issue. As such, the Lambeth Conference of 1988 discussed women in the episcopacy and made several resolutions on that issue. Lambeth resolved that each province should respect the decision and attitudes of other provinces on the ordination and consecration of women to the episcopate, that bishops should exercise courtesy and maintain communications with bishops who may differ, and that a commission should be appointed by the Archbishop of Canterbury to study the matter further. Lambeth suggested that the unity of the Communion, provinces and dioceses was the primary consideration and whatever steps necessary to ensure that unity should be taken. Finally, it admonished the church to exercise pastoral sensitivity and patience toward all concerned in the matter.[2]

An international commission was appointed by the Archbishop of Canterbury. It produced a report for the church in 1989. In that report, the commission said that it:

Reaffirms its unity in the historical position of respect for dioc-

esan boundaries and the authority of bishops within these
boundaries; and in light of the above affirms that it is deemed
inappropriate behaviour for any bishop or priest of this Communion to exercise episcopal or pastoral ministry within another
diocese without first obtaining the permission and invitation of
the ecclesial authority thereof.[3]

In conclusion, the commission admonished all provinces and individuals to remain in relationship committed to unity despite obvious differences of opinion and practice on the issue toward the end of deeper
koinonia in the Communion.[4]

ANGLICAN CHURCH OF CANADA

As in the larger Communion, there has been no turning back for the
Anglican Church of Canada. Although it took fifteen years, eventually
every diocese in the Canadian church accepted and implemented the
ordination of women to the priesthood. Table 22 shows the timeline of
these ordinations. Beginning after the first 18 ordinations discussed in
the main body of this study, this table traces the journey of the Anglican
Church of Canada, by diocese, showing in chronological order the first
ordinations of women to the priesthood in each of the remaining 20
dioceses.

Table 22 confirms the notion that there was no regional relationship
in this issue. The timeline shows that dioceses all over the country ran-
domly ordained women with no specific concentration in one part of the
country at any given time. The table also reinforces our stress on the
importance of episcopal leadership. After the first ordinations, following
almost immediately after the Lambeth Conference of 1978, the ordination of women in each diocese (in most cases) did not occur until bishops who had maintained opposition had retired and been replaced by a
bishop with a different attitude on the issue.

The only significant issue left to resolve at the national level after
1978 was the issue of the Conscience Clause. In May, 1982, the synod of
the diocese of Athabasca asked the church to reconsider the Conscience
Clause. In response, the National Executive Council, the chief administrative committee of the national church, appointed a task force to review the operation of the Conscience Clause. That task force came back
with the following recommendation:

We recognize and affirm the continuing validity of the Conscience Clause for those who belonged to the Anglican Church of Canada at the time it was passed. While continuing to recognize the rights of individual consciences, we believe that those who now come to membership in our Church must recognize and accept that the ministry of women priests must also be protected conscientiously as the expressed will of our Church. Christian charity cannot be legislated, but needs to be implemented more effectively in the future than in the past in order to realize the community which belongs in the Body of Christ.[5]

At the recommendation of the National Executive, the General Synod discussed the Conscience Clause the following year. A motion to approve the above statement was defeated. A motion was presented which stated that the Conscience Clause should continue in effect. Several amendments were proposed to the motion. One of these added the hope that the Synod looked forward to the day when the Conscience Clause could be dropped. That amendment was defeated by the House of Bishops. Ultimately the General Synod of 1983 passed a somewhat amended motion which stated that the Conscience Clause should be maintained.[6]

Three years later at the General Synod of 1986, the Conscience Clause was rescinded. Two clergy wrote a motion that the clause be rescinded and replaced by a position statement. Ultimately, that motion was carried in amended form but not before several proposed amendments had failed. Among them was a motion that the position statement apply only to those henceforth entering the ordained ministry. That amendment was defeated, and ultimately a position statement was adopted for the whole church. It read as follows:

That subject to the continued applicability of the 1975 Conscience Clause to those who have heretofore availed themselves of its provisions regarding ordination, this General Synod rescind the Conscience Clause and adopt the following position statement: this General Synod reaffirm its acceptance of ordination of women to the priesthood; no action which questions the integrity of any priest or postulant on the grounds of sex alone can be defended; this General Synod honours all priests, upholds them in its prayers and desires that God's will may be done in and through all priests regardless of sex; while Christian love cannot be legislated, it needs to be practised and demonstrated in the Body of Christ.[7]

With the passage of this motion, the General Synod put to rest all doubt about the acceptance of women in the priesthood in the Anglican Church of Canada. By June of 1991, all dioceses of the Canadian church had echoed that acceptance through the reception of the ministry of ordained women in their churches.

The full admission of women to the three-fold order of the ministry in the Canadian church was realized with the consecration of the Reverend Victoria Matthews to the episcopacy on 12 February 1994. Victoria Matthews was the first woman to be elected to the office of bishop in the Anglican Church of Canada. A synod of the Diocese of Toronto elected her as one of its suffragan bishops on 19 November 1993.

CHURCH OF ENGLAND

The 1978 decision by the General Synod not to accept women as priests was not the end of the story. In a very real sense, it was just the beginning. The 1978 rejection of the proposed legislation to allow women in the priesthood served as a catalyst for a much more aggressive lobby toward that ultimate end. The AGOW transformed itself into the Movement for the Ordination of Women (MOW). MOW, with a full-time staff, became a much more formidable opponent to the anti-ordination lobbyists than its predecessor had been. The opposition also continued to gather strength consolidating on two fronts, the Cost of Conscience clergy organization, and Women Against the Ordination of Women (WOW), a group of lay women who rejected the idea of women in the priesthood. The journey from 1978 to the decision of the General Synod on 11 November 1992 to prepare the way for women as priests, was a long and tumultuous one for both sides.

After six years of aggressive lobbying on the part of MOW, those who supported the ordination of women were successful in their attempts to get proposed legislation back on the agenda for Synod. Six years after the 1978 defeat of a motion, the General Synod of 1984 passed a motion asking the Standing Committee to bring forward legislation to permit the ordination of women to the priesthood. That was the first stage in a legislative process which culminated in the success of 11 November 1992, and the first actual ordinations of women to the priesthood 12 March 1994.

While the 1984 motion was being voted on in diocesan synods, the General Synod focussed its attention on related but distinct issues. In 1985, the Synod passed final legislation enabling women to be ordained as deacons. That success was preceded by the other necessary stages of the Church of England legislative process and culminated in the passage of the legislation by the English parliament in 1986, and the first reception of women in the diaconate in the Church of England in 1987. Interestingly, the women who were ordained deacons, as in the Canadian case, were those already serving the church as deaconesses. Not all deaconesses chose to be so received but all who wanted that option were given the opportunity. The number ordained to, or received in the diaconate on a full-time stipendiary basis was 439. There were many others who were non-stipendiary. The exact number of these was unrecorded. As of 1994, MOW estimated the number of women deacons at 1,300, but it was not possible to give an absolutely accurate account. Also in 1986, the General Synod failed to pass legislation allowing women ordained abroad to officiate in England. The whole ordination of women matter was then passed on to the House of Bishops for further study. In 1987, the General Synod passed draft legislation which included two measures at the request of the House of Bishops. The first measure enabled women to be ordained to the priesthood but not to the episcopacy, with safeguards written in for bishops and parishes opposed to the ordination of women. The second measure made a financial provision for relief of hardship for those resigning from ecclesiastical service because of opposition to the ordination of women. It was these two measures which were approved by the General Synod of 1992.

As a final measure, the requisite two-thirds majority in each house was required on 11 November 1992. That two-thirds majority was comfortably achieved in the House of Bishops and Clergy, but only barely in the House of Laity. The figures were: bishops, 39 for and 13 against; clergy, 176 for and 74 against; laity, 169 for and 82 against.[8] With the passage of this legislation, financial compensation for opposing clergy who planned to leave the Church of England was also guaranteed. Before the ordination of women to the priesthood could be implemented, the legislation had to be passed by Parliament.

The period between 1978 and 1994 was characterized by often dramatic and public debate on this issue. The English press focused on the conflict, making dire predictions of a drastic schism in the Church of England. The Movement for the Ordination of Women maintained throughout that, while the opposition was vocal and publicized, it did not represent the mind of the church at large. After the results of the vote were announced, the press reported that it had sources which placed the number of opposing clergy at 3,500.[9] Prior to the vote, MOW placed the figure at 1,000. Prior to the vote, they stressed that their major fear, however, was not the clergy but the laity. It was not that most lay people were opposed. History demonstrated quite the opposite. As a lobby group, however, MOW had failed to pay as close attention as it might have to that group, feeling confident of its support. That left more room for the political manoeuvring of the opposition among that group as delegates for the Synod were selected at the diocesan level.

When legislation successfully passed in the Church of England, it was led by a man who actively promoted the ordination of women. After the November vote Archbishop of Canterbury George Carey said, "I would have doubted my own leadership abilities if the Synod had not voted in favour of women priests."[10] The successful legislation had also been brought by the House of Bishops who, in the 1980s, themselves actively assumed an initiatory role in the debates.

The ordination of women to the priesthood and the episcopate is here to stay in Anglicanism. Perhaps what is happening in the Anglican Communion will be also a harbinger of what is to come in other parts of Christendom. We see in this story Anglican participation in transformation. Beyond the rigid demarcation of men and women into separate spheres of labour because of gender, lies a whole new world. Beyond the walled garden, there is the promise of a new era of healing mutuality in the work of servant discipleship. Beyond the walled garden, there is hope that women and men can together celebrate the intrinsic beauty of shared vocations. There, in that new land of promise, is the potential for life.

Endnotes

1. *Anglican Journal*, 119, no. 1 (Jan. 1993), p. 1.
2. Report of the Archbishop of Canterbury's Commission on Communion and Women in the Episcopate, ACC, 1989, p. 5.
3. Archbishop's Commission, 1989, p. 25.
4. Archbishop's Commission, 1989, p. 29.
5. Minutes of the National Executive Council, November, 1982, pp. 2, 8, 27.

6.   G.S. *Journal of Proceedings*, 1983, GSA83, pp. 30-38.
7.   G.S. *Journal of Proceedings*, 1986, pp. 114-117.
8.   *Anglican Journal*, 118, no. 10 (December 1992), p. 1.
9.   *The Independent* 12/11,92.
10. *Sunday Times*, 15/11/92.

APPENDIX
REFERENCE TABLES
&
BIBLIOGRAPHY

Table 1: Ordination of Women — In Global Perspective — August 1970

	Africa		Asia		Australia		West Europe		East Europe		North America		Latin America		Totals	
	Do	Do Not	Do	Do Not	Do	Do Not	Do	Do Not	Do	Do Not	Do	Do Not	Do	Do Not	Do	Do Not
Anglicans		5		3		2		4				2		2		18
Baptist	1	1		3	1*		1	1		1	2	2			4+1*	8
Congregational		2		1u	3*	1u	4				2				5+3*	2
Disciples	1			1	2		1				2				6	1
Independent		1		1												22
Lutheran		4		2			6	4	3	6	1			2	10	10
Methodist	1	3/1p	1	1	2		1*	2			3	1		3	7+1*	10
Pentecostal														2		2
Old Catholic								4		2		1				7
East Orthodox		1		2				3		7		3				16
Orient. Orthodox		2		4						1		1				8
Reformed	1	10	5	11/3u	1	4	11	3	2	2/1p	2	3	1		23	33
Roman Catholic																
United	2	2	2	5			1	2	1	1	1+2*	2	1	1u	7	12
Others		2					2	2		p			2*	1u	3+2*	4
Totals	6	33	8	33	9	6	27	25	6	20	15	15	1	11	72	143

* = in principle but not yet in practice   u = unknown at time of completion   p = probable

Source: figures provided by a study on ordination of women by World Council of Churches, 1970

Table 2: Numbers of Women in Paid Labour and Active Clergy in the Anglican Church of Canada in 1947

Type of Work	Number	Relative Proportion (%)
Ordained Women	0	0
Deaconesses	42	17
Chaplains' Assistant	2	1
Female Religious	43	17
Home and Overseas Missionaries	40	16
Other Church Workers	120	49
TOTAL	247	100
CLERGY	1780	
Women as a % of the Church's paid labour force		13.4

Source: *These estimated figures on women's work have been compiled from the* Canadian Council of Churches Report on Women Workers, *1947 and oral history interviews. The clergy figure has been calculated from names recorded in the* Church of England in Canada Year Book, *1948.*

Table 3: Relative Proportion of Women in Paid Labour in the Church of England in Canada in 1947

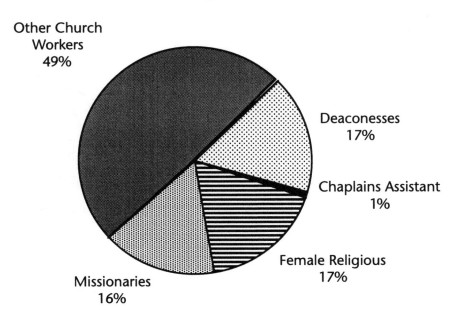

Other Church Workers 49%

Deaconesses 17%

Chaplains Assistant 1%

Female Religious 17%

Missionaries 16%

Table 4: Deaconesses in the Anglican Church of Canada
1961 – 1978

1961	28	1970	26
1962	30	1971	11
1963		1972	11
1964	32	1973	15
1965	26	1974	13
1966		1975	16
1967	29	1976	9
1968	23	1977	3 active (8)**
1969	15*	1978	4 active (7)

* move to diaconate, first one in 1969 and others the following year
** numbers in parentheses are total numbers including retired deaconesses

Source: Figures are taken from Anglican Church of Canada Year Book, 1961-1979

Table 5: Women as a percentage of the Canadian Labour Force
1921–1981

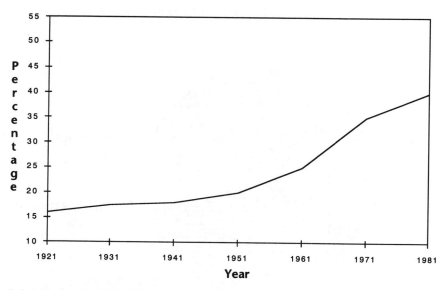

Excludes Newfoundland 1921–1961

Source: Based on F. H. Leacy, ed., Historical Statistics, 2nd ed. (Ottawa: Statistics Canada, 1983); Statscan Cat. 71-201, 1971 and 1981.

Table 6: Time Chart of the First Eighteen Ordinations of Women to the Priesthood in the Anglican Church of Canada 30 November 1976 to 31 December 1977

	Time	Women	Background	Diocese	Bishop
i.	30 November 1976	Patricia Reed	Social Worker, Deacon	Cariboo	John Snowden
	30 November 1976	Mary Mills	Deaconess, Deacon	Huron	David Ragg
	30 November 1976	Elspeth Alley	Housewife, Deacon	New Westminster	David Somerville
	30 November 1976	Virginia Bryant	Deaconess, Deacon	New Westminster	David Somerville
	30 November 1976	Mary Lucas	Student, Deacon	Niagara	John Bothwell
	30 November 1976	Beverley Shanley	Deaconess, Deacon	Niagara	John Bothwell
ii.	19 December 1976	Ina Caton	Deaconess, Deacon	Saskatoon	D. Ford
iii.	6 January 1977	Kathleen Hill	Bishop's Messenger	Brandon	John Conlin
	6 January 1977	Margery Keenon	Bishop's Messenger	Brandon	John Conlin
	6 January 1977	Joy Ruddock	Bishop's Messenger	Brandon	John Conlin
	6 January 1977	Thelma Tanner	Bishop's Messenger	Brandon	John Conlin
iv.	9 January 1977	Dorothy Daly	Deaconess, Deacon	Calendonia	Douglas Hambidge
v.	7 March 1977	Phyllis Locke	Deaconess, Deacon	Athabasca	Frederick Hugh Wright Crabb
	7 March 1977	Enid longwell	Deaconess, Deacon	Athabasca	Frederick Hugh Wright Crabb
vi.	25 April 1977	Virginia Lane	Office Admin., Deacon	Huron	Davis Ragg
vii.	22 May 1977	Margery Pezzack	Deaconess, Deacon	Toronto	Lewis Garnsworthy
viii.	5 June 1977	Ruth Matthews	Deaconess, Deacon	Quebec	A. Gooding
ix.	18 November 1977	Sr. Rosemary Anne Benwell	SSJD, Deaconess, Deacon	Toronto	Allan Reed

Table 7: Summary of Diocesan Decision-Making Processes
10 Categories, 1968–1978

No Mention of the Issue	Bishop & Synod in Favour	Bishop in Favour Synod Undecided	Bishop Opposed and Undiscussed by Synod	Bishop Undecided & Synod Opposed
Artic British Columbia Calgary Eastern Newfoundland Keewatin Western Newfoundland	Algoma Athabasca Caledonia Cariboo Edmonton Huron Nova Scotia Rupert's Land Saskatoon Toronto	Brandon Montreal New Westminister	Kootenay Ontario Yukon	Frederiction Saskatchewan
Bishop & Synod Opposed	**Bishop Opposed & Synod in Favour**	**Bishop in Favour & Synod Opposed**	**Bishop Undecided & Synod in Favour**	**Bishop in Favour & Synod Passes Conscience Clause**
Moosonee	Ottawa Qu'Appelle	Quebec	Central Newfoundland Rupert's Land	Niagra

Table 8: Total Numbers of Authorized Women in Ministry in the Church of England, 1920–1939

	With District Visitors (unpaid)	Without District Visitors (paid)
1920	71332	2,263
1921	70,272	2,101
1922	67,984	2,052
1923	67,387	2,040
1924	67,558	2,026
1925	67,416	2,013
1926	67,379	1,996
1927	67,285	1,715
1928	66,063	1,890
1929	63,777	1,856
1930	62,899	1,845
1931	62,556	1,802
1932	62,446	1,769
1933	61,823	1,732
1934	61,818	1,704
1935	62,640	1,657
1936	61,700	1,573
1937	62,087	1,610
1938	61,367	1,589
1939	60,231	1,443

Source: Statistics compiled from Church of England Year Book, 1920–1940.

* figures include deaconesses, lay workers, Church Army Sisters, social workers and female religious, district vistors, and licensed women workers from 1937

Table 9: Total Numbers of Women in Paid Ministry in the Church of England, 1956–1978

(includes deaconesses, lay workers, church army sisters, social workers, and religious)

1956	1,449
1958	not available
1960	2,742
1962	3,058
1963/4	3,193
1965	3,444
1966	3,490
1967	3,105
1968	3,010
1969	2,686
1970	not available
1971	2,650
1972	2,638
1973	2,581
1974	2,537
1975	2,553
1976	2,380
1977	not available
1978	2,520

Source: Figures are taken from the Church of England Year Book, 1956–1980.

Table 10: Full-Time Paid Deaconesses in the Church of England 1920–1978

1920	387	1940–1955	*
1922	350	1959	119
1924	331	1961	109
1926	328	1963/4	80
1928	268	1966	78
1930	227	1968	78
1932	242	1971	78
1934	240	1973	97
1936	225	1975	85
1938	189	1978	144

Source: Statistics are compiled from the Church of England Year Book, 1920–1980.

*   No statistical record kept from 1956. A statistical supplement to the Church of England *Year Book* provides the information.

** From this point until 1939, paid and voluntary deaconesses are counted together.

Table 11: Percentage of Paid Women Workers Represented by Deaconesses, in the Church of England

1920	17.1%	1939	12.4%
1922	17.1%	1960	2.4%
1924	16.4%	1962	2.6%
1926	16.5%	1965	2.3%
1928	14.2%	1967	2.7%
1930	12.3%	1969	3.0%
1932	13.7%	1972	3.6%
1934	14.1%	1974	3.7%
1936	14.2%	1976	4.1%
1938	11.9%		

Source: Percentages are calculated from statistics in the Church of England Year Book, 1920–1979

Table 12: Total Number of Authorized (District Visitors — Voluntary, Others — Paid) Women in the Church of England

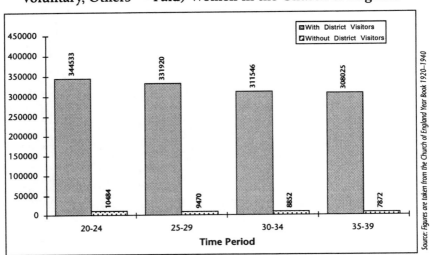

Source: Figures are taken from the Church of England Year Book 1920–1940

Figures include deaconesses, lay workers, Church Army Sisters, social workers, female religious district visitors.

Table 13:Total Number of Authorized Women in Ministry in the Church of England

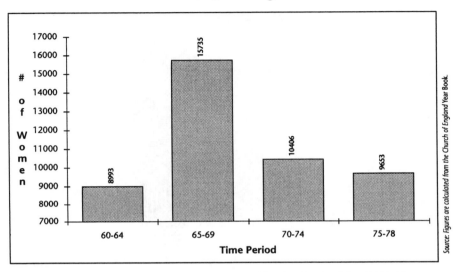

Figures include deaconesses, lay workers, Church Army Sisters, social workers, female religious district visitors.

Table 14: Percentage of Authorized Women Workers Represented by Deaconesses in the Church of England

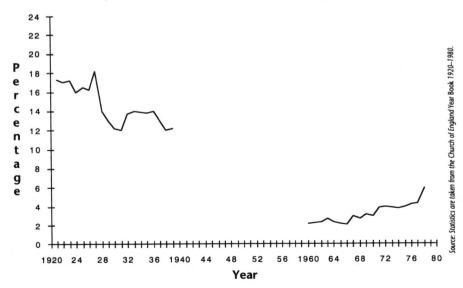

No data is available for the years 1940 through 1959.

Table 15: Women Workers and Deaconesses in the Church of England, 1978

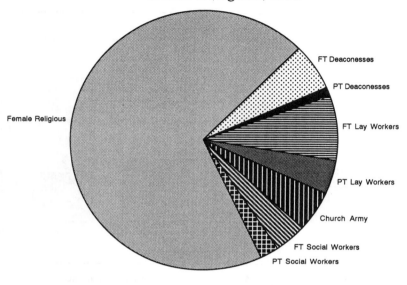

Source: Percentages are compiled from the Church of England Yearbook, 1980.

| FT Deaconesses | 6% | PT Deaconesses | 1% | FT Lay Workers | 8% | PT Lay Workers | 4% |
| Church Army | 5% | FT Social Workers | 4% | PT Social Workers | 2% | Female Religious | 69% |

FT stands for full-time and PT stands for part-time.

Table 16: Full-Time Paid Deaconesses in the Church of England 1920–1978

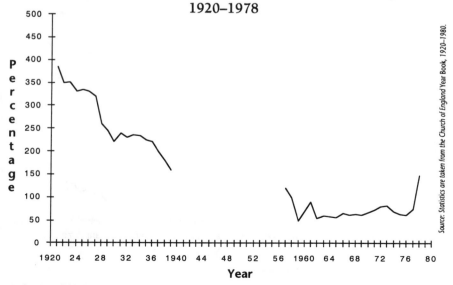

Source: Statistics are taken from the Church of England Year Book, 1920–1980.

No data is available for 1940–1955.

Table 17: Full-Time Paid Deaconesses in the Church of England 1920–1978

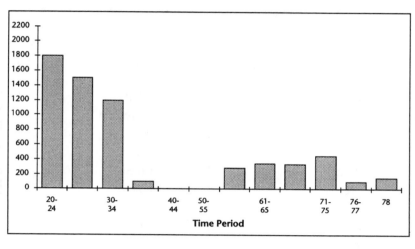

Source: Statistics are taken from the Church of England Year Book, 1920–1980.

No data is available for 1940–1955.

Table 18: Paid Women Workers and Deaconesses in the Church of England, 1978

Deaconesses	
Full time	144
Part time	35
Lay workers	
Full time	195
Part time	96
Church Army	127
Social workers	
Full time	101
Part time	45
Female religious	1,681
Female lay readers	487

Source: Figures are taken from the Church of England Year Book, 1979–1980.

Table 19: Full-Time Deaconesses in the Church of England in 1978, by Diocese

1.	Bath & Wells	0	23.	London	22
2.	Birmingham	2	24.	Manchester	3
3.	Blackburn	1	25.	Newcastle	0
4.	Bradford	0	26.	Norwich	4
5.	Bristol	4	27.	Oxford	4
6.	Canterbury	2	28.	Peterborough	0
7.	Carlisle	0	29.	Portsmouth	1
8.	Chelmsford	11	30.	Ripon	1
9.	Chester	3	31.	Rochester	1
10.	Chichester	3	32.	St. Albans	9
11.	Coventry	1	33.	St.Edms & Ipswich	0
12.	Derby	3	34.	Salisbury	1
13.	Durham	6	35.	Sheffield	2
14.	Ely	4	36.	Sodor & Man	0
15.	Exeter	3	37.	Southwark	23
16.	Gloucester	0	38.	Southwell	3
17.	Guildford	2	39.	Truro	0
18.	Hereford	0	40.	Wakefield	5
19.	Leicester	1	41.	Winchester	1
20.	Lichfield	4	42.	Worcester	4
21.	Lincoln	0	43.	York	4
22.	Liverpool	6			

Source: Statistics are taken from the Church of England Year Book, 1979–1980.

Table 20: Numbers of Women Currently Serving in the Priesthood in the Anglican Communion by June, 1992 (by Country)

Country	Number	% of Total Number
Australia	10	.73%
Burundi	2	.15%
Brazil	5	.35%
Canada	158	11.50%
Hong Kong and Macao	2	.15%
Ireland	7	.51%
Kenya	3	.22%
New Zealand	120	8.70%
North India	2	.15%
Philippines	1	.07%
South India	1	.07%
Uganda	36	2.60%
U.S.A.	1,031	74.80%
West Africa	1	.07%
Total	1,379	100.00%

Source: The figures in this table are calculated on the basis of information released by the Anglican Worldwide Communications office in London, England, June, 1992.

Table 21: Church of England Results of Diocesan Voting, 1973–1975

DIOCESE	1st Motion FOR	AGAINST	ABST.	2nd Motion FOR	AGAINST	ABST.	Amendment FOR	AGAINST	ABST.
1. CANTERBURY	CARRIED			CARRIED			LOST		
Archbishop	1			1			1		
Clergy	48	11	1	29	26	1	30	29	
Laity	46	1	1	35	19	1	22	35	1
2. YORK	CARRIED			CARRIED			LOST		
Archbishop	1			1			1		
Clergy	64	25	5	56	32	1	32	54	2
Laity	69	22		63	25		30	58	
3. LONDON	LOST								
Archbishop	1								
Clergy	56	82	3						
Laity	77	67	10						
4. DURHAM	CARRIED			LOST					
Bishop	1			1					
Clergy	43	37	2	39	41	1			
Laity	61	19	2	57	20	3			
5. WINCHESTER	CARRIED			LOST			LOST		
Bishop	1			1			1		
Clergy	46	35	2	30	35	2	41	30	2
Laity	45	21		45	21		21	44	1
6. BATH & WELLS	CARRIED			LOST			LOST		
Bishop	1				1		1		
Clergy	42	27	5	36	32	2	30	36	3
Laity	59	14	4	52	21		23	52	1
7. BIRMINGHAM	CARRIED			LOST			LOST		
Bishop	1				1		1		
Clergy	65	17	3	58	20	1	21	57	1
Laity	64	6	2	67	9	2	10	74	
8. BLACKBURN	LOST								
Bishop		1							
Clergy	38	40	1						
Laity	38	27	1						
9. BRADFORD	CARRIED			LOST			LOST		
Bishop	1			1			1		
Clergy	31	27	1	25	33		31	26	
Laity	36	15		31	19		16	35	

DIOCESE	1st Motion			2nd Motion			Ammendment		
	FOR	AGAINST	ABST.	FOR	AGAINST	ABST.	FOR	AGAINST	ABST.
10. BRISTOL	CARRIED			CARRIED			LOST		
Bishop	1			1				1	
Clergy	50	21		36	35		35	35	
Laity	49	27		41	35		35	40	
11. CARLISLE	CARRIED			LOST			LOST		
Bishop	1					1		1	
Clergy	47	33	2	36	39	1	41	36	
Laity	57	18	1	49	24		24	48	
12. CHELMSFORD	CARRIED			LOST			LOST		
Bishop	1			1				1	
Clergy	56	36		43	47		48	39	
Laity	52	39		39	47		53	40	
13. CHESTER	LOST								
Bishop		1							
Clergy	28	29							
Laity	7	22	5						
14. CHICHESTER	LOST			LOST					
Bishop		1			1				
Clergy	46	40		31	54				
Laity	62	28		54	36				
15. COVENTRY	CARRIED			CARRIED			LOST		
Bishop	1			1				1	
Clergy	29	18	3	30	20		20	28	
Laity	53	16	2	53	16	1	16	52	2
16. DERBY	CARRIED			LOST			LOST		
Bishop	1			1				1	
Clergy	35	32		30	36		35	29	
Laity	38	22	2	35	25	2	24	35	
17. ELY	LOST								
Bishop	1								
Clergy	29	34	3						
Laity	46	22	2						
18. EXETER	LOST			LOST					
Bishop									
Clergy	25	24		18	28	1			
Laity	46	13	1	44	18	2			

DIOCESE	1st Motion			2nd Motion			Amendment		
	FOR	AGAINST	ABST.	FOR	AGAINST	ABST.	FOR	AGAINST	ABST.
19. GLOUCESTER — LOST									
Bishop	1								
(Tewkesbury)									
Clergy	26	29							
Laity	51	22							
20. GUILDFORD — CARRIED / LOST / LOST									
Bishop	1				1				1
Clergy	51	20		34	43	1	43	33	
Laity	48	14	2	38	30	1	28	38	2
21. HEREFORD — CARRIED / LOST / LOST									
Bishop	1				1		1		
Clergy	43	23	1	33	28	2	28	35	2
Laity	56	16	2	56	18	3	16	50	1
22. LEICESTER — CARRIED / LOST									
Bishop	1				1				
Clergy	44	28	1	44	33	2			
Laity	49	19	1	53	19				
23. LICHFIELD — LOST / Voting on amended motion CARRIED									
Bishop		1		1			1		
Clergy	38	23	5	34	25	3	34	26	3
Laity	34	26	7	38	25	1	38	25	1
24. LINCOLN — CARRIED									
Bishop									
Clergy	135	25							
Laity									
25. LIVERPOOL — CARRIED / LOST / LOST									
Bishop	1			1				1	
Clergy	30	24		25	31		30	26	
Laity	40	19		38	22		23	36	
26. MANCHESTER — CARRIED / CARRIED / LOST									
Bishop	1			1				1	
Clergy	60	23	1	46	23	3	12	50	7
Laity	59	21	1	57	15		10	57	3
27. NEWCASTLE — CARRIED / LOST / LOST									
Bishop	1			1				1	
Clergy	31	26	1	18	37		32	21	
Laity	35	16		31	20		20	32	

DIOCESE	1st Motion			2nd Motion			Amendment		
	FOR	AGAINST	ABST.	FOR	AGAINST	ABST.	FOR	AGAINST	ABST.
28. NORWICH	LOST			LOST			LOST		
Bishop									
Clergy	65	34	2	56	36	3	39	58	3
Laity	60	20		56	25		23	54	4
29. OXFORD	CARRIED			CARRIED			LOST		
Bishop	1			1			1		
Clergy	43	24		38	21		21	37	
Laity	72	10		61	13		14	60	
30. PETERBOROUGH	LOST								
Bishop		1							
Clergy	25	45	1						
Laity	34	30							
31. PORTSMOUTH	CARRIED			CARRIED			LOST		
Bishop	1			1			1		
Clergy	35	9	2	35	13		9	35	1
Laity	40	9	3	40	15		12	40	
32. RIPON	CARRIED			LOST			LOST		
Bishop	1			1			1		
Clergy	35	32		24	40	1	40	25	
Laity	43	17	1	41	21	1	21	41	1
33. ROCHESTER	CARRIED			CARRIED			LOST		
Bishop	1			1			1		
Clergy	55	31	3	49	35	3	37	49	1
Laity	58	11	4	56	19	1	21	55	2
34. ST. ALBANS	CARRIED			LOST			LOST		
Bishop	1			1			1		
Clergy	45	25		36	35		36	35	
Laity	61	20		45	35		35	47	
35. ST. EDMUNDSBURY & IPSWICH	CARRIED			CARRIED			LOST		
Bishop	1			1					1
Clergy	42	13	15	35	22	2	19	35	3
Laity	56	6	5	55	8		9	55	1
36. SALISBURY	CARRIED			CARRIED			LOST		
Bishop	1			1			1		
Clergy	59	31	3	55	32	6	36	54	4
Laity	89	9	3	92	8	2	11	89	1

DIOCESE	1st Motion			2nd Motion			Ammendment		
	FOR	AGAINST	ABST.	FOR	AGAINST	ABST.	FOR	AGAINST	ABST.
37. SHEFFIELD		CARRIED			CARRIED			LOST	
Bishop	1			1				1	
Clergy	38	17	5	33	23		23	28	2
Laity	42	17		36	17		21	33	
38. SODOR & MAN		CARRIED			CARRIED			LOST	
Bishop	1			1				1	
Clergy	17	10	1	16	10		12	16	
Laity	45	24	2	42	22		23	46	
39. SOUTHWARK		CARRIED			CARRIED			LOST	
Bishop (Woolwich)	1			1				1	
Clergy	73	18		68	20		22	67	
Laity	57	25		48	25		25	48	
40. SOUTHWELL		LOST							
Bishop	1								
Clergy	24	24	1						
Laity	30	23							
41. TRURO		LOST							
Bishop		1							
Clergy	24	65	1						
Laity	40	51	1						
42. WAKEFIELD		CARRIED			CARRIED			LOST	
Bishop	1			1				1	
Clergy	54	26	1	48	32	1	31	45	3
Laity	49	16	2	43	24		25	40	
43. WORCESTER		CARRIED			CARRIED			LOST	
Bishop	1			1				1	
Clergy	42	19		45	19		20	45	
Laity	47	17		47	17		17	47	

Source: GS 252

Table 22: The First Ordinations of Women to the Priesthood in the
Anglican Church of Canada in Each of the Remaining 20 Dioceses:
January 1, 1978 to June 16, 1991

DATE	WOMEN	DIOCESE	BISHOP
1 October, 1978	Lettie James	Montreal	R.Hollis
28 October, 1978	Ruth Pogson	Rupert's Land	B.Valentine
	Joan Whiting + GENEVE MURDOCH		
24 June, 1979	Betty Garrett	Qu'Appelle	M.Peers
29 June, 1979	Brenda Jean Pierce	Nova Scotia	L.Hatfield
4 December, 1980	Sara Eaton	Ottawa	E.Lackey
30 November, 1981	Odette Perron	Moosonee	C.Lawrence
18 November, 1982	Christina Oosthuizen	Central Newfoundland	S.Payne
4 September, 1983	Kate Merriman	Yukon	R.Ferris
	Dorothy Thorpe		
28 October, 1983	Jane Moorehouse-Bourcet	Kootenay	R.Berry
17 March, 1984	Kathleen Schmitt	Edmonton	E.K.Clarke
26 February, 1985	Gertrude Gosse	Eastern Newfoundland	M.Mate
21 September, 1985	Susan DeGruchy	Algoma	L.Peterson
13 April, 1986	Margaret Rogers	Ontario	A.Read
20 April, 1986	Janice Speer		
14 September, 1986	Lynn Braye	Western Newfoundland	S.Payne
13 December, 1986	Ray Kiebuzinski	Keewatin	H.Allan
25 March, 1987	Muriel Adey	British Columbia	R.Shepherd
01 March, 1987	Jennifer Lee Walsh	Calgary	B.Curtis
11 June, 1990	Patricia Britton	Fredericton	G.Lemmon
28 April, 1991	Doreen Becker	Saskatchewan	C.Arthurson
16 June, 1991	Anne Lindgren	Arctic	J.Clarke

Source: This table was compiled through personal communication with each of the diocesan officers of the dioceses listed.

Bibliography

I. ARCHIVES OF THE ANGLICAN CHURCH OF CANADA, TORONTO, CANADA

1. Church and daily newspapers

Anglican Churchman, Globe and Mail, Toronto Star, Anglican Magazine

2. Papers

Committee on Women's Work in the Church, 1955–1959, G.S.-75-10. Subcommittee on Deaconess Order and Sisterhoods, G.S.-CWWC.

Women's Auxiliary Papers, G.S.-76-15, Box 25.

Women's Inter-Church Council of Canada Papers, 1973, GS-76-15, Box 26.

Scott Papers, M101.

Manifesto on the Ordination of Women to the Priesthood, 1975, Scott Papers, M101.

Alison Kemper, "Deaconess as Urban Missionary and Ideal Woman," G.S. 76-15, Box 25.

Primate's Papers, GS-81-1, Box 1-4.

3. Proceedings and Minutes

Annual Session — Meeting of the House of Bishops of the Church of England in Canada, 1920–

Annual Session — Meeting of the House of Bishops of the Anglican Church of Canada, 1964–1979.

Synod Journals of the Dioceses of Algoma, Arctic, Athabasca, Brandon, Caledonia, Cariboo, Calgary, Edmonton, Huron, Keewatin, Niagara, Ottawa, Ontario, Toronto, Montreal, Newfoundland (Eastern, Western, Central), Nova Scotia, Rupert's Land, Saskatoon, Saskatchewan, British Columbia, Qu'Appelle, Yukon.

Synod Journals of the Ecclesiastical Provinces of British Columbia, Canada, Ontario, Rupert's Land, 1970–1976.

Anglican Registered Church Workers Association, G.S.-76-15, Box 26.

General Synod, *Journal of Proceedings*, 1921 to 1980.

Council of Full-Time Women Workers Records, 1974–69, G.S.-76-15, Box 25.

4. Reports

House of Bishops, Report on Women's Work in the Church, 1935.

Royal Commission on the Status of Women, G.S.-76-15, Box 26.

Anglican Consultative Council Reports

ACC-1 Limuru, 1971; ACC-2 Dublin, 1973; ACC-3 Trinidad, 1976

Majority and Minority Report of the Primate's Task Force on the Ordination of Women to the Priesthood, 1972.

Sociological Analysis of Women Workers in the Anglican Church of Canada, GS-76-15, Box 26.

II. DIOCESAN ARCHIVES

Diocese of Brandon

- *Synod Journals* 1930–1978

- Records and papers of Bishop's Messengers

Diocese of Huron

- Synod *Journal of Proceedings* 1920–1978

- *Huron Church News*

- Bishop D. Ragg Papers

Diocese of Niagara

- Synod *Journal of Proceedings* 1920–1978

- *Niagara Anglican*
- Bishop J. Bothwell Papers

Diocese of Toronto
- *Synod Journals* 1920–1978

Diocese of Ottawa
- *Synod Journals* 1920–1978

Diocese of New Westminster
- *Synod Journals* 1920–1978

III. NATIONAL ARCHIVES OF CANADA

National Council on the Status of Women Papers

IV. CHURCH OF ENGLAND RECORDS CENTRE, SOUTH BERMONDSEY, ENGLAND

1. Church and daily newspapers _____

Church Times, The Guardian, Yorkshire Post, Times, The Independent

2. Papers _____

Deaconess Papers, CWMC/CDH/DSS/1-8

Deaconess Employment Records, CWMC/EMPL/1

Working Party on Women's Ministry, CWMC/OW/a, CWMC/ow/2-3, CWMC/0W 3/1.

F. C. Eccles Papers, CWMC/FCE/1-5.

Council of Women's Ministry in the Church Papers, CWMC/ALPH/L3, CWMC/ACPH/L1, CWMC/ACPH/G1, CWMC/ALPH/A1-A6, CWMC/ALPH/L4-P5, CWMC/ALPH/P6, CWMC/ ALPH/T1, CWMC/ALPH/W2.

Church of England Diocesan Files on Women: (42), CWMC/D10/1-10, CWMC/D10/11-20, CWMC/D10/21-30, CWMC/D10/31-42.

Council of Women's Ministry Correspondence, CWMC/COU/C/1-7.

Council of Women's Ministry Historical File, CWMC/HIST/1.

Advisory Committee on the Church's Ministry Files, ACCM/OW/1-8, ACCM/DSS/9, ACCM/ MIN/WP/3, ACCM/SEC/5, ACCM/PUBNS/Box 1-2.

Working Papers for the Commission on Women and Holy Orders, AC/1963/1/m/1-2.

"Women in the Professions," ACCM1

Lampe, G. W. H., The Church's Tradition and the Question of the Ordination of Women to the Historic Ministry, 1968, ACCM/PB/81.

Savard, John, The Case Against the Ordination of Women, ACCM/PB.

Anonymous, Women in the Priesthood? ACCM/PB/188.

Greenacre, Roger, Christian Unity and the Ordination of Women, 1978, ACCM/PB/94.

Mascall, E. L., Women Priests? Church Literature Association, 1972, ACCM/PB/94.

3. Proceedings and Minutes _____

Council of Women's Ministry Minutes, up to 1969, CWMC/COU/M/2.

Journal of Proceedings for the Dioceses of Canterbury, Chelmsford, London, Oxford, Southward, 1968–1978.

Canterbury Chronicle of Convocation, 1968–1978.

Church Assembly Report of Proceedings, 1920–1969.

General Synod Report of Proceedings, 1970–1980.

York Journal of Convocation, 1968–1978.

4. Reports _____

Council of Women's Ministry Publications, CWMC/PUBNS/1-5, CWMC/PUBNS/6-9.

Report of the Archbishop's Commission on Women and Holy Orders, 1966.

Gender and Ministry Report, 1962.

Women and the Ordained Ministry, Report of an Anglican-Methodist Commission on Women and Holy Orders, 1968, (p) 262.14.

GS 104, The Ordination of Women to the Priesthood: A Consultative Document Presented by the Advisory Council for the Church's Ministry.

GS Misc 26, The Ordination of Women to the Priesthood, References to the Dioceses.

GS Misc 53, The Archbishop of Canterbury's Correspondence with Leaders of Other Churches on the Ordination of Women.

GS Misc 86, The Ordination of Women: Report of the Anglican/Orthodox Joint Doctrinal Commission.

GS Misc 87, The Ordination of Women: Arrangements for the November 1978 Debate.

GS 281, The Theology of Ordination: A Report by the Faith and Order Advisory Group of the Board for Mission and Unity.

GS 764, The Ordination of Women to the Priesthood: A Report by the House of Bishops of the General Synod of the Church of England, 1987.

GS 829, The Ordination of Women to the Priesthood: A Second Report by the House of Bishops, 1988.

GS 549, Ordination of Deaconesses to the Diaconate Report by the Standing Committee, 1982.

Women's Work in the Church, 1942, by the Committee of the Archbishops of Canterbury and York, London, 1943, CWMC/PUBNS/6-9.

Women in the Church, 1948, CWMC/ALPH/63.

V. DIOCESAN ARCHIVES/RECORDS OFFICES

Diocese of Canterbury
- *Synod Journals* 1973–1976
Diocese of Chelmsford
- *Synod Journals* 1973–1976
Diocese of London
- *Synod Journals* 1973–1976
Diocese of Oxford
- *Synod Journals* 1973–1976
Diocese of Oxford
- *Synod Journals* 1973–1976

VI. LAMBETH PALACE LIBRARY

Fisher Papers
   v. 122, pp. 250–4.   Deaconesses
   v. 211, pp. 56–60.   Lay Women
   v. 221, pp. 246–248., v. 232, pp. 178–198.
   v. 1, pp. 132–133   Ordination of Women
   v. 11, pp. 67–130, v. 27, pp. 239–245, v. 44, pp. 11–22
   v. 69, pp. 182–191, v. 177, pp. 295–300, v. 188, pp. 116–121
   v. 190, pp. 232–240, v. 202, pp, 105, 225, 308–357, v. 226, pp. 335–338
Lang Papers
   v. 18, pp. 41–42, pp. 152–165, pp. 216–222   Deaconesses
   v. 93, pp. 118–225, v. 95, pp. 76–69, v. 109, pp. 306–310
   v. 110, pp. 135–141, v. 169, pp. 151–158, v. 176, pp. 57–60, v. 182, pp. 86–94

v. 93–94.   Ministry of Women in the Church of England,

v. 98, pp. 299–305   1920–42

v. 103, pp. 257–261, v. 122, pp. 274–187

Lambeth Conference Papers

LC114, pp. 198–209   1920

LC 130, pp. 12–20, LC 136, pp. 1–78

Letitia Fairfield, "Women and Lay Ministries, LC 1920, cxxxvii, pp. 61–70.

LC168, pp. 27, 29, 32 1930

Temple Papers

v. 18, pp. 56–70   Deaconesses

v. 36, pp. 228–33   Ordination of Women

v. 59, pp. 131–44.   Women Church Workers

VII. PUBLIC RECORDS OFFICE

The White Paper

VIII. SARAH FAWCETT LIBRARY

1. Papers _____

AGOW Papers (Anglican Group for the Ordination of Women) ORE/AEOW/A, B1-B5, Box 556, ARG/AGOW/B6-B12, Box 557.

Women in the Church, Box 1 and 2.

Society for the Ministry of Men and Women in the Church Newsletters, 1929–1978.

Lace, Jessie, *The Ordination of Women to the Historic Ministry of the Church*, London, 1958, 262.14.

Burgon, J. W., *Woman's Place: A Sermon*. London, 1871, 361.12.

Fairfield, Zoe, *The Women's Movement and the Family*. London, 1913. Women in the Church, Box 1.

IX. DIOCESE OF SOUTH CHINA AND HONG KONG

Synod Journals, 1942–1972

Papers of Bishop R. O. Hall

Papers of Bishop D. Baker

ORAL HISTORY INTERVIEWS
I. CANADA

Aimee, The Reverend Beth (Diocese of Brandon). Deacon, 1974, and later one of the first women ordained to the priesthood in the Diocese of Brandon.

Alley, The Reverend Elspeth (Diocese of New Westminster). Deacon and later one of the first women ordained in the Diocese of New Westminster.

Benwell, The Reverend Sr. Rosemary (Diocese of Toronto). Religious of the Sisters of Saint John the Divine, and one of the first women ordained to the priesthood in the Diocese of Toronto.

Bothwell, Archbishop John (Diocese of Niagara), Bishop of the Diocese of Niagara who ordained the first women to the priesthood.

Caton, The Reverend Ina, (Diocese of Saskatoon). Deaconess, and later the first woman ordained to the priesthood in the Diocese of Saskatoon.

Crabb, Archbishop Hugh Wright (Diocese of Athabasca). Bishop of the Diocese of Athabasca who ordained first woman to the priesthood in his diocese.

Daly, The Reverend Dorothy (Diocese of Caledonia). Deaconess, and later the first woman ordained to the priesthood in the Diocese of Caledonia.

Gooding, Bishop Allan (Diocese of Quebec). Bishop of Quebec who ordained that diocese's first woman to the priesthood.

Kennon, The Reverend Margery (Diocese of Brandon). Bishop's Messenger who later became one of the first women ordained to the priesthood in the Diocese of Brandon.

Lane, The Reverend Virginia (Diocese of Huron). Deacon, who later became one of the first women ordained to the priesthood in the Diocese of Huron.

Lightbourne, Francis. Layworker and field secretary of the AWTC.

Matthews, The Reverend Ruth (Diocese of Quebec). Deaconess and later the first woman ordained to the priesthood in the Diocese of Quebec.

Maybee, Mrs. Diane. Layworker in the Anglican Church of Canada and member of the Anglican Registered Church Workers Association in the 1960s–70s.

Mills, The Reverend Mary (Diocese of Huron). Deaconess, and the first woman ordained to the priesthood in the Diocese of Huron.

Mother Frances Joyce. Sisters of Saint John the Divine, Mother Superior.

Pogson, The Reverend Ruth (Diocese of Rupert's Land). Deaconess and later one of the first women ordained to the priesthood in the Diocese of Rupert's Land.

Ragg, Bishop David (Diocese of Huron). The Bishop of Huron who ordained the first women to the priesthood in that diocese.

Reed, The Reverend Patricia (Diocese of Cariboo). Deaconess, and later the first woman ordained to the priesthood in the Diocese of Cariboo.

Scott, Archbishop Edward (Primate). Primate of the Anglican Church of Canada during the ordination of women debates.

Seaborn, Archbishop Robert (Diocese of Eastern Newfoundland and Labrador). Member of the Wider Ordained Ministry Committee.

Shanley, The Reverend Beverley (Diocese of Niagara). Deaconess and later one of the first women ordained to the priesthood in the Diocese of Niagara.

Shore, Mrs. Edith. Layworker in the Anglican Church of Canada and founding member of the Anglican Registered Church Workers Association.

Somerville, Archbishop David (Diocese of New Westminster). Bishop of New Westminster who ordained the first women to the priesthood in that diocese.

II. ENGLAND

Brooke, Dr. George (MOW). Layperson, member of the Anglican Group for the Ordination of Women to the Priesthood.

Byatt, Deaconess Margaret (Diocese of Southwark). Deaconess serving in the Diocese of Southwork.

Coggan, Archbishop Donald (Diocese of Canterbury). Archbishop of Canterbury in 1978.

Cope, The Reverend Olive (Diocese of London). Deaconess in the Diocese of London in 1978, who was later made a deacon.

Denzil Octavia, The Reverend Sr. (Diocese of London). Deaconess with the Community of Saint Andrew in the Diocese of London, who was later made a deacon.

Evans, The Reverend Gwen (Diocese of London). Deaconess in the Diocese of London, who was later made a deacon.

Finder, Deaconess Patricia Constance (Diocese of Southwark). Deaconess in the Diocese of Southwark.

Gurney, The Reverend Anne (Diocese of London). Deaconess in the Diocese of London, who was later made a deacon. She was also Head Deaconess of Gilmore House in the 1970s.

Helena Mary, Sr. Deaconess (Diocese of London). Deaconess with the Community of Saint Andrew in the Diocese of London.

Howard, Dame Christian (General Synod). Member of General Synod and writer of GS104.

Howard, Deaconess June (Diocese of London). Deaconess in the Diocese of London.

Hunt, The Reverend Jessie (Diocese of Chelmsford). Deaconess in the Diocese of Chelmsford who was later made a deacon.

Ingram, The Reverend Emily (Diocese of Chelmsford). Deaconess in the Diocese of Chelmsford, who was later made a deacon.

Judith, The Reverend Sr. (Diocese of London). Deaconess with the Community of Saint Andrew in the Diocese of London, who was later made a deacon.

Kroll, The Reverend Dr. Sr. Una (Diocese of London). Deaconess in the Diocese of London, who was later made a deacon. Founding member of the Christian Parity Group.

Lillian, The Reverend Mother (Diocese of London). Deaconess with the Community of Saint Andrew in the Diocese of London, who was later made a deacon.

Lloyd, The Reverend Pamela (Diocese of Canterbury). Deaconess in the Diocese of Canterbury, who was later made a deacon.

McClatchey, The Reverend Diana (MOW). Deaconess in the Diocese of London, also a member of the AGOW, who was later made a deacon and became head of MOW.

Parsons, The Reverend Anne (Diocese of Southwark). Deaconess in the Diocese of Southwark, who was later made a deacon.

Parsons, The Reverend Mary (Diocese of Oxford). Deaconess in the Diocese of Oxford in 1978, who was later made a deacon.

Patricia, The Reverend Sr. (Diocese of London). Deaconess with the Community of Saint Andrew in the Diocese of London, who was later made a deacon.

Speer, The Reverend Gwen (Diocese of Southwark). Deaconess in the Diocese of Southwark, who was later made a deacon.

Theresa, The Reverend Sr. (Diocese of London). Deaconess with the Community of Saint Andrew in the Diocese of London, who was later made a deacon.

Trillo, Mrs. John (Diocese of Chelmsford, per Bishop A. John Trillo). Wife of the Bishop of Chelmsford.

Wensley, The Reverend Beryl (Diocese of Southwark). Deaconess in the Diocese of Southwark, who was later made a deacon.

Winfield, The Reverend June Mary (Diocese of Southwark). Deaconess in the Diocese of Southwark, who was later made a deacon.

Wintle, The Reverend Ruth (Diocese of London). Deaconess in the Diocese of London, who was later made a deacon.

PUBLISHED WORKS
I. ANGLICANISM — GENERAL

Bradshaw, Paul F., *The Anglican Ordinal, Its History and Development from the Reformation.* London: SPCK Alwin Club, 1971.

Davies, Rupert Eric, *The Testing of the Churches, 1932–82.* London: Epworth, 1982.

Echlin, Edward P., *The Story of the Anglican Ministry.* Slough: St. Paul Publishers, 1974.

Howe, John, Highways and Hedges, *Anglicanism and the Universal Church.* Toronto: Anglican Book Centre, 1985.

Sykes, Stephen, ed., *Authority in the Anglican Communion*. London: SPCK, 1988.

Wand, J. W. C., *Anglicanism in History and Today*. London: Weidenfield and Nicolson, 1967.

II. THE CHURCH IN CANADA

Boon, T. C. B., *The Anglican Church from the Bay to the Rockies*. Toronto: Ryerson, 1962.

Bibby, Reginald W., *Fragmented Gods: The Poverty and Potential of Religion in Canada*. Toronto: Irwin Publishing, 1987.

Carrington, Philip, *The Anglican Church in Canada*. Toronto: Collins, 1963.

Crysdale, Stewart and Les Wheatcroft, eds., *Religion in Canadian Society*. Toronto, MacMillan, 1976.

Ervin, Spencer, *The Political and Ecclesiastical History of the Anglican Church of Canada*. Ambler, Pennsylvania: Trinity, 1967.

Grant, Jown Webster, *The Church in the Canadian Era*. Burlington: Welch Publishing Co., 1988.

Handy, Robert T., *A History of the Churches in the United States and Canada*. New York: Oxford University Press, 1979.

Lower, A. R. M., *Canadians in the Making: A Social History of Canada*. Toronto: Longmans, 1958.

Millman, Thomas R. and A. R. Kelley, *Atlantic Canada to 1900: A History of the Anglican Church*. Toronto: Anglican Book Centre, 1983.

Moir, John S. and C. T. McIntire, eds., *Canadian Protestant and Catholic Missions, 1820s–1960s*. New York: Peter Lang, 1988.

Moir, John S., *The Church in the British Era*. Toronto: McGraw-Hill/Ryerson, 1972.

Peake, F. A., *The Anglican Church in British Columbia*. Vancouver: Mitchell, 1959.

Slater, Peter, ed., *Religion and Culture in Canada/Religion et Culture au Canada*. Toronto: Canadian Corporation for Studies in Religion, 1977.

III. WOMEN IN CANADA

Acton, Janice et al., eds., *Women at Work: Ontario 1850–1930*. Toronto: Canadian Women's Press, 1974.

Anderson, Margaret, *Mother Was Not a Person*. Montreal: Black Rose Books, 1972.

Armstrong, Pat, *The Double Ghetto: Canadian Women and Their Segregated Word*. Toronto: McClelland and Stuart, 1978.

Bourne, Paula, *Women's Paid and Unpaid Work*. Toronto: New Hogtown Press, 1985.

Canadian Advisory Council on the Status of Women, *Integration and Participation: Women's Work in the Home and in the Labour Force*. Ottawa: Canadian Advisory Council on the Status of Women, 1987.

"Canadian Women and Church Missionary Societies in the Nineteenth Century: A Step Toward Independence," in *Atlantis*, 2 (Spring, 1977), 2–11.

Cook, Ramsay and Wendy Mitchison, eds., *The Proper Sphere — Women's Place in Canadian Society*. Toronto: Oxford University Press, 1976.

Fox, Beryl, *The Visible Woman: A History of Women and Women's Rights in Canada*. Toronto, 1975.

Headon, Christopher, "Women and Organized Religion in Mid and Late Nineteenth Century," in *Journal of the Canadian Church Historical Society*, Vol. 20: 1,2 (March–June 1978), 3-18.

Kealey, Linda, ed., *A Not Unreasonable Claim: Women and Reform in Canada 1890s–1920s*. Toronto: Canadian Women's Press, 1979.

L'Esperance, Jeanne, *The Widening Sphere — Women in Canada, 1870–1940*. Ottawa: Public Archives, 1982.

National Council of Women in Canada. *Women of Canada, Their Life and Work*. Ottawa: National Council of Women in Canada, 1975.

Phillips, Paul and Erin, *Women's Work: Inequality in the Labour Market*. Toronto: J. Lorimer, 1983.

Prentice, Alison L., *Canadian Women — A History*. Toronto: Harcourt Brace Jovanovich Canada, 1988.

Prentice, Alison and Susan Mann Trofimenkoff, eds., *The Neglected Majority: Essays in Canadian Women's History*. Toronto: McClelland Stewart, 1985.

Prentice, Alison, "Writing Women into History — The History of Women's Work in Canada," in *Atlantis*, 32, 2 (Spring, 1978), 72–83.

No Primary Author, *The Proper Sphere — A Woman's Place in Canadian Society*. Toronto: Oxford University Press, 1976.

Cook, Ramsay and Wendy Mitchison, eds., *The Proper Sphere: Women's Place in Canadian Society*. Toronto: McClelland and Stewart, 1986.

Pierson, Ruth Roach, *They're Still Women After All: The Second World War and Canadian Womanhood*. Toronto: McClelland and Stewart, 1986.

Reilly, Heather, *Some Sources for Women's History in the Public Archives of Canada*. Ottawa: Public Archives, 1974.

Silverman, Elaine Leslau, "Writing Canadian Women's History, 1970–82, an Historical Analysis," in *Canadian Historical Review*, 63, 4, 1982, 513–533.

Strong-Boag, Veronica and Anita Clair Fellman, eds., *Re-Thinking Canada — The Promise of Women's History*. Toronto: Copp Clark Pitman, 1986.

IV. THE CHURCH IN ENGLAND

Edwards, David L., Christian England. V. 3 and 4. Michigan: Erdmanns, 1980.

Field-Bibb, Jacqueline, *Women Towards Priesthood: Ministerial Politics and Feminist Praxis*. Cambridge: Cambridge University Press, 1991.

Fullalove, Brenda, "The History of Women in the Church of England 1919–1970." M.Phil. Thesis, University of Manchester at Manchester, 1986.

Heeney, Brian, "The Beginnings of Church Feminism: Women and the Councils of the Church of England, 1897–1919," in *Journal of Ecclesiastical History*, 33. (1982), 89–109.

Heeney, Brian, *The Women's Movement in the Church of England 1850–1930*. Oxford: Clarendon Press, 1988.

Heeney, Brian, "Women's Struggle for Professional Work and Status in the Church of England 1900–1930," in *Historical Journal*, 26, (1983), 329–347.

Humphry, Ellen F., *Ministries of Women During 50 Years in Connection with the SPG London: Society for the Propogation of the Gospel, 1915*.

Leonard, Graham, *The Speech to the General Synod on the Ordination of Women*. London: Church Literary Associations, 1978.

Moorman, J. R. H., *A History of the Church in England*. London: A and C Black, 1986.

Reffold, A. E., *A Noble Army of Women; Marie Carlisle and the Church Army Sisters*. London: Church Literary Association, 1947.

Temple, William, "How the Women's Movement May Help the Cause of Religion," in *The Religious Aspect of the Women's Movement*. London: Church Literature Association, 1912.

Webb, R. K., *Modern England*. New York: Harper and Row, 1980.

Welsby, Paul A., *A History of the Church in England, 1945–1980*. Oxford: Oxford University Press, 1986.

V. WOMEN IN ENGLAND

Adam, Ruth, *A Woman's Place, 1910–1975*. United Kingdom: Readers Union, 1976.

Fanner, Barbara, ed., *The Women of England: Interpretive Bibliographical Essays*. Hamden: Anchor Books, 1979.

Harrison, Brian, *Separate Spheres: The Opposition to Women's Suffrage in Britain*. New York: Holmes and Meier, 1978.

Lewis, Jane, *Women in England 1870 – 1950: Sexual Divisions and Social Change*. Bloomington: Indiana University Press, 1984.

Nicolas, Suzanne, *Bibliography on Women Workers 1861–1965*. Geneva: International Labour Office, Central Library and Documentation Branch, 1970.

Roebuck, Janet, *The Making of Modern English Society from 1850*. London: Routledge and Kegan Paul, 1982.

Smith, Harold L., ed., *British Feminism in the Twentieth Century*. Massachusetts: University of Massachusetts Press, 1990.

Wilson, Elizabeth, *Only Halfway to Paradise: Women in Postwar Britain, 1945–1968*. London: Tavistock Publications, 1980.

No Primary Author, *Women in English Religion 1700–1925*. New York: Edwin Mellen Press, 1983.

VI. ORDINATION OF WOMEN, GENERAL

Anglican Roman Catholic Inter-Church Commission, The Final Report. Cincinnati: Forward Movement Publications, 1982.

Baker, John Austin, *The Right Time*. London: The Movement for the Ordination of Women, 1981.

Chapman, Jennifer, *The Last Bastion: Women Priests, the Case For and Against*. London: Methuen, 1989.

Chittister, Joan, *Winds of Change — Women Challenge the Church*. Kansas City: Sheed and Ward, 1986.

Craston, Colin, *Evangelicals and the Ordination of Women*. Bramcole: Grove Books, 1975.

Dicken, Helene, *Women and the Apostolic Ministry*. London: Church Literature Association, 1978.

Eberhard, Peggy, *From Subordination to Ordination*. Toronto: Faculty of Law, University of Toronto, 1975.

Ermarth, Margaret Sittler, *Adam's Fractured Rib — Observations on Women in the Church*. Philadelphia: Fortress Press, 1970.

Furlong, Monica, ed., *Feminine in the Church*. London: Society for the Propogation of Christian Knowledge, 1984.

Hannon, Vincent Emmanuel Sister, *The Question of Women and the Priesthood*. London: Church Literature Association, 1976.

Heyer, Robert J., *Women and Orders*. New York: Paulist Press, 1974.

Jewett, Paul King, *The Ordination of Women — An Essay on the Office of Christian Ministry*. Grand Rapids: Erdmanns, 1980.

King, Ursula, ed., *Women in the World's Religions*. New York: Paragon House, 1987.

Lehman, Edward, *Women Clergy: Breaking Through Gender Barriers*. New Brunswick: Transition Books, 1985.

Maitland, Sarah, *A Map of the New Country: Women and Christianity*. London: Routledge and Kegan Paul, 1983.

No Primary Author, New Women, New Church, New Priestly Ministry. Proceedings of the second conference on the ordination of Roman Catholic Women. Rochester: Women's Ordination Conference, 1980.

Panton, Ethel and Dorothy Batho, *The Order of Deaconesses, Past, Present and Future*. London: Student Christian Movement Press, 1937.

Parvey, Constance, *Ordination of Women in Ecumenical Perspective*. Faith and Order Paper no. 105, Geneva: World Council of Churches, 1980.

Peberdy, Alyson, *Women Priests?* London: Marshall Pickering, 1988.

Peck, Jack, *The Ordination of Women to the Priesthood*. Toronto: Anglican Book Centre, 1975.

Smythe, Paul Rodney, *The Ordination of Women*. London: Sheffington, 1939.

Weidman, Judith L.,*Women Ministers: How Women are Re-Defining Traditional Roles*. New York: Harper and Row, 1981.

No Primary Author, *Why Not? Priesthood and the Ordination of Women*. Berkshire: Marcham Manor Press, 1976.

No Primary Author, *Women and Priesthood*. London: Longmans, 1930.

No Primary Author, *Women Priests, Obstacles to Unity?* London: Catholic Truth Society, 1986.

VII. WOMEN IN AMERICAN CHURCH AND SOCIETY

Bellamy, Nelle V., "Participation of Women in the Public Life of the Church from Lambeth Conferences 1867–1978," in *The Historical Magazine of the Protestant Episcopal Church*, 51 (1982), 81–98.

Bird, David John, "The Anglican Communion Occupies a Special Place," Ph.D. Thesis, Dusquesne University, 1987.

Donovan, Mary S., *A Different Call: Women's Ministries in the Episcopal Church 1850–1920*. Wilton: Morehouse-Barlow, 1986.

Donovan, Mary S., *Women Priests in the Episcopal Church — the Experience of the First Decade*. Cincinnati: Forward Movement Publications, 1988.

Douglas, Ann, *The Feminization of American Culture*. New York: Knopf, 1977.

Flexner, Eleanor, *Century of Struggle: The Women's Rights Movement in the United States*. New York: Atheneum, 1973.

Gaylor, Christine Camille, "The Ordination of Women in the Episcopal Church in the United States — A Case Study," Ph.D. Thesis, St. John's University, 1982.

Harkness, Georgia Elma, *Women in Church and Society*. Nashville: Abingdon Press, 1972.

Hardesty, Nancy, *Women Called to Witness: Evangelical Feminism in the Nineteenth Century*. Nashville: Abingdon Press, 1984.

Harris, Barbara, *Beyond Her Sphere: Women and the Professions in American History*. Westport: Greenwood Press, 1978.

Huyck, Heather, "To Celebrate a Whole Priesthood: The History of Women's Ordination in the Episcopal Church," Ph.D. Thesis. University of Minnesota, 1981.

Kelly, Arthur James, "The Response of the Episcopal Church to Social Change and Social Issues 1960–1978," Ph.D. Thesis, New York University, 1981.

Marrett, Michael McFarlene, "The Historical Background and Spiritual Authority of the Lambeth Conferences and Their Impact on the Protestant Episcopal Church in the U.S.A., with Particular Emphasis on the Ordination of Women to the Priesthood," Ph.D. Thesis, New York University, 1980.

Reumann, John Henry Paul, Ministries Examined — Laity, Clergy Women and Bishops in a Time of Change. Minneapolis: Augsburg Press, 1987.

Ruether, Rosemary and Rosemary Skinner Keller, ed., *Women and Religion in America*, v.3. San Francisco: Harper and Row, 1986.

Sartori, Shirley Larmour, "Conflict and Institutional Change: The Ordination of Women in the Episcopal Church," Ph.D. Thesis, State University of New York at Albany, 1978.

Scott, John Morgan, "A Survey of Attitudes Toward Female Leadership in the Church in the Diocese of Pennsylvania." D.Min. thesis, Eastern Baptist Theological Seminary, 1987.

Verdesi, Elizabeth Howell, *In But Still Out: Women in the Church*. Philadelphia: The Westminster Press, 1976.

Welter, Barbara, "The Cult of True Womanhood," in *American Quarterly* 18 (Summer, 1966), 151–174.

VIII. WOMEN AND HISTORY, GENERAL

Banks, Olive, *Faces of Feminism: A Study of Feminism as a Social Movement*. Oxford: Martin Robertson, 1981.

de Beauvoir, Simone, *The Second Sex*. Harmondsworth: Penguin, 1953.

Bourne, Paul, ed., *Women's Paid and Unpaid Work: Historical and Contemporary Perspectives*. Toronto: NewHogtown Press, 1985.

Burnet, Jean, ed., *Looking into My Sister's Eyes: An Exploration in Women's History*. Toronto: Multicultural History Society of Ontario, 1986.

Carr, Anne E., *Transforming Grace: Christian Tradition and Women's Experience*. San Francisco: Harper and Row, 1988.

Dowell, Susan, *Dispossessed Daughters of Eve — Faith and Feminism*. London: Society for the Propogation of Christian Knowledge, 1987.

Fox, Margaret A. F., *Women's Speaking*. London: Pythia, 1989.

Franklin, Ursula M., et al, eds., *Knowledge Reconsidered — A Feminist Overview*. Ottawa: Canadian Research Institute for the Advancement of Women, 1984.

Gramsci, Antonio, "Problems in History and Culture — The Intellectuals," in *Selections from the Prison Notebooks*. New York, 1971.

Hirshcon, Renee, ed., *Women and Property — Women as Property*. London: Croom Helm, 1984.

McLaughlin, Eleanor and Rosemary Ruether, eds., *Women of Spirit: Female Leadership in Jewish and Christian Traditions*. New York: Simon and Schuester, 1979.

Sacks, Karen, *Sisters and Wives, the Past and Future of Sexual Equality*. Westport: Greenwood Press, 1976.

Stanton, Elizabeth and Susan B. Anthony, *History of Woman Suffrage*. New York: Fowler, 1981.

Tavard, George H., *Women in Christian Tradition*. Notre Dame: University of Notre Dame, 1973.

Wine, Jeri Dawn and Jamie L. Ristock, eds., *Women and Social Change*. Toronto: James Lorimer, 1991.